COLLABORATIVE CREATIVITY

Contemporary Perspectives

Edited by
Dorothy Miell
and
Karen Littleton

FREE ASSOCIATION BOOKS

First published in 2004 by
FREE ASSOCIATION BOOKS
57 Warren Street
London W1T 5NR

www.fabooks.com

A catalogue record for this book is available from the British Library

ISBN 1 85343 763 8

10 9 8 7 6 5 4 3 2 1

Designed and produced for the publisher by
Chase Publishing Services, Sidmouth, EX10 9QG
Printed and bound in the European Union by
Antony Rowe Ltd, Chippenham and Eastbourne, England

Collaborative Creativity

Contents

Acknowledgements

The editors would like to thank colleagues at The Open University who formed part of the stimulating research environment which encouraged us to embark on this project and to see it through: in particular the members of the *Processes in Collaboration, Communication and Creativity* Research Group and of the *Educational Dialogue Research Unit.* We would also like to thank Raymond MacDonald for the cover artwork inspired by the notion of collaborative creativity and Sue Jefcoate for her generous assistance in preparing the manuscript. Finally many thanks are due to the editorial team at Free Association Books who were so helpful and efficient throughout the production process.

Acknowledgements

1
Collaborative Creativity: Contemporary Perspectives

Karen Littleton and Dorothy Miell

Taking a view of creativity as fundamentally and necessarily social, and in many cases an explicitly collaborative endeavour, can bring new and important insights to our understanding of both the processes and outcomes of creative activities. This approach to creativity as social, derived in part from socio-cultural theory and research, is one that has gained ground in the academic literature in recent years (John-Steiner, 2000; Montuori & Purser, 1999; Sawyer, 2001, 2004; Sawyer et al., 2003). It is an approach which is opening up exciting new methods of study and theoretical insights for contemporary researchers from many traditions studying creativity in a range of domains. The current volume builds on the growing interest in this area by offering a set of chapters which apply the ideas inherent in this approach to a wide range of contexts such as music, business, school-based creative writing and art, fashion design, architecture and web-based collaborations. The central tenet of the volume is that if we are to characterise human creativity we need to study and understand the socioemotional, interpersonal and cultural dynamics which support and sustain such activity. We also need to understand the use of cultural tools and technologies and examine the ways in which interpersonal and institutional contexts for creativity are enabled and resourced. The volume offers a distinctive and valuable contribution to this growing field of scholarship by presenting a balance between new empirical findings, reviews and critiques of existing literature, and practice-based reflections.

Inherent in these contemporary approaches to collaborative creativity is an emphasis on studying the processes involved rather than a sole focus on examining the quality of the product of creative endeavours. It is not only cognitive processes that are implicated in creative work. Creating collaboratively can be a highly emotionally charged and deeply personally meaningful process – involving the construction of subjectivities and relationships as well as ideas and artefacts. Recognising the centrality of affect, motivation and identity work challenges researchers to develop rich methodological tools for studying these emergent processes and conceptualising their role within collaborative creativity. Underpinning many researchers' interest in exploring and conceptualising the nature of creative collaboration is the need to understand how better to support such endeavours, in order to most effectively foster opportunities for creative work. Whilst there is agreement about the value of trying to establish supportive contexts for collaboration, there is also a recognition that any attempts at intervention need to reflect the requirements and preferences of particular groups and communities. There is no simple agreed formula that can be applied to promote creativity.

The contributions in this volume are grouped into two parts which reflect the salient issues considered above; the first examining the ways in which identity, affect and motivation are implicated in creative collaboration and the second considering ways in which collaborative creativity might be enabled and supported.

In any area of research, ideas develop through collective as well as individual efforts. The present volume emerged out of a continuing dialogue about the nature of creativity and how to facilitate and enhance it which took place between researchers working collaboratively at The Open University on interdisciplinary research projects spanning diverse subject domains. In these studies (of music making, teacher training, online student project work, business teams and children engaged in classroom creative writing) we were led to question existing definitions of and methods for studying creativity and to identify the essentially collaborative nature of all creative endeavour. The chapters subsequently commissioned for this volume (from both members of this original research community and beyond it) have enabled us to continue interrogating the nature of collaborative creativity across a range of domain areas and from a number of contemporary perspectives. The chapters illustrate the ways in which ideas are argued over, contested, borrowed and shared as our collective understanding is advanced. Negotiating and constructing shared understanding is an inherently creative phenomenon, and its achievement a fundamentally social and collaborative process. In contributing to the wider academic and practice-based debates on the nature of collaborative creativity, this volume can be seen as an illustration of its own thesis.

THE CONTRIBUTIONS

Here, we highlight some of the key themes, questions and issues being considered in the book, drawing mainly on the contributions from within it. In presenting this synopsis we have used the voices of the contributors themselves to summarise the key themes and issues emerging from their chapters. Unless otherwise specified, references to contributors refer to their contributions to the present volume.

Part I of the book is concerned with 'Identity, affect and motivation' and opens with a contribution from Seana Moran and Vera John-Steiner who discuss: 'how collaboration in creative work affects and is affected by identity and motivation, which have been particularly understudied in our individual, cognitive-focused age' (Moran & John-Steiner, p.11). Recognising that: 'creative work involves the transformation of a domain's raw materials…into something qualitatively novel yet appropriate' (p.11), the work discussed in Chapter 2 highlights that collaborative creativity is so powerful precisely because it has the potential to change the way people conceive of themselves. As Moran and John-Steiner, citing Josselson (1996), comment: 'Identity is the ultimate act of creativity – it is what we make of ourselves' (p.13). Thus inherent in creative work is identity work involving the continual negotiation and re-negotiation of subjectivities.

Particularly striking accounts of such negotiated and contested processes of identity construction are given by Sibelius Academy piano-solo students in the material presented in Chapter 3 (Sini Wirtanen & Karen Littleton). In considering how the interpretation of a piece from the canon can be seen as a creative process, Wirtanen and Littleton's analyses explore 'how students' identity projects are mediated within and in relation to the interpretative work they undertake with their teacher' (p.27). They are motivated to undertake such work not simply to master and reproduce a particular cultural tradition, but also to transform that tradition by infusing the music with their own unique interpretation. The extracts presented in the chapter testify to both the difficulty and necessity for students of: 'finding their own voice' (p.38) in their interpretations and of: 'telling their own story whilst working in a way which recognises and respects established traditions' (p.38). It is the expressions of self and a life lived and experienced, that Wirtanen and Littleton argue, seem to be associated positively with students' confidence as soloists and: 'which are legitimated, sanctioned or prohibited in the context of the creative relationship between a student and their teacher' (p.38). The experience of students working at this advanced level suggests that in some cases the teaching–learning relationship may be characterised as a creative collaboration, although conflicts and tensions may frequently be experienced within it.

Chapter 4, by Helen Storey and Mathilda Marie Joubert, characterises the processes and practices of creative collaboration as an 'emotional dance'. Drawing on material from an autobiographical interview with Helen Storey about her involvement in interdisciplinary projects, we hear 'from the inside' how creative collaborations are lived and experienced. It is clear from Storey's reflections that, as echoed in Moran and John-Steiner's chapter, creators often struggle to work out new, more adequate forms of symbolic expression (Gardner, 1993, p.34), and Storey describes how she and her collaborators not only: 'had to create a new language for the audience', but that they also had to: 'keep on creating a unique new language to facilitate cross-disciplinary collaboration, since no one party carries the other worlds' language fully' (p.45). This struggle to create a shared discourse was a crucial and yet demanding part of the creative process. Storey also identifies risk-taking as an inherent part of creative work although: 'a mutual relationship of trust' is recognised as being 'key when collaborating creatively' (p.46). Issues of risk-taking and trust are inextricably interwoven within the intimacy between and the mutual vulnerability of close collaborators. Close collaboration can lead to extraordinary interactions between partners and thus conversations can be exhausting as: 'you can only stay that vulnerable for so long' (p.47). Yet the important thing about collaboration is seen to: 'be the ability to be mutually vulnerable…you have to take each other to the edge of what you individually thought you were capable of' (p.47).

Storey comments on the 'shared' ownership of the collaborative projects she was involved in. Whilst it was not part of Helen Storey's experience of collaboration, for some creative partnerships: 'the desire for owning one's efforts can become a source of conflict when apportioning credit' (Moran & John-Steiner, p.19). Collaborative creativity is seen as having had a significant impact on Storey's own identity. Rather than describing the strengthening of her own sense of self and personal achievements Storey notes that: 'The key moments are far more important than having any identity. Having less of a personality is actually more enabling. Through collaborative creativity you overcome the need to have a personality, which is amazingly freeing. I feel that through my creative work over the last seven years I became more and more invisible. I feel a strangely pleasing disembling of my identity rather than a reinforcing or a clarification of what I used to be' (p.49). This notion of invisibility rooted in interdependence rather than independence of self seems to resonate with Moran and John-Steiner's description of 'integrative collaborations' (p.21) in which collaborators temporarily become almost a single entity. For some collaborators it would appear that, either momentarily or for more extended periods of time, the envelope of the self is extended such that one 'loses' oneself.

The importance of creating trust and taking risks in the context of creative collaborations is further highlighted by Cordelia Bryan in Chapter 5. Bryan suggests that in the context of learning relationships '...creative collaboration does not, by and large, just happen either with staff or with students. The process needs to be modelled, practised and nurtured so that group members gradually feel safe enough to participate fully and ultimately to take risks' (pp.54–55). Over the course of the chapter Bryan describes a three-stage approach to the development and assessment of creative collaboration in the performing arts, highlighting the importance of creating an environment of trust, the exploration of group dynamics and the challenges of assessing group skills. Crucially she emphasises the importance of an environment in which trust is fostered through workshop-based activities and productive creative 'controversy' is centred: 'around task related problems rather than personal opinions or abilities (Johnson & Johnson, 1994, pp.310–311)'. She also suggests that it is only: '*after* group participants have experienced working collaboratively in a safe environment and applying some basic group dynamic theory that formal assessment should be considered' (p.60). Such assessment may involve: 'attempting new ways to involve students in their own assessment process' (p.62), emphasising creative *processes*, not just *products*.

The constraints and pressures associated with the formal assessment of creative work is an issue that is also raised in Chapter 6 by Fred Seddon. Having analysed the collaboration between university-level jazz students preparing for a gig, Seddon suggests that their prior experiences of being assessed may have impacted on the collaborative communication observed (even in the situations he studied where the students were not being assessed). Seddon notes that the type of 'empathetic attunement' (for a definition see p.68) that is experienced by professional jazz musicians and which enables them to create collaboratively was not evident in the collaborations between the students he observed and interviewed. He suggests that one of the reasons for this may be that: 'the students were usually continuously assessed during group performance and this can add pressure. This pressure can undermine congeniality and inhibit feelings of safety and security, which would not be conducive to collective risk-taking. Thus it is possible that a lack of trust or feeling insecure in assessment situations...may have had consequences for the collaborative interactions observed here...' (p.76). It is also possible that the relative lack of shared personal and musical history and experiences of playing together, may have: 'inhibited decentering, introspection and the development of trust' (p.76) which Seddon sees as being necessary pre-cursors to empathetic attunement.

Seddon's work clearly emphasises the importance of non-verbal behaviour in mediating collaborative interactions and the need for understanding beyond words – attunement – between collaborators. This need to go beyond words is also highlighted by Eva Vass in Chapter 7. Focusing on the analysis of primary school children's collaborative creative writing Vass highlights the 'centrality of emotions in the processes of creative writing' (p.91) showing, for example, that children's evaluations of their ideas are based equally on the appeal of an idea (emotion) – mediated in part through grins, smiles, an excited tone or playful exaggerated intonation – and their appropriateness (reason). This emphasis on affect sits at the heart of Vass' work and leads her to critique accounts of collaborative creative work focusing solely on explicit argumentation and reasoning in talk – a critique that is re-visited later in the volume by Teresa Dillon (see Chapter 11).

Throughout the volume, different authors' contributions demonstrate the multiplicity of ways in which one can conceptualise the notion of collaborative creativity. Many authors focus on what Moran and John-Steiner describe as 'real-time collaborations between living people who depend on each other and contribute jointly to a common goal of transforming their domain, which neither could do alone' (p.12). Typically these collaborative relationships are seen as being established between peers but, in some cases, the relationship between a tutor and a student can constitute a creative collaboration (see Wirtanen & Littleton, Chapter 3) – in which collaboration is characterised as: 'a fundamentally different kind of interaction from the simple exchanges that occur among work acquaintances (Schrage, 1990). Social interaction involves two or more people talking or in exchange, cooperation adds the constraint of shared purpose, and working together often provides coordination of effort. But collaboration involves an intricate blending of skills, temperaments, effort and sometimes personalities to realise a shared vision of something new and useful' (Moran & John-Steiner, p.11). The chapter by Gabrielle Ivinson (Chapter 8), however, highlights how collaboration can be seen as central to the achievement of most creative acts, even those that initially appear to be solitary. For example, the art student sitting silently in the still life art examination is characterised by Ivinson as collaborating: 'with the community of artists who developed the conventions of still life drawing in the past; with the school through her recognition of what counts as legitimate subject practice and with her family as she tries to fulfil their expectations through her performance' (p.96).

Crucially, the chapter highlights how: 'the past, in the form of dominant social representations about art, exerts a ubiquitous influence over the development of adolescents' "artistic identities"' (p.96) and how, through collaborative processes students can find: 'the symbolic resources needed to make sense of art and to resolve conflicting social representations of art' (p.108).

Part II of the book, 'Enabling Creative Collaborations', opens with a contribution from Stephen O'Hear and Julian Sefton-Green (Chapter 9) which explores how computer technology enables new forms of creative collaboration and mediates the social worlds of creative communities. These authors analyse the structural features of an Internet message board and its use to consider: 'how various kinds of collaboration can act as a kind of creative infrastructure' (p.124). Focusing on one young man's use of an online message board, dedicated to the band 'Interpol', O'Hear and Sefton-Green investigate how the social and technological features of the forum supported this young man's growth as an artist and discuss how such casual, culturally motivated online communities could potentially afford a different model of a 'learning community'. Interestingly, whilst it was clear that his artistic work was developing through his participation in the forum, the young man himself resisted any notion that his involvement with the forum constituted any form of 'work' or 'learning'. For Tom himself participation in the forum was 'fun' and O'Hear and Sefton-Green suggest that it shows us 'how being able to put yourself in situations where you can take risks, where not so much hangs on each action or event and...trust in friendly camaraderie...[creates] a rich and necessary creative environment' (p.122). In exploring the implications of such experiences for formal education O'Hear and Sefton-Green suggest that it is not appropriate to make art-school more like the forum, rather the: 'forum and Art-School *together* provide the right kind of learning infrastructure' (p.122 emphasis added). Their consideration of the identity work in such environments further highlights the need to continue to pay attention to the role of identity in conventional learning situations.

The exploration of technologically mediated creative collaborations continues in Chapter 10. Here Maarten De Laat and Vic Lally discuss how researchers collaborate creatively to write an academic paper using the Internet and they attempt to characterise, through the analysis of computer-archive data from their own joint work, what a creative collaboration 'looks like'. Their work suggests that the analysis of software archives has the potential to develop our understanding of such collaborative creativity, particularly by opening up possibilities for analysing collaborative interactions and relationships as they develop over time (the need to study collaboration over the long-term was highlighted earlier in the volume by Moran and John-Steiner). The authors also point to the range of software tools available for resourcing collaborations at a distance, considering how these tools are flexibly deployed to resource creative collaboration.

The work reported in Chapters 9 and 10 clearly highlights that the computer is an artefact which is not only capable of supporting collaborative creative endeavour, but also has the potential to uniquely transform the way in which such collaborative activity is organised. It thus has the potential to re-organise the social processes of collaborators' collective activity and this is one of the reasons why the central role of the computer in framing and mediating joint activity needs to be conceptualised. Teresa Dillon's work (Chapter 11), which explores how young people create music together using the computer software *Dance eJay*, highlights the crucial role that this software plays in 'scaffolding' the interactions between collaborators. Dillon describes *eJay* as having a strong visual interface, which provided a distinctive scaffold for novice partners since they could see the available samples easily and watch their compositions unfold. The nature of this visual interface is such that it signalled powerfully possible ways of interacting with the software, thereby framing the young people's interpretation of the task they had been set. Note also that the availability of such software means that a degree of technical proficiency with a musical instrument is no longer a pre-requisite for participation in creative musical collaborations (cf., the contributions from Wirtanen & Littleton and Seddon), potentially opening up new opportunities for those who might not otherwise have the skills to participate in collective music-making.

Chapters 12 and 13 (by Jane Henry and Rosalind Searle respectively) extend the discussion of collaborative creativity by considering collaborations in organisational settings. Drawing on a wide range of research studies, conducted in diverse contexts, the authors consider the ways in which organisations have attempted to facilitate, develop and sustain creativity and innovation. Both contributions emphasise how within organisational literature there has been a shift away from considering creativity solely in terms of a quality that emanates from an individual, towards the adoption of approaches focused on facilitating and promoting productive interaction between people. The permeability of organisational boundaries and the value of collaboration *across* organisations are also highlighted. That said, Henry's contribution reminds us of the dangers of over-generalising our conceptions of collaborative creativity from research undertaken in Western contexts. The Western cultural frame for creativity, which privileges individual innovation: 'does not seem to be shared by those in more collaborative cultures. Countries like Japan have an excellent record of continuous improvement in their products and processes, perhaps because they recognise that creativity is very much about collaboration over time and not just breakthroughs by a few individuals' (p.170). This reminds us that descriptions of creative processes and practices in one cultural context should not, and cannot, become prescriptions for promoting creativity in another. Searle also points to the need for a holistic approach to promoting innovation and creativity in teams suggesting that such efforts are: 'likely to be rewarded not just with economic growth, but also improved job-satisfaction and well-being amongst team members' (p.185).

The final contribution, from Tim Sharp and Jim Lutz invites us to think outside the (music) box and consider the multiplicity of ways in which one can conceptualise collaborative relationships, using the example of music and architecture. A central tenet of Sharp and Lutz's argument is that: 'the collaboration of sound and space contributes significantly to experienced meaning as musical performance meets architectural structure' (p.189). Building on a theme raised earlier in the volume regarding the necessity of constructing a shared discourse to mediate interdisciplinary collaborations, Sharp and Lutz suggest that whilst at first sight the disciplines of architecture and music may appear different, they are in fact allied arts and that correspondences exist at a fundamental level with notions such as structure, rhythm, harmony/dissonance and time providing a common language facilitating collaboration. In support of this thesis three historical accounts of collaborations between architects and musicians with synergistic results are offered in which, Sharp and Lutz argue: 'sound and space inform one another through a vocabulary shared by musician and designer' (p.196). It is this collaboration of sound and space which produces a type of 'chamber music' where: 'the real experience of the sounds and meaning of the music is captured within all of the participating elements of the "performance chamber"' (p.202).

REFERENCES

Gardner, H. (1993). *Creating minds*. New York: Basic Books.

John-Steiner, V. (2000). *Creative collaboration*. New York: Oxford University Press.

Johnson, D.W. & Johnson, F.P. (1994). *Joining together: Group theory and group skills*. London: Allyn & Bacon.

Josselson, R. (1996). *Revising herself: The story of women's identity from college to midlife*. New York: Oxford University Press.

Montuori, A. & Purser, R.E. (1999). *Social creativity* Vol. 1. Cresskill, NJ: Hampton Press.

Sawyer, R.K. (2001). *Creating conversations: Improvisation in everyday discourse*. Cresskill, NJ: Hampton Press.

Sawyer, R.K. (2004). *Group creativity: Music, theatre, collaboration*. Mahwah, NJ: Lawrence Erlbaum Associates.

Sawyer, R.K., John-Steiner, V., Moran, S., Sternberg, R.J., Feldman, D.H., Nakamura, J. & Csikszentmihalyi, M. (2003). *Creativity and development*. New York: Oxford University Press.

Schrage, M. (1990). *Shared minds: The new technologies of collaboration*. New York: Random House.

Part I
Identity, Affect and Motivation

2
How Collaboration in Creative Work Impacts Identity and Motivation

Seana Moran and Vera John-Steiner

Being roped together on a mountaintop, recalled Cubist painter Georges Braque. Finely tuned instruments resonating into a singular harmonic symphony, reflected feminist psychologist Carol Gilligan. Such metaphors are how these well-known creators described the experiences of their long-term collaborations that led to creative breakthroughs.

Although collaboration, cooperation, social interaction and working together are used nearly interchangeably as psychologists increasingly explore the social factors in human development, cognition, and behaviour (e.g., Abra, 1994; Rogoff, 1990), we hold collaboration to a higher standard. Collaboration is an 'affair of the mind' (John-Steiner, 2000). It is a fundamentally different kind of interaction from the simple exchanges that occur among work acquaintances (Schrage, 1990). Social interaction involves two or more people talking or in exchange, cooperation adds the constraint of shared purpose, and working together often provides coordination of effort. But collaboration involves an intricate blending of skills, temperaments, effort and sometimes personalities to realise a shared vision of something new and useful.

This chapter explores how collaboration in creative work affects and is affected by identity and motivation, which have been particularly understudied in our individual, cognitive-focused age. Creative work involves the transformation of a domain's raw materials (e.g., paint and canvas) into something qualitatively novel yet appropriate (Amabile, 1996). At its most influential, creativity actually changes the way people conceive the domain: following Einstein, people thought about space and time differently (Gardner, 1993). Identity involves how people form themselves through what activities and roles they choose to 'make their own'. Motivation focuses on the conditions and forces that affect how people direct their energy and resources toward a purpose. How does creative collaboration impact identity and motivation?

Recently, collaboration has been of considerable interest to researchers in extending our understanding of creativity beyond the individual. How is it that 'two heads are better than one'? To a certain extent, all creativity is collaborative in that it draws from the ideas and products of past creators as raw materials, and depends on publications, audiences, collectors, etc. to propagate the new idea (Abra, 1994; Bakhtin, 1982; Becker, 1982; Csikszentmihalyi, 1996). In this discussion we focus on real-time collaborations between living people who depend on each other and contribute jointly to a common goal of transforming their domain, which neither could do alone.

Studies of creative collaboration use both experimental/observational and case study methodologies. Experiments place children or adults into teams to improvise, solve a problem, or generate ideas to be completed in one or two short sessions (Abra & Abra, 1999; Amabile, 1996; Granott, 1993; Kabanoff & O'Brien, 1979; Purser & Montuori, 1999; Rogoff, 1990; Sawyer, 1992, 1997). These studies have helped determine when individuals versus when groups produce more creative results as well as the dynamics of interaction that impact creative output (see Brophy, 1998 for review). However, neither interactions over longer time frames nor emotional aspects of collaboration, both which support the emergence of trust and synergy, have been explored thoroughly.

Case studies (Chadwick & Courtivron, 1996; John-Steiner, 1997, 2000) help bring the hidden mental processes of well-known creative collaborations into the public realm through actions, dialogues, use of tools, and works-in-progress (Engeström, 1987; Granott, 1993; Moran & John-Steiner, 2003). While they outline the contours of collaboration over time, they often are limited by collaborators' lack of conscious awareness regarding some of the dynamics of collaboration, and by retrospective bias as collaborators may not have kept detailed notes while their ideas were in development.

Our approach emphasises the border-crossing nature of both creativity – in terms of stepping beyond the bounds of the known – and collaboration – in terms of a permeable boundary between individuals in terms of perspective, purpose, and energy. We examine identity and motivation in light of three characteristics of collaboration:

- *Complementarity*. Collaborators are not homogeneous people, but rather individuals with different perspectives, expertise, conceptualisations, working methods, temperaments, resources, needs, and talents (John-Steiner, 1997; John-Steiner et al., 1998). The interaction of these differences forms the foundation for the dynamics of collaboration to unfold.
- *Tension*. Collaboration's goal is not to reach consensus, as such agreement does not lead to learning or challenge (Johnston & Thomas, 1997). Not only are tensions between vulnerability and security, doing and getting done, jumping in and stepping back, and collaborators' personal differences not eliminated, but preferably they are taken advantage of as a mechanism for bringing out latent opportunities of the domain. As Francis Crick, co-discoverer of DNA, quipped, 'Politeness…is the poison of all good collaboration' (quoted in Abra, 1994, p.8). This opportunity is especially apparent when partnerships cross cultural boundaries, as Picasso the Spaniard collaborated with Braque the Frenchman, or Plath the American with Hughes the Englishman. Collaboration is not absence of tension, but fruitful cultivation of tension.
- *Emergence*. Collaboration can lead to outcomes that could not be predicted solely from the additive power of people working as a group

(Sawyer, 2003). As people become more interdependent across the stages of the creative process (e.g., problem finding vs. problem solving vs. elaboration; Getzels & Csikszentmihalyi, 1976; Wallas, 1926) and the lifespan of the collaborative relationship (e.g., the first vs. fifth project), the relationship and product can qualitatively change. Schrage (1990) distinguished conceptual collaboration in framing a problem and technical collaboration in problem representation and solution. Granott (1993) described nine types of collaboration based on differences in collaborator expertise, activity synchronisation, and attention allocation. John-Steiner (2000) categorised collaboration based on roles, working methods, and levels of commitment.

We focus on two types of collaborations – complementary, common among scientists and academics, and integrated, most likely to be found in literature and the arts. To illustrate, we use well-known, successful creative collaborations that have demonstrated domain transformation.

COLLABORATION AND IDENTITY

'Who am I?' is the basic question of identity, which has been studied along three lines of thought. Sociologists, such as Goffman (1959) and Bourdieu (1993), represent identity as what one's self presents to others based on roles and public actions within social structural relations. Identity provides social positioning. Psychologists, such as Erikson (1968) and Marcia (1966), focus on the developmental trajectory of a person, with identity representing the unification of elements of the self from the past, present, and anticipated future within cultural constraints (Wenger, 1998). Identity provides continuity of self over time. Anthropologists and feminist researchers, such as Holland et al. (1998) and Goldberger et al. (1996), explore the multiplicity of context-dependent identities people have as they negotiate both social position and self-meaning in their worlds. Thus, identity comprises the flexible construction and reconstruction of both productive social relations and psychological integrity.

Identities continue to develop throughout life (Pulkkinen & Kokko, 2000) and are significantly affected by culture (Markus & Kitayama, 1991) and social power structures (Goldberger et al., 1996; Jordan et al., 1991) – a process that is even more pronounced for individuals who are marginalised. If one's experiences are unusual for the dominant culture, marginalisation can be harnessed for creative purposes, particularly for those pioneers willing to be 'firsts' (Gardner, 1993; Helson, 1985, 1990; Hurtado, 1996; Richie et al., 1997). Helson's (1990; Helson & Pais, 2000) longitudinal research of women and Richie et al.'s (1997) study of African-American women show how identity and creative processes co-develop. In the past, creativity scholars (e.g., Gruber, 1974) focused mostly on how creators externalise their cognitive processes into creative products or artifacts. They failed to emphasise how the creative process leads also to the *internal* construction of identity, as Josselson (1996) suggests: 'Identity is the ultimate act of creativity – it is what we make of ourselves' (p.27).

How does collaboration aid this reciprocal creativity-identity process? In many studies, identity is framed as a predictor variable of creative problem solving. Identity can provide some of the raw materials from which the collaborative work grows. Relationships require a certain stability for participants to anticipate preferences and acts and to find common ground: if people act erratically, it is difficult to know and work with them. For example, as Sylvia Plath's mental illness led her marriage to break up and her identity to unravel, her husband Ted Hughes found it increasingly difficult to understand or work with her despite their ongoing love of poetry (John-Steiner, 2000).

Collaborations do not start from scratch: during their formative years, the collaborators' initial identities provide the foundation for both the relationship and the creative product. Marie Curie's negotiator personality and Pierre Curie's attention to details and scientific reputation underpinned their scientific collaboration. Will Durant's contemplation and writing experience and Ariel Durant's youthful bohemianism framed their co-authorship of the multi-volume *The Story of Civilization* (John-Steiner, 2000). The complementarity of differences in identity sets the stage for the developmental trajectory of the creative endeavour.

Collaborators' identities can remain distinct over the course of the collaboration, contributing their particular strengths and taking the lead at different stages, as tends to occur in complementary collaborations: one writer might be stronger in action and the other in emotional insights, as writers Henry Miller and Anaïs Nin were. Or identities can temporarily merge, as in highly intense integrated collaborations: Picasso and Braque both describe how they effaced their personalities, signed their paintings on the back, and became fused with each other's thinking and painting during Cubism's birth (John-Steiner, 2000). Similarly, many collaborators, such as Jean-Paul Sartre and Simone de Beauvoir, talk about how they 'share a brain', finish each others' sentences, and often know what their partner will say before it's articulated (John-Steiner, 2000). Their identities have comingled.

Over time, creative collaboration can become a vehicle for identity development, allowing different aspects of identities to come to the fore, differentiate from, and integrate with other emergent identities (Bateson, 1990; Goldberger et al., 1996; Holland et al., 1998). From a Vygotskian perspective, creativity not only transforms objective materials into creative products, it also transforms the creator (Helson & Pais, 2000; Moran & John-Steiner, 2003): 'In fulfilling the activity, the subjects also change and develop themselves. The transforming and purposeful character of activity allows the subject to step beyond the frames of a given situation and to see it in a wider historical and societal context. It makes it possible for the subject to find means that go beyond the possibilities given' (Engeström et al., 1999, p.39). In particular, collaboration affects a creator's identity through connection, reflection, flexibility, and stability.

The interpersonal *connection* creates an identity that is bigger than both individuals. It provides a 'figured world' (Holland et al., 1998) or meaning-making system that is intersubjectively constructed between collaborators. In effect, there are at least three 'players': each collaborator and the relationship itself, born from true empathy or shared subjectivity (Clinchy, 1996; Jordan, 1991). When the collaboration breaks up, the shared identity is lost; collaborators grieve for the loss of part of their larger selves. People from marginal groups – such as women, people of colour, and immigrants – are much more likely than people in the dominant culture to recognise this larger-than-self identity as supportive of growth and creative success (Goldberger et al., 1996; Richie et al., 1997). Sometimes, collaboration can 'effervesce' (Durkheim, 1912) into a creative movement, bringing a formerly subjugated group identity into a more influential position within the dominant culture, as happened with African-American artists in the Harlem Renaissance of the 1920s (Wintz, 1996).

Creative collaborators can become more *reflective* by serving as 'revealing mirrors' to each other (John-Steiner, 2000). Because collaborators must communicate with each other, collaborators' inner speech – their condensed stream of thought that generates creative associations – must be shared. Collaboration provides a zone of proximal development (Vygotsky, 1978) for collaborators to learn about their own hidden assumptions and unexamined beliefs (Polanyi, 1966). For example, the researchers on psychologist Carol Gilligan's team examining girls' development became more reflective about their subjects and also discovered, at both the intellectual and the emotional level, much about themselves from their work interactions with the girls (John-Steiner, 2000). Thus, awareness of contrasting assumptions in the course of collaboration can breed deeper understanding of both the other person and oneself (Johnston & Thomas, 1997).

Collaboration also increases mental, and sometimes social, *flexibility*. Collaborators come to the partnership with a specific set of sensitivities – for example, to rhythm in language, connotative meanings, or character contours for writers (John-Steiner, 1997). The complementarity of these sensitivities can open a shared space for collaborators to experience writing in a new way. This process often happens in advertising as visual-based designers and verbal-oriented writers collaborate (Schrage, 1990). By sharing in each others' expertise and experience, the boundaries of their identities expand (John-Steiner, 2000). Such flexibility also extends to overcoming institutionalised social constraints: scientist Marie Curie as well as authors Ariel Durant and Nan Lyon moved beyond the confines of the caretaker and helpmate feminine roles by collaborating with their husbands (John-Steiner, 2000). By providing an 'ally' for their 'deviant' work opportunity (Asch, 1956; Kiesler et al., 1966), collaboration kept these women from foreclosing too quickly into a normative identity. Instead, they followed their hearts and minds toward creative achievement.

Furthermore, by working with others, individuals can become more truly themselves, *stabilising* their own developing sensitivities, interests, and preferences (John-Steiner, 2000). As Vygotsky theorised, people become more individualised through close social interaction (Moran & John-Steiner, 2003). Collaboration gives people the safe foundation and encouragement to share themselves with others. Henry Miller's encouragement to publish her personal diaries made Anaïs Nin more willing to take risks. The more differentiated her identity became, the more capable she grew in her contribution, which helped transform literature and the studies of women.

Also regarding stability, collaboration can provide a safety net against mental breakdown or identity diffusion. Creators often are in danger of and sometimes succumb to mental illness as they struggle to break the boundaries of their current knowledge (Jamison, 1989; Rothenberg, 1990): 'These are the times that try the mettle of the creator. No longer do the conventional symbol systems suffice; the creator must begin, at first largely in isolation, to work out a new, more adequate form of symbolic expression...' (Gardner, 1993, p.34). At least one sympathetic person seems necessary for the person to endure the tribulations of the creative process: Freud had his friend Wilhelm Fliess, Einstein had his friend Marcel Grossmann (Gardner, 1993; John-Steiner, 2000).

Although support may come from various sources (e.g., family, friends, co-workers), collaborative support emphasises that individuals are not alone in their struggle to create. Their collaborators not only recognise but also accept *and co-participate in* the uncertainty, ambiguity, and challenge of the creative path. Collaboration can fill the gap usually taken up by established, institutionalised structures and practices to relieve anxieties inherent in uncertain situations (Jaques, 1955). It can temper the rigidification of identifying commitments that happens to many people as they become locked into jobs, ideas, or conventional work methods. Collaboration keeps minds and hearts and identities supple, open to wider possibilities. Therefore, it provides emotional scaffolding as well as intellectual scaffolding for creative work (John-Steiner, 2000). It sets up a safe space to hear criticism, explore ideas that most of the field would consider eccentric, receive encouragement when work is not going well, and both accept one's personal limitations yet move beyond them with the help of the other.

COLLABORATION AND MOTIVATION

'Why am I doing this?' is the basic question of motivation, which has been researched primarily in three ways. Through experimental manipulation, the behaviourists focused on how external rewards, punishments, incentives, or directives affect the effort people invest in a task, including creative work (Skinner, 1953). The psychoanalysts (Freud, 1958) and drive theorists (McClelland, 1967) emphasised how people's effort stemmed from an unmet need: creators make their innermost fantasies public via creative products to earn the admiration of others or as a drive for achievement. More recent cognitive research has conceptualised motivation in terms of self-regulation that transforms social values into personal values so that the locus of effort comes from inside the person (Ryan & Deci, 2000). As with identity, motivation has mostly been considered a predictor or control variable for studies of collaboration: how much does a person's motivation level contribute to collaborative effectiveness? Several studies show that people who focus on a task they love (Amabile, 1996) and strive for continuous improvement (Dweck, 2000) tend to perform better in creative or other tasks.

Although motivation often is considered an individual attribute, several studies have examined how working in groups affects task motivation and product creativity. Most of this research concludes that working alone produces higher motivation and more creative products. Performance in groups tends to peak at the level of the least motivated or proficient rather than rise above the separate contributions of the individuals (Abra & Abra, 1999; Paulus, 1999; Purser & Montuori, 1999). However, these studies bring together virtual strangers for a very short time to work on problems not necessarily within the participants' scope of expertise. Thus, the groups studied did not satisfy the three characteristics of true collaboration described above – complementarity, tension, and emergence – that occur in real-life creative collaborations. For this reason, we focus on motivation dynamics that appear in actual, well-known collaborations. These include: multiplying motivational energy resources available for creative work; widening the scope of intrinsic motivation; and generating a new type of motivation stemming from the relationship itself.

Collaborators can build on each others' excitement as well as each others' ideas in a *multiplicative* way. Collaboration not only doubles energy resources by putting together two or more people's efforts toward a shared goal, but also the synergies of collaboration create a further reserve of energy. Collaboration can provide a kind of 'insurance policy' against quitting as it smoothes the ups and downs of the creative process. Psychologist Howard Gruber recalls that, had he or his wife, Doris Wallace, been working alone on their book, difficult passages probably would have been discarded rather than worked through toward further insight. He explains, 'By spreading the risk, [collaboration] encourages you to take more chances' (John-Steiner, 2000, p.19).

Abra and Abra (1999) suggest that collaboration bolsters 'unstable self-discipline' because one becomes attached and responsible to the other collaborator as well as the work. Such dual orientation lessens the loneliness of creative work and reduces the fears of going against field norms: as Sartre once said to de Beauvoir, 'You gave me a confidence in myself that I shouldn't have had alone' (John-Steiner, 2000, p.15). Motivational energy comes both from challenge, as with Bohr's love to be contradicted by colleagues to propel him to go deeper into a problem, and from confirmation that one's work is interesting to another person. Both can bolster confidence, as occurred between the choreographer Suki John and director Bill Conte (John-Steiner, 2000). Collaboration increases the chances that both collaborators reach the goal: as one moves forward, so do they both (Paulus, 1999).

In addition, collaboration may *widen the scope of intrinsic motivation*, which Amabile (1996) showed correlates with creative performance. Intrinsic motivation derives from a person's affinity for the particular aspects and properties of the task – for love of the work itself. Compared to extrinsic motivation as a response to rewards and evaluation, intrinsic motivation has an internal, emotional source and often seems to be stronger in solitary pursuits (Amabile, 1996; Csikszentmihalyi, 1996; Ryan & Deci, 2000). But intrinsic motivation is fragile: if both extrinsic and intrinsic motivation are present in a situation, people tend to attribute their engagement to extrinsic sources (Amabile, 1996).

Another person being present can seem to affect one's balance of intrinsic and extrinsic motivation, and a person's behaviour will tend toward conformity (Simonton, 1994). As a result, some scholars suggest that collaboration would bring extrinsic motivation to the fore as partners influence and critique each others' efforts (Abra, 1994).

Creative collaborators, however, usually describe themselves as intrinsically motivated (John-Steiner, 2000). Although the collaborator is present during creative work periods, collaboration seems to allow development of a joint intrinsic motivation because of the shared sense of purpose (Abra & Abra, 1999). Collaborators can provide difficult criticism to their partners without being perceived as controlling. For example, Ivan and Nan Lyons, authors of the popular novel, *Someone is Killing the Great Chefs of Europe*, sometimes had to walk away from the work and go for a drive to deflate the tension criticism brings. Neither these collaborators, nor others John-Steiner (2000) interviewed, felt their partners were trying to control them. Control of the project came from the integrity of the project itself – an intrinsic motivator.

Not only is intrinsic motivation widened in collaboration, but intrinsic and extrinsic motivators can cooperate rather than compete with each other. Most studies have shown that extrinsic motivators, especially expectation of evaluation, tend to reduce the power of intrinsic motivation not only during the current situation but also later in similar situations (Amabile, 1996). But shared passion and wanting to not let each other down can lead toward creative results; in this way, criticism stimulates rather than detracts from creative performance. Ryan and Deci (2000) suggest that when communication and feedback improve feelings of competence, they can enhance intrinsic motivation as long as such communications do not threaten the other's sense of autonomy or internal volition. They must affirm and confirm the other (Clinchy, 1996). This emotional connection can also affect motivation in terms of collaborator support when the current aspect of the work is not intrinsically interesting to the other collaborator. Affection can bolster rather than reduce intrinsic motivation and help keep the less intrinsically motivated collaborator engaged in the project.

Finally, we propose that collaboration itself generates its own kind of motivation which we refer to as *connective motivation*. Whereas both intrinsic and extrinsic motivation focus on the outcome of the partnership – the energy behind reaching a goal or creating a product – connected motivation emphasises the partnership process itself. As people work together, the interaction can provide them with a mutually satisfying experience akin to friendship and love. Although Henry Miller and Anaïs Nin did not co-write a common book, their support of each other's individual work and their enjoyment of their relationship were crucial to their collaboration (Nin, 1986). In this sense, identity and motivation are related: motivation focuses on the connection with the other person; it is not limited to the goal.

This connected motivation may be more apparent in non-Western cultures and among women in Western culture. Women's interdependent ways of working contribute to a collaborative process in which both connectedness and achievement sustain their motivation (John-Steiner, 2000; Richie et al., 1997). In addition, cultural researchers show how people from societies where identities are construed more interdependently, as in China, Japan or Africa, are motivated less from the need for self-expression than from responsiveness to others, empathy, and social dynamics (Iyengar & Lepper, 1999; Markus & Kitayama, 1991). Motivation is less contingent on task and more on relationship. Even Ryan and Deci's (2000) theory admits that people are most motivated in situations of mutuality not isolation, and several researchers address how autonomy is not the absence of relationship but a more differentiated-yet-integrated way of emotionally connecting to others (Goldberger et al., 1996; Helson, 1985; Jordan et al., 1991; John-Steiner, 2000; Moran & John-Steiner, 2003). Collaboration, in summary, can both stabilise and maximise the energies that partners bring to their projects. Creators' love for the work and for each other moderate the inherent difficulties that can occur when working together.

CHALLENGES OF WORKING TOGETHER

If collaboration can provide so many benefits to creative work, why has the literature been so critical of its potential? Several researchers point out the pitfalls of working with others: lower performance (Brophy, 1998); anxiety, stress and control issues (Pritzker & Runco, 1997); conformity of thought (Janis, 1972); imbalance of the workload (Jackson & Padgett, 1982); personality clashes (Nolan, 1978), and competition (Johnson & Johnson, 1989). Potential endogenous problems with collaboration revolve around four core issues:

- *Impatience.* Collaboration takes a lot of time. In addition to the work itself, time and effort must also be directed to the relationship, which is almost like an additional partner. If people see this time and effort as a cost rather than an investment, problems are more likely to arise that can short-circuit the collaborative process, as illustrated in the final days of the 'Group Theater' (John-Steiner, 2000). Such impatience is more troublesome in close, integrated collaborations in which partners have a large and complex vision. The intensity of the challenge can result in a premature dissolution of the partnership. As a result, integrated collaborations are more vulnerable than complementary ones that have more space between the partners (Bennis & Biederman, 1997; John-Steiner, 2000).
- *Ownership.* Identification with one's work is a powerful motivator in intellectual and artistic work. But in collaboration, the desire for owning one's efforts can become a source of conflict when apportioning credit. When individuals are not fully committed to their joint efforts, resentment and possibly sabotage can occur (Abra, 1994; Pritzker & Runco, 1997). Even when everyone agrees to joint ownership, pragmatic concerns can arise due to conventions of the field, such as in academia where listing author names implies differential contribution to the article. Belenky and her co-writers (1986) recognised this tension in their book's preface: 'this book is not separated into parts that we wish to attribute to one or the

other of us...the book as a whole is the product of our joint efforts and interchange of ideas' (p. xxv). They chose to list their names alphabetically. In a later jointly authored work, they switched the order to reflect the weight of their individual contributions (Goldberger et al., 1996).

- *Conflict*. In a lot of teams, conflict is considered something to be avoided (Pritzker & Runco, 1997). Groups that emphasise consensus rather than working on an effective synthesis of multiple perspectives tend to depress creativity. But in effective collaborations, conflict is another tool to deepen understanding (Piaget, 1932). It wards against groupthink (Janis, 1972) and competition as collaborators work out their differences. The intense dance partnership of Martha Graham and Erick Hawkins is an example of a relationship where conflict was not addressed and the partnership could not survive the sexual, professional, and creative competition that seethed below the surface (John-Steiner, 2000).

- *Unfriendliness*. There is a general notion that people who work together should like each other. Studies with children show that friends produce better musical compositions than non-friends, however the effects may dissipate with age (MacDonald et al., 2002; Miell & MacDonald, 2000). These findings highlight the importance of dialogue and trust in more effectively settling disagreements. However, not all collaborators need to be friends to produce great works. For example, the musical composition team Rodgers and Hammerstein suggests that in some situations the power of the work can override the lack of friendship ties (Nolan, 1978; Rodgers, 1975).

What do these influences mean for collaborators' identities and motivation? Identity negotiation often concerns a balance of agency (expressing oneself) and communality (appropriating from others) (McAdams, 1993). Identity and motivation crises can revolve around too much agency or too much communality within collaborations. Too much agency involves collaborators being too self-absorbed, heightening their own achievement and power at the expense of others (Pritzker & Runco, 1997). Too much communality involves fusion or overidentification with one's partner that can lead to psychological suffocation by either collaborator. When either of these extremes occurs, partners may feel that the collaboration has been compromised and either lose motivation or quit. What is ideal seems to be autonomy (Abra, 1994; Harrington, 1990), which is the bringing of a flexible self into partnership that neither overpowers nor is overpowered by the other. Each creator contributes a unique perspective to the social arena of collaboration (Gruber, 1998).

Such agency and communality do not occur in a vacuum. Many collaborative problems in the literature may be the result less of endogenous than of exogenous problems or interference from external sources, such as deadlines, social customs, or directives from funders. Collaborators lose their identification with and commitment to their work and partners when they do not have the power and control to choose the purpose and methods of their work (Pritzker &

Runco, 1997). Psychological freedom and a sense of control are key moderators of collaborative success.

We argue that the benefits of effective collaboration and the challenges of flawed collaboration point to two critical underlying factors for creative work: sharing and trust. One notion of sharing focuses on a division of labour in which each participant is protected from carrying the whole burden. But another notion of sharing is akin to 'joint tenancy', as when two people get married or sign a lease together. In this case, each partner is responsible for 100 per cent of the benefits, debt, and risk of the venture. If one person does not carry through, the other person is liable for the entirety. This second notion is how we use sharing in relation to collaboration. Collaboration is an open-ended process in which sharing requires flexible integration of individual effort. This flexibility is especially relevant to creative work where partners don't know in advance what the final product will be (Belenky et al., 1986).

Trust consists of respect for another person's different perspective, an expectation of good will, and confidence in the other's ability to contribute to the common purpose (Burke & Stets, 1999; Dooley & Fryxell, 1999). Trust is the foundation for collaboration that makes possible the development of true sharing, openly negotiated conflict, and a long-term relationship despite the uncertainties and risks. It sets up conditions for cooperation and higher performance to occur (Dirks & Ferrin, 2001) by creating a comfortable shared social space and understandings (Johnson & Johnson, 1989; Pritzker & Runco, 1997; Rogoff, 1990). Trust often develops into friendships, which may explain why friends tend to collaborate better. It moderates conflict, turning destructive tension into constructive controversy by forming a type of mutual regulation that creates bridges between different perspectives (Johnson & Johnson, 1989). Without trust, tension becomes an impassable chasm so that true collaboration cannot emerge, and the participants are left with conflict and unrealised dreams.

DIRECTIONS FOR FUTURE RESEARCH

Collaboration creates an environment where the partners can push the boundaries of themselves and integrate their differing personal characteristics. Interactions among partners create new properties that build on each other toward creative outcomes, identities, and relational possibilities. Identity and motivation – both what the collaborators come into the collaboration with and what develops from the collaboration itself – keep the work process flexible, which can lead both to personal transformation and to domain transformation.

In complementary collaborations, the partners remain distinct while they work together; they orbit around each other and their shared purpose. Their identities do not fuse but do become defined in terms of or in relation to each other (Harding, 1996). Their motivation results from what each individually contributes as well as the force of their collaborative interaction. In integrative collaborations, the two collaborators temporarily become almost a single entity. The partnership can be all consuming as the collaborators do not perceive themselves as whole without the other. They share an identity and motivational base. Sometimes the pressure can become too intense or other life events can interfere, which results in the collaboration collapsing.

More research remains to be done to understand how identities and motivations develop over the course of a collaboration. We have suggested dimensions to explore including identity connection, reflection, flexibility, and intensity; the dynamics of intrinsic, extrinsic, and connected motivations; and sharing and trust. As yet, we understand little about how such dimensions function. Our work has focused on documented collaborations in the middle of their lifespans – after they have been operating for a while among people who are already successful in their fields. It is particularly difficult though important also to study a collaboration from its inception. In addition, more data are needed on the collaborators themselves and their decisions regarding the continuity of their work together. Another critical area requiring further study involves changes in the collaborative process itself and not just on its end products. The challenge for future researchers will be to come together from different fields and work as collaborators themselves. They may find they become the best subjects for their own studies. Endeavours of this kind will expand our knowledge and provide us with deeper insights into the social and personal practices of dynamic societies.

REFERENCES

Abra, J. (1994). 'Collaboration in creative work: An initiative for investigation'. *Creativity Research Journal, 7* (1), 1–20.

Abra, J. & Abra, G. (1999). 'Collaboration and competition'. In M.A. Runco & S.R. Pritzker (eds), *Encyclopedia of creativity* (pp.283–293). San Diego: Academic Press.

Amabile, T. (1996). *Creativity in context.* Boulder, CO: Westview Press.

Asch, S.E. (1956). 'Studies of independence and conformity: A minority of one against a unanimous majority'. *Psychological Monographs, 70*, 416.

Bakhtin, M.M. (1982). *The dialogic imagination.* Austin: University of Texas Press.

Bateson, M.C. (1990). *Composing a life.* New York: Plume/Penguin.

Becker, H. (1982). *Art worlds.* Berkeley: University of California Press.

Belenky, M.F., Clinchy, B.M., Goldberger, N.R. & Tarule, J.M. (1986). *Women's ways of knowing.* New York: Basic Books.

Bennis, W. & Biederman, P.W. (1997). *Organizing genius: The secrets of creative collaboration.* Reading, MA: Addison-Wesley.

Bourdieu, P. (1993). *The field of cultural production.* New York: Columbia University Press.

Brophy, D.R. (1998). 'Understanding, measuring, and enhancing collective creative problem-solving efforts'. *Creativity Research Journal, 11* (3), 199–229.

Burke, P.J. & Stets, J.E. (1999). 'Trust and commitment through self-verification'. *Social Psychology Quarterly, 62* (4), 347–360.

Chadwick, W. & Courtivron, I.D. (eds). (1996). *Significant others: Creativity and intimate partnership.* London: Thames & Hudson.

Clinchy, B.M. (1996). 'Connected and separate knowing: Toward a marriage of two minds'. In N. Goldberger, J. Tarule, B. Clinchy & M. Belenky, *Knowledge, difference, and power: Essays inspired by 'Women's Ways of Knowing'* (pp.205–247). New York: Basic Books.

Csikszentmihalyi, M. (1996). *Creativity: Flow and the psychology of discovery and invention.* New York: HarperCollins.

Dirks, K.T. & Ferrin, D.L. (2001). 'The role of trust in organizational settings'. *Organization Science, 12* (4), 450–467.

Dooley, R.S. & Fryxell, G.E. (1999). 'Attaining decision quality and commitment from dissent: The moderating effects of loyalty and competence in strategic decision-making teams'. *Academy of Management Journal, 42* (4), 389–402.

Durkheim, E. (1912/1965). *The elementary forms of the religious life* (J.W. Swain, trans.). New York: Free Press. (Original work published 1912.)

Dweck, C.S. (2000). *Self-theories*. Philadelphia: Taylor & Francis.

Engeström, Y. (1987). *Learning by expanding: An activity-theoretical approach to developmental research*. Helsinki: Orienta-Konsultit Oy.

Engeström, Y., Miettinen, R. & Punamaki, R-L. (1999). *Perspectives on activity theory*. Cambridge: Cambridge University Press.

Erikson, E. (1968). *Identity: Youth and crisis*. New York: Norton.

Freud, S. (1958). *Creativity and the unconscious* (edited by B. Nelson). New York: Harper & Row.

Gardner, H. (1993). *Creating minds*. New York: Basic Books.

Getzels, J. & Csikszentmihalyi, M. (1976). *The creative vision*. New York: Wiley.

Goffman, E. (1959). *The presentation of self in everyday life*. Garden City, NJ: Doubleday.

Goldberger, N., Tarule, J., Clinchy, B. & Belenky, M. (1996). *Knowledge, difference, and power: Essays inspired by 'Women's Ways of Knowing'*. New York: Basic Books.

Granott, N. (1993). 'Patterns of interaction in the co-construction of knowledge'. In R.H. Wozniak & K.W. Fischer (eds), *Development in context* (pp.193–207). Hillsdale, NJ: Erlbaum.

Gruber, H.E. (1974). *Darwin on man: A psychological study of scientific creativity*. New York: Dutton.

Gruber, H.E. (1998). 'The social construction of extraordinary selves: Collaboration among unique creative people'. In R.C. Friedman & K.B. Rogers (eds), *Talent in context: Historical and social perspectives on giftedness* (pp.127–147). Washington, DC: American Psychological Association.

Harding, S. (1996). 'Gendered ways of knowing and the "epistemological crisis" of the West'. In N. Goldberger, J. Tarule, B. Clinchy & M. Belenky, *Knowledge, difference, and power: Essays inspired by 'Women's Ways of Knowing'* (pp.431–454). New York: Basic Books.

Harrington, D.M. (1990). 'The ecology of human creativity: A psychological perspective'. In M.A. Runco & R.S. Albert (eds), *Theories of creativity* (pp.143–169). London: Sage.

Helson, R. (1985). 'Lives of women who became autonomous'. *Journal of Personality, 53* (2), 257–285.

Helson, R. (1990). 'Creativity in women: Outer and inner views over time'. In M.A. Runco & R.S. Albert (eds), *Theories of creativity* (pp.46–58). Newbury Park, CA: Sage.

Helson, R. & Pais, J.L. (2000). 'Creative potential, creative achievement, and personal growth'. *Journal of Personality, 68* (1), 1–27.

Holland, D., Lachicotte, Jr., W., Skinner, D. & Cain, C. (1998). *Identity and agency in cultural worlds*. Cambridge, MA: Harvard University Press.

Hurtado, A. (1996). 'Strategic suspensions: Feminists of color theorize the production of knowledge'. In N.R. Goldberger, J.M. Tarule, B.M. Clinchy & M.F. Belenky (eds), *Knowledge, difference, and power: Essays inspired by 'Women's Ways of Knowing'* (pp.372–392). New York: Basic Books.

Iyengar, S.S. & Lepper, M.R. (1999). 'Rethinking the value of choice: A cultural perspective on intrinsic motivation'. *Journal of Personality and Social Psychology, 76* (3), 349–399.

Jackson, J.M., & Padgett, V.R. (1982). 'With a little help from my friend: Social loafing and the Lennon-McCartney songs'. *Personality and Social Psychology Bulletin, 8*, 672–677.

Jamison, K.R. (1989). 'Mood disorders and patterns of creativity in British writers and artists'. *Psychiatry, 52*, 125–134.

Janis, I.L. (1972). *Victims of groupthink*. Boston: Houghton Mifflin.

Jaques, E. (1955). 'Social systems as a defense against persecutory and depressive anxiety'. In M. Klein, P. Heimann & R.E. Money-Kyrle (eds), *New directions in psychoanalysis* (pp.478–498). London: Tavistock.

John-Steiner, V. (1997). *Notebooks of the mind: Explorations in thinking*, 2nd edn. New York: Oxford University Press.

John-Steiner, V. (2000). *Creative collaboration*. New York: Oxford University Press.

John-Steiner, V., Weber, R.J. & Minnis, M. (1998). 'The challenge of studying collaboration'. *American Educational Research Journal, 35* (4), 773–783.

Johnson, D.W. & Johnson, R.T. (1989). *Cooperation and competition: Theory and research*. Edina, MN: Interaction Book Co.

Johnston, M. & Thomas, J.M. (1997). 'Keeping differences in tensions through dialogue'. In M. Johnston with the Educators for Collaborative Change (eds), *Contradictions in collaboration: New thinking on school/university partnerships* (pp.9–19). New York: Teachers College Press.

Jordan, J.V. (1991). 'The meaning of mutuality'. In J. Jordan, A.G. Kaplan, J.B. Miller, I.P. Stiver & J.L. Surrey (eds), *Women's growth in connection: Writings from the Stone Center* (pp.81–96). New York: Guilford Press.

Jordan, J., Kaplan, A.G., Miller, J.B., Stiver, I.P. & Surrey, J.L. (1991). *Women's growth in connection: Writings from the Stone Center*. New York: Guilford Press.

Josselson, R. (1996). *Revising herself: The story of women's identity from college to midlife*. New York: Oxford University Press.

Kabanoff, B. & O'Brien, G.E. (1979). 'Cooperation structure and the relationship of leader and member ability to group performance'. *Journal of Applied Psychology, 64* (5), 526–532.

Kiesler, C.A., Zanna, M. & De Salvo, J. (1966). 'Deviation and conformity: Opinion change as a function of commitment, attraction, and presence of a deviate'. *Journal of Personality and Social Psychology, 3* (4), 458–467.

MacDonald, A.R., Miell, D. & Mitchell, L. (2002). 'An investigation of children's musical collaborations: The effect of friendship and age'. *Psychology of Music, 30* (2), 148–163.

Marcia, J.E. (1966). 'Development and validation of ego identity status'. *Journal of Personality and Social Psychology, 3*, 551–558.

Markus, H.R. & Kitayama, S. (1991). 'Culture and the self: Implications for cognition, emotion, and motivation'. *Psychological Review, 98* (2), 234–253.

McAdams, D.P. (1993). *The stories we live by: Personal myths and the making of the self*. New York: Morrow.

McClelland, D. (1967). *The achieving society*. New York: The Free Press.

Miell, D. & MacDonald, R. (2000). 'Children's creative collaborations: The importance of friendship when working together on a musical composition'. *Social Development, 9* (3), 348–369.

Moran, S. & John-Steiner, V. (2003). 'Creativity in the making: Vygotsky's contemporary contribution to the dialectic of development and creativity'. In R.K. Sawyer et al. (eds), *Creativity and Development* (pp.61–90). New York: Oxford University Press.

Nin, A. (1986). *Henry & June: From the unexpurgated diary of Anais Nin*. San Diego: Harcourt Brace Jovanovich.

Nolan, F. (1978). *The sound of their music: The story of Rodgers & Hammerstein*. New York: Walter & Company.

Paulus, P.B. (1999). 'Group creativity'. In M.A. Runco (ed.), *Encyclopedia of creativity, vol. 1*. New York: Academic Press.

Piaget, J. (1932/1965). *The moral judgment of the child*. Glencoe, IL: Free Press. (Original work published 1932).

Polanyi, M. (1966). *The tacit dimension*. Garden City, NJ: Doubleday.

Pritzker, S.R. & Runco, M.A. (1997). 'The creative decision making process in group situation comedy writing'. In R.K. Sawyer (ed.), *Creativity in performance* (pp.115–142). Norwood, NJ: Ablex.

Pulkkinen, L. & Kokko, K. (2000). 'Identity development in adulthood: A longitudinal study'. *Journal of Research in Personality, 34*, 445–470.

Purser, R.E. & Montuori, A. (eds). (1999). *Social creativity*. Cresskill, NJ: Hampton Press.

Richie, B.S., Fassinger, R.E., Linn, S.G. & Johnson, J., et al. (1997). 'Persistence, connection, and passion: A qualitative study of the career development of highly achieving African American-Black and White women'. *Journal of Counseling Psychology, 44* (2), 133–148.

Rodgers, R. (1975). *Musical stages: An autobiography*. New York: Random House.

Rogoff, B. (1990). *Apprenticeship in thinking*. New York: Oxford University Press.

Rothenberg, A. (1990). *Creativity and madness*. Baltimore: Johns Hopkins University Press.

Ryan, R.M. & Deci, E.L. (2000). 'Self-determination theory and the facilitation of intrinsic motivation, social development, and well-being'. *American Psychologist, 55* (1), 68–78.

Sawyer, R.K. (1992). 'Improvisational creativity: An analysis of jazz performance'. *Creativity Research Journal, 5*, 253–263.

Sawyer, R.K. (1997). 'Improvisational theater: An ethnotheory of conversational practice'. In R.K. Sawyer (ed.), *Creativity in performance*. Greenwich, CT: Ablex.

Sawyer, R.K. (2003). 'Emergence in creativity and development'. In R.K. Sawyer et al., *Creativity and development* (pp.12–60). New York: Oxford University Press.

Schrage, M. (1990). *Shared minds: The new technologies of collaboration*. New York: Random House.

Simonton, D.K. (1994). *Greatness: Who makes history and why*. New York: Guilford Press.

Skinner, B.F. (1953). *The science of behavior*. New York: Macmillan.

Vygotsky, L.S. (1978). *Mind in society: The development of higher psychological processes* (edited by M. Cole, V. John-Steiner, S. Scribner & E. Souberman). Cambridge, MA: Harvard University Press.

Wallas, G. (1926). *The art of thought*. New York: Harcourt.

Wenger, E. (1998). *Communities of practice: Learning, meanings and identity*. New York: Cambridge University Press.

Wintz, C.D. (ed.). (1996). *Remembering the Harlem Renaissance*. New York: Garland Publishing.

3
Collaboration, Conflict and the Musical Identity Work of Solo-Piano Students: The Significance of the Student–Teacher Relationship

Sini Wirtanen and Karen Littleton

INTRODUCTION

A soloist studying classical music needs to learn both a range of technical playing skills and how to interpret key pieces from the canon. Being able to interpret rather than simply reproduce works is one of the hallmarks of being an 'artist' rather than simply someone who is technically competent. The creation of individual interpretations can thus be seen as one of the core competencies for a professional solo pianist. It forms a central aspect of their personal musical identity, as it marks their playing out as distinctive and underpins any potential professional career as a soloist. Interpretation can therefore be seen as an inherently creative process. Whilst creativity has traditionally been characterised in terms of individually-based processes, it is as much a cultural and social event as a psychological one (Csikszentmihalyi, 1996, 1999). Thus the creation of a novel interpretation of a piece from the canon cannot be seen solely as an individual product, but also as a socially and culturally constituted and situated act, in which received wisdom, convention and prior interpretations are mobilised and combined with aspects of personal style and preference to inform judgements relating to individuals' musical products. Conceptualising this form of creativity as a social event thereby establishes a dialectic between the individual soloist and the established practices and cultural traditions of a particular musical community. A skilful solo pianist should be able to connect with particular established musical traditions and conventions, whilst also building on this to offer their unique interpretation of a particular piece. Inherent in the negotiated and often contested processes of interpretation are the similarly complex social processes of identity construction. To interpret creatively in relation to the parameters afforded by culturally mediated and legitimated conventions, is to position oneself as a skilled solo pianist and member of the established classical music community.

In this chapter we use thematic analysis of individual interviews with ten piano-solo students (aged 18–27 years) at the Sibelius Academy, Finland to explore solo pianists' identity work and consider, through an analysis of the students' accounts, how their identity projects are mediated within and in relation to the interpretative work on the canon which they undertake with their teacher. In this chapter identity is conceptualised as something, which is 'relational', being constructed and negotiated within and in relation to specific relationships which are in turn embedded in particular social, cultural and historical contexts. Identity work is assumed to be ongoing (MacDonald & Miell, 2002; O'Neill, 2002) and dynamic, which means that identities are continually changing across diverse relationships and contexts and also over time. Identities are also assumed to be multiple with: 'different relationships between the individual and other people enabling different identities to emerge and take priority at any one time for the person concerned' (MacDonald & Miell, 2002, p.168). Through the analyses presented as part of this chapter we aim to understand some of the processes through which aspiring solo pianists negotiate an emergent identity as soloist. We highlight the significance of an identity 'as soloist' in relation to other ongoing musical identity projects, such as that of 'popular musician' and 'band member', recognising that different communities and contexts often present competing demands and interests which need to be negotiated and reconciled by an individual as part of the processes involved in constructing subjectivities. We suggest that the process of negotiating a solo pianist's identity is a complex event mediated by communication that is socially, culturally, and historically situated (Wertsch, 1991) and where the teacher represents and mediates the voice of an official educational institution and the associated established music culture and traditions (Bakhtin, 1986). Thus, in the analyses of the teacher–student relationship presented here, we aim to be sensitive to the ways in which the particular institutional and cultural context of the Sibelius Academy affords opportunities for and places constraints upon interaction and personal identity work.

Teachers often work in a directive, didactic mode, however, with more advanced students, such as those participating in this research, there is evidence that at times the teacher–student relationship can be truly characterised as a creative collaboration. As Moran and John-Steiner, this volume, note:

> Collaboration is an 'affair of the mind'…Social interaction involves two or more people talking or in exchange, cooperation adds the constraint of shared purpose, and working together often provides coordination of effort. But collaboration involves an intricate blending of skills, temperaments, effort and sometimes personalities to realise a shared vision of something new and useful. (p.11)

In this chapter we suggest that at times both student and teacher work together to create an interpretation that is something qualitatively different from previous interpretations yet still appropriate (Amabile, 1996) and that these processes are implicated in identity work. Our work also highlights the conflicts, and problematic identity positions, which emerge in the creative relationship between teacher and student where visions and insights are not necessarily shared.

Music education and music culture in Finland

Music is one of the most popular hobbies amongst school-age children in Finland and the music school network is comprehensive and effective. In addition, there is the National 'Junior Academy', which is directed at young, exceptionally gifted music students of school age, and is affiliated to the Sibelius Academy, the only music academy in Finland. The Junior Academy accepts students considered by the board to possess the potential for a professional career in music. As well as music schools that educate children aged between 4 and 18 years, there are 14 colleges and institutions of music in Finland. In these institutions education is organised up to Bachelor's degree level.

In Finland the institutionally organised education in classical music can be characterised in terms of what Sloboda (1996) has described as the 'classical conservatoire culture'. Definitions of 'good musicianship' are constituted largely within this culture, where the emphasis is on musical artworks within the formal, classical tradition. The focus is on accuracy, the 'faithful' interpretation of a printed score and 'controlled' performance, rather than improvisation or composition. An essential characteristic is the development of a repertoire of extremely technically difficult compositions and conceptions of mastery are based on the ability to perform works from a small, core set of compositions. Changes within a domain are not adopted unless they are sanctioned by 'gate-keepers' (such as teachers, critics and competition jury members) (see Csikszentmihalyi 1996, 1999). Competitive events are an important part of the conservatoire culture. In competitions performers are compared directly by experts on their ability to perform identical or very similar pieces. These judgements form an important element in the assessment of progress. One route towards membership of the established classical music community is participation in both national and international competitions and master-classes. Summer courses are also 'places to be seen' – students 'get to know and be known' and 'keep in touch' with other musicians and Academy teachers.

The Sibelius Academy

The Sibelius Academy is the only music academy in Finland and one of the biggest in Europe. Internationally, it is held in high esteem as an institute of music. Thus, perhaps not surprisingly, the Sibelius Academy maintains a dominant position within Finnish music culture. In addition to providing the highest level of education in the field of music, Academy staff and students regularly perform and undertake artistic activities and research. The Sibelius Academy is committed to fostering Finland's musical culture and heritage, and various kinds of concerts and festivals are arranged under its auspices.

There are over 1,500 students at the Academy and the yearly intake is approximately 145 students. Students admitted to the Academy are entitled to take the degree 'Master of Music' but they may also take a Bachelor's degree. The degree programme is divided into eight instrumental groups, one of them being piano (for information on the Academy and admissions data see: http:// www.siba.fi).

Music studies in the Department of Piano Music

The Department of Piano Music in the Sibelius Academy, the site being studied here, was designated as a top unit for artistic activity (2001–03) by the Finnish Ministry of Education. In 2001 the number of applicants to the department of Piano Music was 82, nine of whom were accepted. At the moment there are approximately 70 piano-solo students in total in the Sibelius Academy. Whilst only approximately ten solo pianists gain entry to the Sibelius Academy yearly, there is a surplus of high level professional solo pianists in Finland and thus there is huge competition and a high level of skill and ability amongst professional solo pianists.

Music studies in the Department of Piano Music are based on the Western classical music tradition and students' achievements are predominantly assessed via a programme of work collected from different classical traditions. All major instrument studies are organised and focused around solo work within intensive one-to-one private lessons. Personal solo practice also takes place in addition to and in preparation for these lessons. Throughout their studies at the Academy, students work with just one teacher and changing teachers happens only in exceptional circumstances. Whether group lessons, peer-critique sessions and/or other kind of collaborative groups are organised in major instrument studies depends largely on the teachers' own inclinations. Such sessions are not part of the formally recognised degree requirements or curriculum. Students frequently participate in master classes and other courses on a voluntary basis. They also participate in piano competitions. Whilst not required as part of the formal curriculum, students are encouraged to enter these competitions and are supported in their preparation for them. Thus there are students who enter competitions annually for the duration of their Academy studies.

THE RESEARCH APPROACH

Ten Finnish classical piano-solo students, three men and seven women, aged 18–27 years, were interviewed. At the time of the interview the average age of interviewees was 23 years 6 months and the average length of their studies was 5 years 8 months. The students were all registered within the Sibelius Academy's Department of Piano Music.

Six of the interviewees had been studying mainly in music schools before they began their studies within the Sibelius Academy's Masters Program for Piano Music (of these six, three had also studied partly in conservatoires). One of the interviewees had completed a Bachelor's degree in the conservatoire in order to qualify as a teacher. Three of the interviewees came to the Sibelius Academy from the Junior Academy. They had started studying in the Junior Academy when they were approximately 10 years old. Prior to the Junior Academy they had been studying in music schools. All interviewees began their 'formal' piano lessons when they were approximately 6 years old (between 4 to 11 years). Over the years, all students had worked with a number of different male and female teachers.

The data were collected through semi-structured themed interviews in which individual students were given the opportunity to talk about their backgrounds and to discuss their experiences associated with learning music. Nine of the interviews were conducted in piano practising rooms at the Sibelius Academy in Helsinki and one was undertaken at the interviewee's home. Interviews lasted approximately 2–3 hours. The interviews were carried out during the summer of 1998 and the spring of 2001. The interviews were designed to be interviewee-centred, with the interviewer taking a predominantly facilitative role. Each interview was based around a discussion of key focal topics (for example, music at home, peer influences, teachers, studies, practising, competitions, performing, the future) which the interviewer and interviewee explored freely. For each interview the specific line of questioning emerged from the immediate context. This means that the interviewer picked up on and developed particular issues as an interviewee raised them, encouraging them to offer further reflections and provide examples and personal narratives. All the interviews were audio-recorded and transcribed for analysis. The interviewer also made impressionistic notes concerning each interview.

Analysis of the interviews was undertaken through repeated listening to the audio-recordings and associated close reading of the corresponding transcripts. This resulted in the emergence of numerous key themes relating to the students' soloist and musical identity work. Here we focus solely on the significance of the student–teacher relationship for identity work and discuss three associated themes in detail in the section that follows. Our analyses focus on developing an understanding of the identity work inherent in the complex processes involved in the *collaborative construction of interpretations*, the *struggle between accepted interpretations and personal creativity* and *engagement with other musical genres*. The themes presented demonstrate how the students' developing interpretations of key pieces and the student–teacher interactions regarding those interpretations constitute crucial sites within which a student's identity as soloist is negotiated and re-negotiated. We argue that through their tutoring, evaluations and sanctioning of particular interpretations with respect to convention, teachers are crucial mediators of students' 'identity projects', projects which involve the reconciliation of tradition with personal aspirations, style and creativity. We will also show how in some circumstances the envisaged reactions of the teacher and the associated risk of troubled identity positions problematises students' engagement with popular forms of music-making.

SOLOIST IDENTITY WORK: THREE THEMES

Theme 1: Collective and collaboratively constructed interpretations

In Extract 1, Elina is talking about the different kind of teacher–student relationships she has had. In her current tutorial relationship processes of interpretation are represented neither as lone, creative individual responses to a piece, nor as the reproduction of the teacher's mediated interpretation. Rather, the processes of interpretation emerge as an interweaving of tradition (as represented in and mediated through the guidance of the teacher) and the student's own creative interpretations. Interpretation is thus characterised as involving subtle negotiation, and the joint construction and agreement of shared meaning and understanding.

Extract 1

E: Now it starts to be more, like, collegial discussion and not, like, authoritarian.

I: Whose opinion is stronger?

E: Oh, it depends a little bit.

I: It's not a clear thing?

E: She doesn't assume or say things like 'you must do it like this', but on the other hand you want to know why...or it is good to know about different traditions, how some well-known pieces are played before you start to work, because otherwise I just play in my own way. Then you don't start to invent your own way otherwise there would be no point in going to the lessons, otherwise you could produce everything by yourself...I think it is possibly the most important thing, I have learned many important things...but then in some phases there has come, however, a kind of certainty with my own playing, because she doesn't tend to dictate in an authoritarian way, like the first teacher. I did not understand why things are like they are, but I had to carry them out, following her particular way, but we tend to analyse things together and then we think and we discuss things and this way it becomes part of my own understanding, why I do this like that and why I want...they are partly my ideas and partly hers and that way is constructive learning and that way I become more confident.

In this extract Elina explains how work with her current teacher has started to be more collegial, rather than authoritarian (in striking comparison to the situation with an earlier teacher). Note that she feels that it is valuable and important to know how some well-known pieces are played before starting to work on them and cites this as one of the reasons for going to lessons. However, she also points out that she has come to have more certainty about her own playing as a result of the collective analysis she has undertaken with her teacher. By thinking through and discussing interpretations, Elina has come to understand 'why things are like they are'. Conventions, or particular ways of playing, are not simply unthinkingly reproduced. Rather, they have been appropriated, becoming part of her own understanding, framing and mediating her interpretative work. In Elina's case, this collegial and collaborative approach to interpretation, and the associated understanding that has come with it, seems to have fostered professional growth and enhanced confidence. Confidence with respect to musical expression seems to have strengthened this student's artistic confidence and her identity as a soloist who is capable of producing creative interpretations within professionally accepted parameters.

Such collaborative approaches to interpretation were often characterised as involving forms of musical communication, where ideas regarding interpretation are shared and mediated through music. This is evident in Meri's account of being 'accompanied' on another piano as she herself played (see Extract 2).

Extract 2

But then Antti himself was terribly good at interpreting and playing...he often accompanied me on the other piano, many times. And I suppose his method, in that phase, at least at that time was such that...try to provide inspiration from there. (Meri)

Meri's comments are made in the context of a broader discussion about how, when she was having lessons at the conservatoire, her teacher was encouraging her to be more expressive. Taken in the context of this broader discussion, we come to understand that the teacher's playing was not undertaken simply to demonstrate a rendition of a piece to be copied or emulated. Rather, Meri suggests the accompaniment was intended to provide 'inspiration' for her own interpretative work. Music was thus the medium within which the interdependent processes of creative interpretation and identity construction were mutually constituted.

Theme 2: The struggle between personally meaningful, creative interpretations and accepted interpretations

Extracts 1 and 2 highlight that there is the potential for an empowering reconciliation of the innovative and the traditional within interpretative acts and processes. However, many students' accounts emphasised the struggle and conflict inherent in interpretation and the difficulty and necessity of successfully negotiating one's identity as soloist within the context of an established social milieu. In relation to this, a key theme in the data concerned the struggle between the student's individual creative interpretation of a piece and the teacher's 'sanctioning' of this with respect to an, often implicit, accepted interpretation within the wider musical community. In these accounts interpretation emerges as a highly contested achievement, in which students are expected to comply with a tutor's guidance. The struggle and conflict inherent in interpreting a piece with the guidance of a tutor can be seen in Extracts 3, 4 and 5.

In Extract 3 Tuomas talks emotively of his teacher's evaluation of his response to, and playing of, particular pieces. His comments are made in the context of a discussion relating to the judging of students' work as part of the 'competition circuit'.

Extract 3

I: But is it not that the evaluation is based on the idea that you have to understand music somehow...?

T: No, there is a teacher who tells you how to do it. Play more loudly here and more quietly here. And one of the biggest things, that disturbs me is, unbelievably, in so many places, the damned precision when preparing the final interpretation...that it, that a high tone can be heard, everything can be heard, but not even a bit of discussion of why this is so.

In this extract Tuomas rejects the idea that evaluation is based on the student's own understanding of the piece. He strongly asserts that there is a teacher who 'tells you how to do it'. He comments that he is disturbed by the precision inherent in the process of interpretation. Tuomas finds it unbelievable that the teacher's emphasis is repeatedly on such precision and he expresses both frustration and incredulity about this. He uses the example of tonality to evoke the often implicit nature of the teaching process he experiences where there is no explicit discussion or explanation of experiences.

Tuomas's struggle to interpret and construct his response to the piece is crucially framed and constrained by the comments of his teacher who is keenly aware of the constraints imposed by the wider musical culture, and in particular, the expectations associated with the judging process in the 'competition circuit'. The struggle to create meaning is thus regularly contested within the site of routine practice and rehearsal. In this extract the construction of a musical interpretation and Tuomas's identity as a creative soloist are contested in an uncomfortable dynamic in which the teacher's stance is a powerful one (see Nielsen, 1999).

In Extract 4, Tuomas talks further about the dilemmas and delicate processes involved in negotiating a position between the teacher's suggested interpretation and one's own creative ideas, particularly in situations when both student's and teacher's reasoning and negotiations are left implicit and tacit. His comments are made in the context of a discussion relating to learning together, with the teacher.

Extract 4

And in reality, if telling it straight now, so, I have very often had a kind of period of what to do when you don't appreciate fully what the teacher says? It is quite dangerous. And even if you have a different opinion of things and you would like to do it another way...so you know that when you go to the next lesson, so, you play according to your own ideas but that is not, like, right either. However, it is quite an uncomfortable situation when it doesn't...like, how do you make sense of it that you play how another person wishes? It is the biggest possible deception that can exist. Let them play then like that...but of course you have to consider that there surely is a good idea behind it, but digging it out then. (Tuomas)

In 'telling it straight' Tuomas discloses his dilemma about what to do when he does not fully embrace the perspective on interpretation the teacher is advocating. He characterises this as a dangerous situation, although he does not expand on the potential losses or risks inherent in it. If he plays according to his own interpretation, it is deemed 'not right'. It is an uncomfortable situation. Tuomas suggests that to play how another person wishes involves deception and perhaps a betrayal of one's own self – it is the biggest possible deception that can exist. He struggles towards understanding the rationale for the teacher's advocacy of his particular stance and uses the archaeological metaphor of having to uncover, through 'digging out', the reasons underpinning the interpretation that his teacher is advocating.

Again there is a sense of the student wanting to understand what is currently left tacit and implicit. Tuomas struggles to give voice to his own interpretations. However, his own creative interpretations are in direct conflict with the guidance being given by the teacher who is working with the student within the framework afforded by a particular system of assessment carrying the weight of historical tradition, oriented to the forms of expression valued by an established classical music community. To adhere unquestioningly to these valued forms of expression is somehow considered by Tuomas to be dishonest – and creates a situation in which inherent in the simple, unquestioning adoption of an interpretation, is the risk of taking on a troubled identity. The struggle to reconcile tradition with the telling of 'ones own story' also has tangible consequences for performance as Tuomas articulates in Extract 5.

Extract 5

For example, I have been listening to my own recording from Dublin. I tried to play this according to the advice I was given and everybody said in the competition you have to ensure that you play carefully. You have to concentrate that it goes right and other things. It sounds quite, hellishly boring when you listen to it. I have possibly never played or...I surely have played...but you can't listen to it for a long time especially when there are mistakes. I tried to concentrate on it and ensured that I played carefully. Then it all disappeared, there was not even a little of my own thinking, there was no confidence and it was, like, too careful [laughs] and it crashed...there must be your own story there.

But what Häkkinen said about this piece is that if this would have been a concert you could play this as you wish, but it is worth bearing in mind that you should not do anything too extreme because she knows that within the jury are people to whom keeping tempo is a really important concern and you should bear this in mind. But, of course, perhaps it can also be the case that if you do something a little different that is exactly the thing that will influence them. I think that says a lot about the system. (Tuomas)

In this extract Tuomas reflects on the recording made of his performance in a piano competition in Dublin. He explains how he tried to play in the competition, in accordance with all the advice he was given, such that he played carefully and according to the stated concerns and expectations of jury members. However, Tuomas's evaluation was that his playing sounded very boring. 'It all disappeared' such that there was none of his own interpretation of the piece and he felt he produced a cautiously executed performance lacking in confidence – his 'own story' was missing and he felt the performance 'crashed'. Invoking the advice of his teacher and the others, Tuomas indicates that the performance of a piece must be occasioned – an interpretation that is suitable for a concert recital and an interpretation that is suitable for a piano competition are different. Yet there is an inherent conundrum – within the competition circuit, with its strong emphasis on technical precision, there is always the possibility that if a performer does 'something a little different', that will be the very thing that influences the jury positively. There is a delicate balancing act here, where innovation can be pivotal and the mark of an accomplished soloist, yet the balance can only be successfully achieved within certain strict parameters and providing certain other criteria are met. The notion of 'telling your own story' is a powerful one which hints at the importance of lived experience, emotional expression and the potentially personally meaningful nature and, for some, the therapeutic value of musical expression and interpretation (Davidson, 2002; O'Neill, 2002, pp.103–104). This notion is extended and elaborated in Extract 6.

Extract 6

> I remember when Kirsi became furious because of my playing, because at that time somehow, there was no control. I remember it was in the peer-critique session when she…at that time the older students were not there…quite, like, became furious – 'it is not permitted to play like that!'…that I have to have a kind of control. I did not know then what she meant when she said that. Terribly difficult to understand what she meant. I feel, yes I feel that I always have…I remember when I was thinking for a long time, like, that life is a little bit, like, filtering my own playing or…also the opposite. They are two big things which are feeding each other all the time. While playing you are able to…all those things that you have experienced, are somehow filtering through playing. Somehow, I had thoughts like this. It is perhaps like that with dancers too…that part which is therapeutic. (Taru)

In Extract 6, Taru recalls her teacher's furious reaction to her playing and the accompanying publicly voiced evaluation in a peer-critique session that her playing was out of control. At that point, however, Taru felt she did not know what 'out of control' meant (although by commenting that she did not know 'then' what that meant hints that she perhaps has some subsequent understanding). For Taru, within her interpretation and musical expression there are imprints of a life lived and a life experienced. It was her lived experience that was filtering through her music in a way that was therapeutic. Taru seemed to have the holistic notion that life and playing the piano are interconnected and that they reciprocally influence each another. She represented her experiences, including the personal difficulties discussed at various points in the interview, as having permeated and infused her playing – the ultimate fusion of self and musical expression. In Taru's case her identity as a solo pianist and the associated expressive interpretation she values as therapeutic risk being 'spoiled' by the notion that her way of playing is somehow out of control. The teacher prohibits her form of playing – deeming it unacceptable. There is thus a tension here between what is personally meaningful for the student and what is acceptable to or expected by the teacher. This theme is explored further in the next section.

Theme 3: Other musical genres and other musical identity projects

In recent discussions of musical identities conceptualisations of identity as plural and multiple (MacDonald & Miell, 2002) have highlighted both the relational aspects of identity work and the significance of other people's expectations. Identity is both performative and situated and it is therefore important to be sensitive to the ways in which an individual negotiates and manages multiple identity projects within different contexts and relationships. The complex negotiation and management of multiple musical identities was evident in the students' accounts. A particularly striking example of this considered management of multiple musical identity projects is captured in Extract 7 where we hear Tuomas talking about the decision he made, immediately prior to an important piano competition, not to tell his teacher about his participation in a folk band. Inherent in this decision not to talk to Matti is the expressed concern that Tuomas would not be regarded as 'serious'. The challenge to his seriousness could arise in part because band rehearsals may be seen as detracting from the time available for competition preparation. However, the challenge may also arise partly because this particular form of folk music is often derided – being regarded as trivial, harmless 'oompah' music (see Extract 8) and therefore being active on the folk scene is perhaps not a form of musical engagement expected from a 'serious' piano soloist.

Extract 7

> Actually, I have to say here that I have actually made the decision not actually to talk to Matti before the competition because I thought that he, like, would have the attitude that I am not serious so I don't know, it could be and probably troubles me a little bit that I have not said anything about it because now it is a little tough. (Tuomas)

In this extract Tuomas orients to the implicit assumption that being a serious piano-solo student within the Academy requires total dedication and commitment. He also orients to and resists the troubled identity of 'someone who is not serious'. Tuomas appears to have consciously decided not to discuss his participation in a folk band with his teacher in order to be perceived as behaving in accordance with that which the teacher would expect from a serious student. Tuomas's strategy effectively enables him to retain his own interests and still fulfil the teacher's expectations by managing multiple identities: one accepted and valued by the teacher and others arising from his other musical interests. Yet attempting to manage his identities as classical piano soloist and folk musician and band member, places him in an uncomfortable dynamic with his teacher that 'troubles' him and makes things 'a little tough'. It is perhaps because his identities as folk musician and band member are so personally meaningful that Tuomas was prepared to accommodate his feelings of unease – such feelings may be less uncomfortable than risking the teacher's disapproval, particularly in the run-up to a competition.

Tuomas talks passionately about his experiences with the folk band. In Extract 8 he also underscores his commitment and dedication to the band and his music making in this context, noting that his participation in the band has involved him in lengthy rehearsal time. Whilst in the beginning he felt that playing with the band would be 'nice' and 'come a bit easier', Tuomas describes a clear recognition that his folk band-work needed to be done 'properly' if it were to be something other than 'oompah' music. Through positing the idea that he saw 'extremely clearly that something had to be done properly' Tuomas underscores that his engagement with this popular form of music is not to be taken lightly. In doing so he is resisting an unwanted and undesirable identity-position of someone engaged in something meaningless – 'harmless oompah'.

Extract 8

At the moment I would defend body and soul why I have gone there. It was only for me...my attitude to it in the beginning...when I was thinking that it is nice that I get to play in the band, I have wanted to for such a long time and it comes a bit easier. But yes we had an unbelievable amount of rehearsal time, we gave, among other things, so much time to that. I saw extremely clearly that you have to do something properly if it is to be something other than a kind of harmless 'oompah' music and then the more I worked the more I understood and started to appreciate that. (Tuomas)

Extract 8 underscores that identity work is a multi-faceted process, embedded in diverse contexts and meeting diverse needs. Although the students interviewed were aspiring professional piano soloists there is evidence that, whilst of central importance, their identity as solo pianist is only one amongst several musical identity projects being negotiated and managed, all of which can be enriching, fulfilling and deeply personally meaningful. Tuomas, for example, had wanted to play in the folk band for a long time, yet he avoids the potentially problematic identity positions associated with his participation by choosing not to disclose his involvement with the band to key people, notably his teacher. He also justifies his decision to participate in the folk band by orienting to possible critiques of his behaviour. He is attempting to manage, reconcile and negotiate a potential clash of cultured worlds, engaging in the musical practices associated with both 'high' and 'popular' culture.

CONCLUDING REMARKS

In this chapter we have argued that the creation of new interpretations of music from an established canon is a socially and culturally mediated creative process and that inherent in the negotiated and contested processes of interpreting musical pieces are the similarly complex socio-cultural processes of identity construction. Our analyses of solo-piano students' accounts of their interactions with, and in relation to, their teachers have revealed these learning relationships to be powerful sites within which the processes of establishing mutual understanding, constructing interpretations, and ongoing identity work are inextricably interwoven. We have also illustrated the multiplicity of these students' identity projects – noting that the ongoing process of constructing an identity as soloist is undertaken in relation to other musical identities and identity projects which too may be personally important and meaningful.

The teacher–student relationship is clearly one that is characterised by asymmetry, both with respect to knowledge and experience. However, with advanced students at this level, teachers adopt a range of teaching strategies and there is evidence to suggest that, at times, the processes of teaching and learning may involve the joint construction of an interpretation. Through sharing, discussing and evaluating ideas, by talking and playing together, the student and their teacher participate in a creative collaboration, the processes of which have significance both for the emergent interpretation and the student's identity as soloist.

Whilst the students interviewed here talked about collectivity and collaboration, their accounts also pointed to areas of conflict and tension in the creative relationship between student and teacher. The analyses presented as part of this chapter suggest that, for students, inherent in such conflicts is the risk of 'troubled', 'spoiled' or 'unwanted' identities, which in many cases they orient to in their accounts. The production of creative interpretations that sustain, resonate with, renew and develop valued, established cultural traditions and practices represents the essence of interpretative work. Such work is a vital part of what it is to be a successful soloist. The analyses presented here suggest that it is in the attempts to reconcile the personal and the established that conflict and tension often arise. The teacher has an important role to play in mediating and inducting the student into the expectations and practices of the established classical music community and the appropriation of such practices is clearly part of a solo-pianist's training. However, the extracts presented in this chapter testify to both the difficulty and the necessity, for students, of finding their own voice and telling their own story whilst working in a way which both recognises and respects established traditions. It is such expressions of self and a life lived and experienced, that seem to be associated positively with students' confidence as soloists, which are legitimated, sanctioned or prohibited in the context of the creative relationship between a student and their teacher.

Clearly the teacher–student relationship, whilst important, is just one context in which a student's identity as soloist is negotiated. Our future research will be extending the work reported here by considering, for example, the significance of family and of peer relationships with other students for the development of musical identities and, in particular, an identity as classical piano soloist. These analyses will be complemented by a more detailed consideration of the salience of cultural practices such as the 'examination system' and the 'competition' circuit and further work on students' engagement with other musical genres.

ACKNOWLEDGEMENTS

We would like to thank the piano-solo students in the Department of Piano Music at the Sibelius Academy who made this research possible. We also wish to acknowledge that the writing of this chapter was made possible by the award, to Karen Littleton, of a Visiting Professorship at the Graduate School, Faculty of Behavioural Sciences, University of Helsinki.

REFERENCES

Amabile, T. (1996). *Creativity in context*. Boulder, CO: Westview Press.

Bakhtin, M.M. (1986). *Speech genres and other late essays* (eds C. Emerson and M. Holquist; trans. V.W. McGee). Austin: University of Texas Press.

Csikszentmihalyi, M. (1996). *Creativity: Flow and the psychology of discovery and invention*. New York: HarperCollins.

Csikszentmihalyi, M. (1999). 'Implications of a systems perspective for study of creativity'. In R.J. Sternberg (ed.), *Handbook of creativity*, (pp.313–335). Cambridge: Cambridge University Press.

Davidson, J.W. (2002). 'The solo performer's identity'. In R.A.R. MacDonald, D.J. Hargreaves & D. Miell (eds), *Musical identities* (pp.97–113). Oxford: Oxford University Press.

MacDonald, R.A.R. & Miell, D. (2002). 'Music for individuals with special needs: A catalyst for developments in identity, communication and music ability'. In R.A.R. MacDonald, D.J. Hargreaves & D. Miell (eds), *Musical Identities* (pp.163–178). Oxford: Oxford University Press.

Nielsen, K.N. (1999). *Musical Apprenticeship. Learning at the academy of music as socially situated*. Psykologisk skriftserie Aarhus universitet 24 (2). Risskov: Psykologisk institut Aarhus Universitet.

O'Neill, S.A. (2002). 'The self-identity of young musicians'. In R.A.R. MacDonald, D.J. Hargreaves & D. Miell (eds), *Musical identities* (pp.79–96). Oxford: Oxford University Press.

Sibelius Academy: http://www.siba.fi

Sloboda, J. (1996). 'The acquisition of musical performance expertise: Deconstructing the "talent" account of individual differences in musical expressivity'. In K.A. Ericsson (ed.), *The road to excellence: The acquisition of expert performance in the arts and sciences, sport and games* (pp.107–126). Mahwah, NJ: Lawrence Erlbaum Associates.

Wertsch, J.V. (1991). *Voices of the mind. A sociocultural approach to mediated action*. London: Harvester-Wheatsheaf.

4

The Emotional Dance
of Creative Collaboration

Helen Storey and Mathilda Marie Joubert

INTRODUCTION

This chapter has been written in quite a different format and style from that which is customary in an academic text like *Collaborative Creativity*. It explores fashion designer Helen Storey's thinking about her collaborative creative projects through the format of an autobiographical interview conducted by Mathilda Marie Joubert. A verbatim transcript was made of the interview. This transcription process was followed by a critical re-reading and associated thematic reorganisation of the material for this chapter. In places the themes emerging from the interview have also been linked to current theoretical discourses about creative collaborations, although the aim was to remain true to Helen's reflections and ideas as expressed in the interview. The interview material is therefore presented here as a first-person, autobiographical account.

This chapter complements the other contributions in this book well. Whereas the majority of the other chapters are written from an 'outsider' perspective, with researchers observing, analysing and describing the creative collaborative process from the outside, the material at the heart of this chapter is written from an 'insider' perspective. Helen Storey is reflecting on her own ideas and practices, which in turn provide us with insights regarding the processes of creative collaboration. This way of investigating creative collaborations has the potential to enhance our understanding of the processes of collaborative creativity by highlighting how such processes are experienced by someone widely regarded as being creative.

CONTEXT

Helen Storey has worked as a fashion designer since 1981, first for fashion houses like Valentino in Italy and then with her own fashion label. Her celebrity clients included Cher, Prince, Janet Jackson, Michael Jackson, Madonna and Liz Hurley. In June 1995 the trading arm of her fashion label closed and she began searching for projects which would not only be ground breaking but would also challenge her skills as an innovator and take her vision of fashion as an educator and communicator to new limits.

She immersed herself in the world of collaborative creativity. In 1996 Helen started the ground breaking project 'Primitive Streak' with her scientist sister, Kate, which brought together the worlds of science and fashion through the creation of a fashion collection reflecting the first 1,000 hours of human life. In 1998 she began work on 'Mental', a scientifically inspired exploration of creativity, emotion and feeling involving over 70 collaborators from different backgrounds, including science, fashion, technology, etc. 'Mental' was not a scientifically inspired fashion collection anymore; it was much broader. It was an interactive multi-disciplinary exhibition and Helen wasn't purely a fashion designer any more, but much more of a producer and an artist.

The process of collaborative creativity is the central theme that runs throughout Helen's account and pervades all the other subsidiary themes presented through first-person reflections in the remainder of this chapter.

THE PROCESS OF CREATIVE COLLABORATION

I have noticed in my life and work that this creative process has been happening increasingly in collaborative settings. My collaborative projects aim to visualise what is in effect intangible, for example what happens in the brain whilst being creative. The process is always more important to me than the product. The product becomes something you need to be professional and responsible about at some stage, particularly for the people who have funded it. But I think what most people recognise in the work that I do, is that in some ways it is a bit like the world of science. It is an experiment and what it will be is what it will be. Its integrity is found in the ability to communicate, rather than in any kind of shiny image at the other end.

I don't think I will ever produce something dead ugly, and I certainly wouldn't do it for the sake of it. But on the whole the process completely determines the outcome, and I don't like to speed that process up or cheat it. There is an awful lot of holding your nerve required when you do that, but it is the most enjoyable bit really; when your mind comes up with something and you haven't got a clue where that came from or where it will lead. But, looking back, you can't cheat that. I wish you could, but there's something about having to do something with virtually no money, with time running out, and you are not sure that you understand what you are doing anyway. You can either produce this terrible mess or something so acute and vital. Luckily what came out with our project had resonance and was regarded as quite vital.

The collaborative creative process is also one of trial and error. All the different collaborations went through lots of small experiments, full of mistakes and roads leading nowhere and then leading somewhere else. There are parts of the process you can explain and there are other parts that are simply just meant to be lived. I think if you try and explain them you are going to miss it.

With both 'Primitive Streak' and 'Mental' there was no overall planned structure to the process of creative collaboration that made sense; the whole thing was run on instinct. You kept pushing forward. A problem comes up, you solve it, you keep pushing forward and it is very much an active juggling to keep the whole thing in the air. The process of getting to the final product is quite invisible, even though you try to unpick it all the time.

I am still finding out what it is that I do now. I spent fifteen years being a fashion designer. I knew it inside out. And now, every single project I do is new. It takes me to areas where I've got to be both open, but very quick off the mark, and very alert. It is also about knowing what is worth pursuing. You need to be astute about what is brave but also do-able. I don't like doing things that are too predetermined; I cannot know exactly where things are going to lead and that is part of the process, but I've got to have a gut feel that it is worth following that path.

A critical reflection upon the processes of my work over the past seven years highlights the following nine themes:

1. Motivation
2. Cross-disciplinarity
3. Recognition of value
4. Fear and risk-taking
5. Relationship of trust
6. Intimacy and mutual vulnerability
7. Facilitating collaboration
8. Ownership
9. Identity and personal growth.

MOTIVATION

I was asked why it was important for me to engage in cross-disciplinary creative collaborative work with other people and not just do it myself. I think that a mixture of internal and external drivers motivate people to collaborate creatively (also called intrinsic and extrinsic motivators by Amabile, 1983).

Personally some external drivers were present, but the internal drivers were strongest. I wanted to continue to scare myself. For example, with 'Mental' I wanted to work with technologies that I thought were really important ones, but I wasn't trained in them. I didn't want my lack of training in those technologies to have a limiting effect on the project. I wanted it to be a multi-faceted project and in order to make it work I had to work with other people – and I was glad to. But the other collaborators also have to be intrinsically motivated to be involved in the project. You have to pick a topic that engages others like 'the mind' in 'Mental' clearly did. Otherwise the collaboration is merely one where you just pay them to fulfil something that you can't do and that is not true collaboration.

If I think back to when I was working in fashion designing 'pure', in some ways I think I was already messing with collaboration there. You do in the sense that when you put on shows you are collaborating with people who are doing makeup, hair, music. There is a central theme and you will all work together on it. In 1996 I started working on 'Primitive Streak', which was my first true collaboration across disciplines. My sister, developmental biologist Dr Kate

Storey, was my motivation for embarking on 'Primitive Streak'. At the time she was at Oxford University (she is now in Dundee) and was invited by the Wellcome Trust to undertake a project to bring scientists and artists together, so she approached me. At the time I felt I had to stop doing fashion and I was looking for something to take me creatively into a new direction. If it wasn't for the Wellcome Trust Sci-Art Initiative we probably wouldn't have done that collaboration. I think everything that they were doing at that stage was a punt, an experiment, and they sort of went with it. I think, in some ways, the Wellcome Trust was ahead of their time by trying that out. Their experimentation enabled our creative collaboration across domains and I can't quite believe that I have been trading off it ever since.

Following 'Primitive Streak', I was searching for ways to continue a new found passion for science and my hunger to question it through art. Back in the autumn of 1998 I was asked a question by a man who needed and deserved an answer. He asked me if I knew what was happening in my mind when I was doing something creative. I didn't, yet I was amazed by my curiosity to look. My fear was that if you 'snooped' at the process by making it conscious, you may ruin it in some way, and yet, I still found it very attractive. So, unsure if I really wanted to know, I sat down at my kitchen table and waited. To begin with I had to ask myself a second question to get myself going. I tried to remember the first time I could recall having an imagination and six states of mind then quite spontaneously suggested themselves. Some were painful, some took me back to as far as I can remember, but all felt true. So the external questioning sparked the internal questioning which in the end led to the creative collaborative project being undertaken and eventually involving more than seventy different collaborators. The collaborators were from a diverse set of backgrounds, including scientists, pattern makers, specialists in interactive computer games, installation specialists, sound designers, etc.

With the project 'Mental', people gradually started to hear about the work being created – I don't know how – but various people found their way to it. The experimental nature of the project enabled greater creative collaboration. Most people that collaborated wanted to, because they felt I'd taken them to the edge of what they in turn thought they were capable of. They liked the idea that this wasn't something that had to be commercially successful. You didn't have to sell it. It didn't have to appear in any shop and wouldn't be judged on sales in any way. But through the collaborations, the work ends up being quite rich and it means that it can go to lots of different audiences and be relevant in lots of ways.

Paradoxically, although 'Mental' was framed as an exploration of an individual creative mind, the project had a very collaborative nature. It would be interesting to perhaps explore this paradox from other people's viewpoints as well. In my view I think different people got involved in the project for different reasons. Some did it just for the experience of it, some recognised that it was going to be one hell of a journey and they just wanted to be part of that journey. Others did it to keep them fresh and connected to the outside world, so that they are not sucked into the day-to-day of what they deal with in their own place of work. 'Mental' was bringing them a different opportunity to revisit their own creativity.

Commercial forces can also drive creative collaborations. After I did a presentation about a proposed project one of the people in the audience, who was in charge of the money, came up and said, 'I think it is wonderful. How much do you want?' So all at once you try everything to make it happen. Before the money was there, the project was merely an idea. But once the money was on the table we had to get the different actors together and we had to collaborate to co-create the project.

There may also be different drivers for creativity for young people. When I reflected on my youth I realised how creativity had become a refuge for me, as for other people; a defence mechanism, for example against bullying at school. As a young person I, however, took refuge in individual creativity whereas I now define myself through collaborative creative activities. Perhaps I needed the individual experience before I could fully participate in collaborative processes. I'm not sure whether this was unique to me or a general characteristic of young people.

CROSS-DISCIPLINARITY

Creativity often depends on cross-disciplinary curiosity and thrives on opportunities to learn from others. As Koestler said in 1964: 'creativity often springs from the unexpected juxtaposition of realms of thought not often combined'. But leaving the security of your own discipline behind can be very frightening. Part of the problem is the uncertainty about where you belong. I became acutely aware of this situation when we tried to place press stories for 'Primitive Streak'. The science pages would say, 'well we can't put dresses in a science page. Forget it.' And the art people would say, 'it's not really art it is fashion'. And the fashion people would say, 'well you can't buy it, it's not fashion'.

I didn't know what we had created either; it almost defies definition or pinning down. I don't consider what I do as art, so I am not looking to people who judge art to tell me whether I am any good or not. I keep using this word 'tools'; I think we are working on communication tools of some kind. The key thing for me is that I want to produce things that have a use and I don't think that is where artists come from. I don't think they come from that place where they want their work to be useful. I think they want a reaction or response. I am somewhere between a designer, who would absolutely have to produce useful and practical objects otherwise it doesn't sell, and an artist.

When I started out on this new path I realised that we had to aim for something new that created its own audience, or we would fail. Slowly, with time, we were able to look back and realise that there is a relationship between collaborative honesty and an audience's appreciation. In the end it had nothing to do with the press, and a new audience and genre was created in spite of any publicity. 'Primitive Streak' was just a direct way of talking about biology in new ways.

We had to create a new language for the audience, but we also keep on creating a unique new language to facilitate cross-disciplinary collaboration, since no one party carries the other world's language fully. For example, when I was working with my sister Kate she had no idea how exhausting it was going to be to explain all the things that she took for granted to somebody who knows nothing about science, which was me at the time. We ended up developing a middle language somewhere between the different disciplines.

RECOGNITION OF VALUE

The difficulty of defining what I do through my creative collaborations could influence how it is regarded or valued by others. Csikszentmihalyi (2001) emphasises the importance of social recognition of creative work, suggesting that work can only be deemed to be creative once the community of interest recognises it as creative. His view is strangely at odds with the art for art's sake debate, which sees the lone artist pursuing his vision irrespective of social recognition. But I found Csikszentmihalyi's view consonant with my own feelings with my collaborative work.

I found that other people had to influence my own feelings of the worthiness of the work I was pursuing; I didn't come to that understanding myself. The first time it dawned on me that what we were doing had value was when the company Pfizer came along and attributed some financial value to it through sponsorship. Although the work wasn't commercially oriented, it strangely started to make me aware of the value of what I was doing. In the end it took quite a lot to persuade me of the significance of what we had created. Partly, that was to do with being absolutely shattered and just focusing on getting the thing done; there was no time to reflect whilst we were working on it. Part of it was that we were perhaps too close to it ourselves to value it and partly the lack of recognition from within was influenced by the fact that I didn't know what we had created.

Social recognition, however, occasionally has a negative side too. After 'Primitive Streak' was completed Kate said that had she known it was going to be in some ways so successful as it was, or get as much attention as it did, she might not have done it, because it opened up a vulnerability in her in terms of how she is perceived in her world. At quite a few stages she could see the science world dividing into those who thought that she was wasting her time (any serious scientist should be at the bench doing the graft, and to fiddle around with textiles and the world of fashion is really a joke), and others who welcomed the idea that you could bring the outside world into science and vice versa. This latter group appreciated that you could take the working and the thinking of a laboratory mind out to the public and, whilst you might lose something, a sort of integrity or detail of it, it was worth it for what you *did* manage to disseminate and communicate.

FEAR AND RISK-TAKING

Fear has been a strong leitmotif since my first foray into the world of cross-disciplinary collaboration, since it involves moving out of your own comfort zone. I now see it as fear tinged with excitement, but my initial reaction was only fear – I just wanted to get to the finish line. There were so many challenges besides designing and producing the work, such as learning the science, getting the rest of the funding, finding a venue, creating a theme, etc. I just remember feeling out of my skin the whole time; sort of wide eyed with the need to get things done. 'Primitive Streak' was also done against the background of my perception of my sister who was incredibly academic and clever and I saw myself as rather watery and stupid. Part of my fear was being 'found out'. The fact that I came through that project and not all scientists were throwing out the work has been such a revelation to me personally. I felt able to take anything on after that.

For the next project, fear returned. I was very frightened about doing 'Mental', because the project was going to be vast, involving so many different disciplines. I had to take many risks and trust other people to get on and do things, for example I haven't a clue how some team members did the multimedia digital game and it would probably take me years to find out how they did it, but the idea of risks was less troubling to me. I actually found I wanted to take the risks and I think a part of it was formed by my personal experiences, like my ex-husband's illness. I got quite brave after it and thought there is nothing to lose really. No one has anything to lose and you should just try things. I suppose it's a faith I have nowadays that I can recover quite quickly from things that knock me down, which allows me to take bigger risks.

RELATIONSHIP OF TRUST

A mutual relationship of trust is key when collaborating creatively. Once you have both decided to trust, you both have a vested interest in it coming out well. There is usually quite a complicated process involved in building this trust between partners. When working with my sister there was no need to build trust, because it was already there. So, we could afford to have quite lethal confrontations and we knew we would be over them the next day. We got on with things far faster, because we didn't have to creep around each other. I think an awful lot of collaborations are taken up by the emotional dance that goes with them, let alone the physical thing or the product that you want to produce. Perhaps Kate and I had gone through that process during our childhood and could now just get on with working together.

Interestingly enough, however, Kate and I didn't have a very close relationship at the time, since we were shaped by our different educations and separate goals. So 'Primitive Streak' was not only a meeting of two disciplines, but a meeting of two siblings who didn't know each other very well at that stage. It felt as if every day I spent with her was as much about finding out who she was nowadays, as it was about how I would internalise and communicate the science. It was just as much a test and an exploration of who we were as women.

When working with people you don't know that well, as in 'Mental', I think part of the success of the collaboration depends on the fact that you need to almost develop a sixth sense about whom you're talking to and be able to very quickly pick up whether they come from a good place within themselves and what their reasons are for wanting to collaborate. The quicker you can pick these things up, the better.

INTIMACY AND MUTUAL VULNERABILITY

I believe a high level of mutual intimacy lies at the heart of successful collaborations and bigger collaborations don't require less intimacy, but more of it. Perhaps this is where the difference comes in between creative and non-creative collaborations or between creatively collaborating and merely working independently together, sometimes called working cooperatively. I don't feel I had to sacrifice any intimacy in the bigger project; I just had a lot more intimate conversations than when I've been working with fewer people. One of the reasons why I was so exhausted after 'Mental' was because of the energy required to sustain the intimacy you get with close collaborations. I was having multiple intimate relationships simultaneously. For example, I was having the most extraordinary conversations with my scientist partner, but we found we could only do it for two hours. Our brains just ached afterwards. Our conversations were exhausting, because you can only stay that vulnerable for so long. Then you put some skin on again.

The important thing I find about collaboration is the necessity to be mutually vulnerable and there can be no high arguments of who is more important than the other. Whether you are the instigator of the project or not, there has to be a levelling of personality that goes on. There has to be an authentic acceptance of this fact, because you both decide to be equal in it. Then you have to take each other to the edge of what you individually thought you were capable of.

FACILITATING COLLABORATION

With 'Mental' I was not only collaborating myself; I was forcing collaborations on other people. The concept determined who talked to whom. There were a lot of other little collaborations happening around me and sometimes I felt I didn't have much to do. I would put the two together and see what happened. When facilitating a new collaboration, what I always try to do is to say: 'This is the project; this is the feel of the overall project', and then to stop talking and to look out and listen for their immediate responses. Then they would ask a question back, they would get more into it and then they would come up with their own solution.

If you are instigating the collaboration, you have to be prepared to open up and to truly take that other person into account, and not become prescriptive to them. And that is where the risk is, because they can come up with something that you don't like. The ideal scenario is that you come up with the third idea that neither of you could have thought of on your own. There is something about the coming together of the two of you that produces something that is unique and when it appears it is unquestionably there. Something is recognised and it usually produces a simultaneous smile.

But the process of facilitating others' collaboration isn't always an easy one. During 'Mental' there were moments when I thought, 'this isn't going to work'. At one point I realised that I had become a choreographer and it felt like I actually lost the ability to influence anything creatively at the source. There were so many cooks there, and it became a balancing act to know when to withdraw and when to let other people collide and use whatever happened in that collision. There were stages in the project where I thought I felt in control and then there were stages where I thought I was simply issuing a recipe for something to be made and on the worst days I felt like I would give the entire project away to someone else to do it and watch it disappear in the distance. The loss and negotiation of 'control' was a difficult thing to come to terms with.

Although I had mixed feelings at one stage during 'Mental', that all I was doing was facilitating other people's creativity, in retrospect I realise that is a pretty wonderful thing to be in the position to do. Ultimately I enjoyed that aspect enormously: giving people the opportunity to see who they are in the bigger scheme of things.

OWNERSHIP

Ownership is another theme that stands out when working in this collaborative fashion. For me it is a completely shared thing; I would never have designed 'Primitive Streak' if I hadn't worked with Kate. Sometimes, however, I felt a current of disowning it within her, but I think it is to do with the fact that she is a very successful female scientist and she doesn't want to be judged negatively by the more cynical elitists in the scientific community. She has worked so hard to get where she is today. From the beginning she saw it as something to help me re-flower in a very generous way and I think she still thinks of it as that. She was a vehicle for me rediscovering my path.

'Mental' was shared with seventy collaborators and I hope the other collaborators all feel they can share the ownership – I do. Although the project started off as a description of the contents of my own mind, I think on the whole they realised quite quickly that I was inviting them to explore their minds and that they had to engage with their own in order to come up with work that was of any value. The process was shared by all and I hope they feel the same about the eventual outcomes.

The opening night for the 'Mental' exhibition was quite difficult for me. There I was supposed to be staking claim for something about me, but it was about seventy other people as well. And yet, they were all looking at me as if I had done it all. The opening party was supposed to be a celebration for everyone, but I was very aware that there were those people who were looking at it as if I had done the whole thing and I really and truly hadn't. It was quite hard. Regarders of 'art' often prefer one culprit!

IDENTITY AND PERSONAL GROWTH

Collaborative creativity has had a significant impact on my own identity. When I started this type of work I knew that it would probably require a new learning and a new negotiation of what I was really capable of. I think you grow immensely as a person, because you risk yourself as a person, or you should risk yourself as a person. I think collaboration makes you braver. The process is a continuous stream of trial and error: you find some connections that are worth following and other diversions that aren't worth following scream out straightaway and you just don't bother with them. But it is not always as clear and you do go down a wrong path at times. No matter what happens, good or bad, collaboration makes you braver.

Collaboration makes you wonder what your identity really is. We piloted one of the projects at a school and it was at that moment I suddenly thought: I am not doing art, I think what I am doing is producing tools, which can be used in different ways. It is not about, 'is it beautiful or not beautiful' or 'do I want it on my living room wall or don't I'. I was actually starting to produce things that might have a social use. That I feel much more comfortable and excited about and it is certainly where my work is going now. Joining that competitive artistic rat race of whether you are producing anything that is provocative or wildly British suppresses the joy for me. I was able to explore these dimensions of my identity only through collaborating with a range of other individuals.

When you work with others there is an endless negotiation about your own power and how much you should have, or how much of it you don't have and you wish you had. I think when you have been through a number of collaborations you realise how much of a distraction that is to the work at hand. The key moments are far more important than having any identity. Having less of a personality is actually more enabling. Through collaborative creativity you overcome the need to have a personality, which is amazingly freeing.

I feel that through my collaborative creative work over the last seven years I became more and more invisible. I feel a strangely pleasing dissembling of my identity rather than a reinforcing or a clarification of what I used to be. I like that. I hope one day to be totally invisible.

CONCLUDING SUMMARY

There are many resonances throughout this chapter with related themes in the literature on creative collaborations and with other chapters in this book. Whatmore (1999) describes how the phenomenon of creativity is increasingly taking place in collaborative settings in a range of domains (from science to architecture and advertising) and predicts that this tendency will continue and increase in future. This chapter supports this view within and across the domains of arts, science and technology. It also complements socio-cultural and situated theories of development (e.g. Vygotsky, 1978; Wertsch, 1977) which stress the importance of recognising that behaviour must be understood within the context of relationships, which are in turn embedded in social and cultural systems. Brown (1989) points out that: 'In studying creativity, many psychologists appear to have committed the "fundamental attribution error", underestimating the role of situational factors and overestimating the role of unique intrapersonal factors' (Brown, 1989, p.29). This chapter avoided this pitfall by providing an insider perspective on interpersonal and cross-disciplinary situational factors of collaborative creativity.

This insider perspective offers a distinctive angle on the creative collaborative process, particularly through the rich use of metaphors. Helen Storey describes the process of learning to collaborate as an emotional dance, which is often the first as well as an ongoing stage of creative collaborations. This links clearly with work by Mercer on the guided construction of knowledge, which postulated that children need to be explicitly taught and inducted into strategies for collaboration through the establishment of ground rules for discourse (Mercer, 1995).

The importance of affect and emotion in creative collaboration stands out as a central theme in this chapter. Topics like the emotional language of collaboration, trust, mutual vulnerability and opening up to others are highlighted through Helen Storey's discourse. Here and in her other work her language for describing these themes gives us food for thought and resonates with other areas of research. She recognises the importance of this new emerging democratic language of collaborative creativity:

We increasingly need new ways of understanding ourselves and our precarious place in the universe. A new and democratic language is emerging, neither elitist or alienating. This emanates when work of purpose is created with the dual enlightenments to be found between the worlds of art and science. In the last few years I have worked and collaborated with many people from very diverse disciplines. In some ways my projects are becoming visualisations of conversations with gymnastic minds that have blown me away with their fluidity and insight. (Storey, 2004)

Yet this insider perspective also exposes a limitation of current research in the field. We need a more inclusive theorising language concerning affect and emotion which are inherent in the process of collaborative creativity. Language used in the field predominantly focuses on cognitive strategies. This knowledge-building language is valuable, but it gives us only part of the picture. Helen Storey's description of her creative practices makes it evident that we need more than just a 'bolt-on' of affect in these creative domains; affect has to move much more to the fore in terms of our analytic enterprises and we need to develop the rich discourse or language to do so.

Understanding and creating climates conducive to creativity is another key theme from this chapter. One of the consequences of creating supporting climates is that it enables greater creative collaboration, which seems to be particularly enabled through collaborations in the creative domain. This could have great implications for other areas of research, including educational, where there are currently big debates about enabling greater creativity within classrooms. A future research agenda could therefore be to study more deeply how collaborators within the creative industries and beyond manage to create these positive climates for creativity and learn how to translate this into the education sector.

One area where Helen Storey's perspective does differ from a lot of the literature on collaboration is her wish for invisibility expressed at the end of the previous section. What is usually found in collaborative projects, is that there is a distinct wish for ownership. Storey's wish for interdependence, not independence is therefore very striking. Csikszentmihalyi (2001) describes only the recognition of creativity as the collaborative process: 'Creativity cannot be recognized except as it operates within a system of cultural rules, and it cannot bring forth anything new unless it can enlist the support of peers... it is the community and not the individual who makes creativity manifest' (Csikszentmihalyi, 2001, p.24). Helen Storey demonstrated that this is a too narrow view. The nature of collaboration goes much further; it shapes the creative product, it determines the creative process and it affects the identity of the collaborator.

REFERENCES

Amabile, T. (1983). *The social psychology of creativity*. New York: Springer-Verlag.

Brown, R.T. (1989). 'Creativity: What are we to measure?' In J.A. Glover, R.R. Ronning & C.R. Reynolds (eds), *Handbook of creativity.* New York: Plenum Press.

Csikszentmihalyi, M. (2001). 'A systems perspective on creativity'. In J. Henry (ed.), *Creative management. Second edition.* London: Sage.

Koestler, A. (1964). *The act of creation.* London: Hutchinson.

Mercer, N. (1995). *The guided construction of knowledge: Talk among teachers and learners.* Clevedon: Multilingual Matters.

Storey, H. (2004). *The Helen Storey Foundation catalogue.* London: Helen Storey Foundation.

Vygotsky, L.S. (1978). *Mind in society: The development of higher psychological processes.* Cambridge, MA: Harvard University Press.

Wertsch, J.V. (1977). *Inner Speech Revisited.* London: Harvester Wheatsheaf.

Whatmore, J. (1999). *Releasing creativity: How leaders develop creative potential in their teams.* London: Kogan Page.

5

Assessing the Creative Work of Groups

Cordelia Bryan

INTRODUCTION

Employers and academics claim to value group-based learning, because of the many transferable skills participants acquire through working collaboratively (Bourner et al., 2001, p.20). However, in higher education the main focus is on learning outcomes and their assessment, thus appearing to privilege task over process. Not surprisingly, students become strategic about their learning and focus on whatever will maximise their chances of gaining the best grades. Sadly, this does not promote group processes nor does it encourage experimentation or risk-taking.

In the performing arts, working in groups is seen as one of the main vehicles for learning. This is acknowledged in the QAA Subject Benchmarking Statements for Dance, Drama and Performance, phase 2, which states that: 'particular emphasis may be placed on collaborative learning and heuristic principles, on "learning through doing" in group contexts' (2002, p.2). The document also states that graduating students should have acquired a range of general transferable skills which include: 'understanding of group dynamics and an ability to implement them in practical contexts' (ibid., p.6). Yet even in this subject discipline, where collaboration is widely acknowledged as essential to 'success', group skills, and the processes whereby they are acquired, rarely attract academic credit.

Initial field research undertaken within the *Assessing Group Practice* consortium[1] found that, although collaboration is often the context of learning, it is rarely a focus of it, due to an almost universal emphasis on task objectives, performance and/or products. Our research also found that students felt that this emphasis on outcomes and product was 'unfair' as it did not differentiate between group members who contributed positively and those who were 'passengers', or worse, had a generally negative influence on the group.[2]

This suggests that we may not be helping to equip students sufficiently with some of the transferable skills that are central to effective collaboration. As Rowntree points out: 'many outcomes of process learning, and many assessment constructs that have not given rise to objectives, do not get expressed in products' (1977, pp.138–139). In the collaborative context, outcomes of process learning which are not expressed in products might include the development of personal and interpersonal team-working skills such as communication, negotiation, self-initiative, resourcefulness and conflict management.

Further investigation revealed that students had little or no knowledge of basic group dynamics. Where we encountered evidence of tutors applying sound pedagogical theories of learning in teams with successful results (Gibbs, 1995; Janis, 1972; Jaques, 2001; Johnson & Johnson, 1994), this was seldom made explicit to students. Comments expressed by students indicated that they generally felt ill-prepared to work in groups. Furthermore, when they were expected to work collaboratively *without* a tutor being present, many expressed frustration at the time wasted through arguments and general poor management of the group and consequently they frequently resorted to requests for tutor help and intervention.

The emphasis on collaborative learning and heuristic principles and on 'learning through doing' in group contexts was clearly not working in ways that might be inferred in the Quality Assurance Agency Benchmarking Statements (2002, p.2). Our research showed that students were clearly not making the most of group learning.

USING ACTION RESEARCH TO
IMPLEMENT CURRICULUM INNOVATION

We subsequently applied Zuber-Skerritt's action research approach as our guiding framework. She defines action research as:

> ...collaborative, critical enquiry by the academics themselves into their own teaching practice, into problems of student learning and into curriculum problems. It is professional development through academic course development, group reflection, action, evaluation and improved practice. (Zuber-Skerritt, 1992, pp.1–2)

In our case, collaborative, critical enquiry was conducted both within *Assessing Group Practice* and outside the consortium thus increasing both the potential base of our data and the possible impact of the curriculum interventions we devised.[3] The consortium encompassed a diversity of institutional sizes, cultures and individuals with varied areas of special interest that enriched the action research process.

The fundamental student learning and curriculum problems identified here could thus be summarised as:

a) lack of student preparation for group work;
b) lack of awareness of group dynamics and techniques and materials to stimulate the development of group skills;
c) scarcity of appropriate and fair methods to allocate credit for group-work-assessed tasks.

The first two problems suggested that students needed to be taught *how* to work in groups. This view was supported by research conducted by Heathfield and Bloxham who showed that by introducing group-work training and induction courses, students became much better at making the most of their group learning (Heathfield & Bloxham, 1996).

The third problem required a systematic review of group assessment methods in practice, followed by action research to select appropriate methods for measuring and evaluating group processes and for identifying individual contribution.

Clearly there would be little point in addressing the assessment issue unless we could offer some 'tried and tested' approaches to raise students' awareness and understanding of group dynamics. In so doing, we hoped to help students to make the most of group learning, and also to reframe assessment as being central to the creative and pedagogic practices in group work.

Assessment methods discussed in this chapter are, therefore, informed by a constructivist pedagogical view of the relationship between learning and assessment that asserts that

- assessment is an essential element in the learning process and must not be treated as a bolt-on extra;
- assessment strategies must be fit for purpose;
- assessment *should* build student self esteem and strengths;
- students take an active part in their own and their peers' assessment;
- assessment *should* be more flexible than is the norm in HEIs (Higher Education Institutions), ideally allowing for student development in their own time;
- assessment *should* value 'process' as much as 'product' and generally allow more room for student diversity;
- ideally assessment methods, particularly in the performing arts, should be capable of rewarding risk-taking and 'legal rule-breaking'.
   (Brown & Glasner, 2000, pp.3–13; Bryan, 2001; Sherpa, 2000)

The consortium team agreed to monitor and evaluate their own group practice using the modes of assessment being trialled with students. These included self and peer evaluation, self and peer grading, forms of individual and group guided reflection as well as external observation and feedback. This process of self monitoring was also externally evaluated and judged to be both rigorous and transformative (Rust, 2003).

Within our action research group we *experienced* for ourselves the inherent paradoxes of recognising group and individual achievement as well as anxiety associated with peer assessment, conflict, risk and failure. We also experienced for ourselves the phenomenon of 'fair play' which recognises that, at its best, the totality of transactions is much greater than the sum of the parts, and consequently, the group as a whole reaps the benefits (Jaques, 2001, p.9). Our first-hand experience mirrored our research findings, that within higher education, this sort of creative collaboration does not, by and large, just happen either with staff or with students. The process needs to be modelled, practised and nurtured so that group members gradually feel safe enough to participate fully and ultimately to take risks.

Whilst we encountered examples of 'successful' group work where evidence of creativity could clearly be seen, this was usually not reflected in the mode of assessment. In other words, creative collaboration happened in spite of the mode of assessment being applied and often as a direct result of skilful and sensitive facilitation on the part of the tutor.

We experienced challenges in common with many curriculum innovators, such as pressures to retain the status quo because any change can be difficult to implement. This was usually due to complex modular systems generating a preference for standardisation. Because of our own first-hand experience of this sort of resistance, we were able to incorporate into our staff development workshops strategies to circumnavigate regulatory constraints when they interfered with or even prevented curriculum innovations being adopted. Similarly, we were able to pool our experience of how and where to locate the champions of change and how to enlist their help (Bryan & Maguire, 2004, pp.33–35).

KEY RESEARCH FINDINGS

Our initial research of staff and student perceptions of group work and its assessment largely conformed to the literature on assessment in general (Boud, 1995; Brown & Glasner, 2000; Jaques, 2001; Johnson & Johnson, 1994; Knight, 1995). For example, some staff felt that an omnipresence of the tutor to help and guide students would be the ideal, a situation in which every aspect in the development of a project could be witnessed. This ideal was shared by many students who would prefer 'professionals' to manage the whole assessment process. Far from welcoming innovative forms of assessment, many students initially resist the current trend that frequently requires them to take an active part in their own and their peers' assessment. A sizeable minority of the students we interviewed appeared to have a forlorn notion that assessment is a precise science, one that can be applied *to* them in all situations by the 'professionals'.

Many tutors we interviewed said they liked the idea of dedicating a protocol mark specifically to successful collaboration, although few managed this in reality. Similarly, there was a general desire to allow more time and space for collaborative projects. What frequently tended to happen in reality was that collaboration was a required strategy for learning (whether in rehearsal and/or performance), rather than an object of assessment in its own right. For example, drama students must work collaboratively (to a greater or lesser degree, depending on the type of production) in order to produce some sort of theatre piece. How well they cooperate, compromise, or negotiate to find creative solutions within their group will affect the final outcome. However, our research revealed that we appear to make little or no distinction (in terms of marks) between those who positively influence the process and those who do not, or who may even affect the process negatively.

The most taxing paradox, which faces all HE study but is particularly elusive within the performing and creative arts, is the necessity to translate quality into numbers – to arrive at a numerical figure which represents, for example, a live performance – and further, to ascertain individual contributions within a group project. Our research revealed that examples of successful practice (where the modes of assessment are well matched to the learning objectives) abound in the assessment of group work. These are predominantly in situations where the main aim is to provide students with formative feedback on both product and, to a lesser extent, on process. However, where the feedback is combined with a need to generate summative grades, it is not surprising that fewer examples exist. Nevertheless, we encountered some innovative assessment strategies, some of which are detailed as case studies and may be viewed at: www.ulst.ac.uk/assessing-groupwork/case_studies.htm

A THREE-STAGE APPROACH TO THE DEVELOPMENT AND ASSESSMENT OF CREATIVE COLLABORATION

The remainder of this chapter describes a flexible three-step approach to improve students' group work by:

a) creating an environment of trust;
b) exploring group dynamics using a Problem Based Learning (PBL) workshop model;
c) assessing group skills.

The approach is, therefore, conceived as a means of developing individual members' sensitivity within groups, and as a means of linking assessment to this process so that the optimum conditions for collaborative creativity may be engendered. We found Adkins's idea of 'community as practice' helpful in that it focuses on group processes:

> I developed the notion that community could be a practice, rather than an entity. It is something about the responsibility of the individual to the whole group. By responsibility I don't necessarily mean 'taking care' of the whole group – it is more like each person in the group having a commitment to the individual experience of every member of the group, including themselves. (Adkins, 2000, p.1)

Creating an environment of trust

In the performing arts, effective learning requires collaboration most of the time. This practical tried and tested method of creating an environment of trust and a sense of group draws from theatre improvisation, games, physical theatre and dance practice using, for example, weight-sharing and physical trust work. Within these 'safe' practices and boundaries, courage to commit fully to the group is developed (see Green, *Trust Workshop*, www.ulst.ac.uk/assessing-groupwork/workshops.html).

Physical trust work can develop into Contact Improvisation (CI), which is a process that demands a physical commitment and intimate collaboration with at least one other person. It is technique beyond the 'daily' state and is ultimately about interdependence through giving into and using body weight in partnership. The *Trust Workshop* uses some basic CI techniques that have been trialled with participants from diverse subject disciplines. Feedback from participants suggests that, with skilful facilitation, CI could benefit groups outside the performing arts by short-circuiting the initial forming and storming stages that can take up an inordinate amount of time. By its nature as improvisation, CI is about spontaneity. Through the impulses from the contact, the student develops the ability to 'physically dialogue' with another person. CI is about the student being able to commit and release his/her weight to realise the potential for moving, as well as developing physical listening to stimuli – receiving and responding and initiating (Bryan & Green, 2003, pp.318–319).

CI as it is employed in Green's *Trust Workshop* is introduced in such a way that the individual group members keep changing partners, and it is this that allows individuals to open up to the group and vice versa. The facilitator directs participants in a very careful way so that the touch is impersonal – it has respect and sensitivity but contact with a body part is simply a contact with support. Workshop participants develop the ability to fall and allow others to fall and then catch them. In CI, students learn that trying to control someone else is futile. If they try to do so by, for example, pre-empting how someone else will react, the improvisation is unproductive and a stalemate will occur physically. As the workshop continues, physical inhibitions even in their most subtle forms, such as someone constantly in the support role, lose their hold and the physical and mental liberation is apparent in most participants. On reflection of the experience of this physical dialogue, the participant often acknowledges how important it is to be open to the unexpected – an aspect of collaborative creativity which cannot be underestimated (ibid., pp.320–321).

The session demonstrates so clearly a group practising being a group; and the link from this physical experience of working with others then needs to be nurtured and followed up with collaborative work, when words become the main medium for communication and expression. If the 'give and take' can work physically, can it be transferred into the rehearsal situation? How might rehearsals be as fluid and open? How might they become as rich in listening and as eloquently communicated?

Feedback from numerous staff development workshops and from student focus groups suggests that by introducing some form of basic physical trust work at the beginning of a new group, participants feel relaxed and in a positive and cooperative frame of mind for the rest of the session. Non-performing arts participants sometimes expressed anxiety at being expected to do physical exercises, mainly because they were unfamiliar with this sort of work. However, once they realised that no technical expertise or special fitness was necessary, and that the tasks could be accomplished by anyone, they joined in wholeheartedly.

When invited to share subsequent feelings and/ or observations after a series of physical exercises, participants' comments were often powerful and quite personal. Since there was no pressure to comment at all, the fact that most participants chose to do so indicates that they felt sufficiently comfortable to share such intimacies with the group. The following comments from participants at three different workshops illustrate the importance of creating an environment of trust:

> I feel completely safe within this group and have a sense that anything I say will be respected.

> I have never liked sharing my experiences in a group in case I show myself up....in this group I feel quite comfortable about it.

> Once you've trusted someone to catch you as you fall, saying something that might be stupid doesn't seem that much of a worry.

Physical trust work can clearly unlock emotions and create a healthy sense of 'group identity' in a relatively short time. It must, however, be sensitively directed. Detailed instruction with accompanying artistic illustrations are intended to enable any sensitive teacher to be able to facilitate Green's *Trust Workshop*. However, unless the facilitator feels completely confident to lead the session, it is probably best avoided.

Exploring group dynamics using a (PBL) workshop model

Our particular workshop approach was adopted for two key reasons. Firstly, it acknowledges research which suggests that it is more productive to centre potential controversy around task-related problems rather than personal opinions or abilities (Johnson & Johnson, 1994, pp.310–311). Secondly, the workshop is a pragmatic approach in response to the view frequently expressed by both staff and students in our research that independent courses or modules intended to teach study skills, profiling, group dynamics or whatever are generally not taken seriously by students. The workshop approach taken here is, therefore, intended to be employed *within existing modules* using group work without any need for major curriculum change.

The workshop can be run as a one-off session or extended over several sessions employing more complex techniques (see Bryan, Workshop: *Developing Effective Group Behaviour*, www.ulst.ac.uk/assessing-groupwork/workshops. htm). The workshop model is simple to set up and run. The structure of the workshop allows for maximum flexibility (having been trialled with participants from 16 different subject disciplines) in that the group *task* or *problem* which students are required to undertake can be supplemented with whatever the tutor determines as key to the course of study. The only proviso is that a) the task must be clearly specified, including the time available in which to complete it; and b) the task must be sufficiently problematic or complex, thus requiring creative collaboration to determine some sort of workable solution. The tutor may also decide whether marks will be allocated at all, whether to emphasise task or to focus mainly on group processes. Structured peer observation is built into this approach using guidelines on how to give and receive feedback in a way that is constructive and non-threatening (ibid., 'how to give and receive effective feedback' and 'observation and feedback prompt', resources linked to *Developing Effective Group Behaviour* workshop).

Put simply, the group is instructed to carry out a task in a specified time. Some students are asked to step outside the activity and to observe the group, making notes based on their observation in response to some key questions. When the task is completed or the time has run out, the group listens (first without responding) to the peer feedback from the observers. The experience of simply receiving feedback and reflecting on this, before justifying, explaining, disagreeing or commenting at all, encourages a deep approach to learning (Bryan & Green, 2003). This is particularly so in the performing arts, where students are constantly placing themselves in a potentially 'dangerous' position in which they lay themselves open to potential ridicule by their peers and/or the audience. Taking risks and experimenting with new ideas and unfamiliar forms takes courage. Two second-year acting students provided insightful reflection on their feelings after their group performed and received oral feedback from their peers based on the observation and feedback prompt:

Before [exploring risk-taking and failure] we've always played safe in our group and got fairly good marks. I learnt so much more from this exercise and the feedback was really helpful, not hurtful as I imagined it could be, but encouraging us to continue trying new ideas.

I'm so glad that we have explored how risk-taking and failure can be seen in a positive way. I would never have dared to experiment as we did, knowing that we were being assessed on the performance. The fact that our working as a group was also being assessed gave me the confidence to experiment.

A pedagogic model where students 'do something' which is observed by their peers before receiving feedback is certainly not radical. Variations of the model were evidenced as common practice within performing arts schools and faculties. What is, however, *not* common practice, is teaching students *how* to maximise the potential learning from group work at the beginning through trust, from observed performance and also at the debriefing stage. We collated a bibliography and developed a bank of resources based on group theories which we found particularly relevant in addressing commonly expressed problems. These included, for example, De Bono's six coloured hats for developing group parallel thinking and dealing with 'difficult' group participants (De Bono, 1994, pp.36–44), and Jaques' group maintenance and group task functions helping students to identify different group roles (Jaques, 2001, pp.28–30). Our intention was that tutors and students might use any of the easily downloadable resources or point students to the source materials in the bibliography to provide some theoretical underpinning of the workshop model. These resources are primarily intended to raise students' awareness of group dynamics so that they are empowered to influence the collaborative process. Thus they learn to recognise when and how they might change the approach to group problem-solving if, for example, one or more members are sabotaging the process. They experience first hand what constitutes effective leadership, how to deal with 'scapegoating', how to utilise the strengths of all group members, and how to move the group through the stages of *forming, storming, norming, performing, mourning* and *retiring* (Tuckman & Jensen, 1977, pp.419–427). Sometimes these phenomena may be learned through a negative occurrence, where group members experience how *not* to lead a group or where they get stuck at the storming stage, thus jeopardising the success of their task. It is essential that the facilitator initiates a full discussion at the debriefing stage so that students learn how to avoid a repetition of the negative experience. By identifying their own strengths and weaknesses and understanding what is going on within their group, students become adept at steering the group in a positive direction when it inevitably enters troubled waters.

It should be noted that 'troubled waters' does not imply and should not be interpreted as the need to avoid conflict at all costs. Our research revealed that both staff and students are frequently afraid of conflict and will go to considerable lengths to avoid it. This is not surprising, since conflict can be destructive and waste valuable time and energy. Added to this, students often interpret 'effective collaboration' as implying a need to avoid conflict and engage in concurrence seeking (Crossley, forthcoming). We, therefore, chose to develop some practical approaches for applying Johnson and Johnson's concept of 'constructive controversy' which they promote as central to group creativity and productivity (Johnson & Johnson, 1994).

To counter this tendency we developed a workshop for staff and students to focus specifically on conflict and controversy in group work and consider ways in which disagreement and difference might lead to constructive and creative outcomes (see Crossley & Dixon workshop: *Addressing Conflict in Group Work* at www.ulst.ac.uk/assessing-groupwork/workshops.htm).

Assessing group skills

It is only *after* group participants have experienced working collaboratively in a safe environment and applying some basic group dynamic theory that formal assessment should be considered. The reader will note that self and peer evaluation, based on observation and reflection, is an integral part of the PBL workshop model. Students are, in fact, practising and developing their own critical and evaluative skills as part of the PBL collaborative process and should, therefore, be partly prepared for formal assessment.

The assessment criteria might be decided by the tutor and explained at the start of the workshop. If the tutor is present throughout, the assessment could be carried out by this person. Alternately, it might be more appropriate to involve the students in their own assessment by engaging them in the process of devising their own assessment criteria. This has two pedagogic benefits. First it aids clarification of the objectives of the session and second, it helps students to de-mystify the whole assessment process by learning how to determine what is or is not important in the exercise and consequently how to allocate the weighting of marks. The following process is a simple way of introducing self and peer assessment and focusing on the difference between group task and group maintenance. Variations of this process were trialled extensively throughout the three and a half years of the project.

Give a mark of 1–5 (5 is the highest) for:
- how well the group achieved the task as stated;
- how well you think *you* contributed to achieve the group task;
- how well the group functioned as a group based on your knowledge of group dynamics;
- how well you think you performed as a group member based on your knowledge of group dynamics.

Grading can be further compared and refined by asking participants to give a mark of 1–5 for group task and group maintenance role for each of their peers. This can be time consuming if all the marks are subsequently shared and full discussion of the variances is allowed.

If the group is relatively new to self and peer assessment *per se*, or to the idea of having their group participation assessed, it can be helpful to leave the whole criteria setting and grading process until the end of a session *after* feedback has been given and discussed fully. If this approach is adopted, it should be emphasised that this is not normal good practice (i.e. to impose assessment criteria *after* the event) but that it is being done for a particular reason, namely, to raise questions about *how* participants might have behaved differently, had they known they would be assessed on their collaborative performance. It can also demonstrate the importance of the mode of assessment being appropriate to the task.

Sufficient time must be allowed for participants to share their feelings as well as their perceptions of assessing and being assessed so that a commonly owned and shared mode of assessment may be developed for subsequent sessions where it is proposed to assess the collaborative process. There are important issues around encouraging student autonomy through involving them in their own assessment and assessment being the ultimate responsibility of the tutor(s). Context is everything in the choice of assessment. Self and peer assessment may not be appropriate in, for example, final year performances where the marks are critical for final degree classification. However, it might be an appropriate form of assessment for certain student-managed rehearsals where the tutor may not be present or for modules where group work is developmental and the final summative assessment could be peer assessed and tutor moderated. The point here is that peer and self assessment methods, as employed in the PBL workshop model, are valid for sound pedagogic reasons. There is a wealth of research which advocates the pedagogic value of involving students in their own assessment (Brown & Glasner, 2000) the most relevant of which in this instance is that students improve their critical judgement and that engaging in the assessment process provides a group identity through a common cause (Lapham & Webster, 2000).

CONCLUSION

Gathering evidence to *prove* that any approach or model for enhancing the quality of learning actually works is notoriously difficult. It is even more problematic when the research has been conducted as action research, where the researchers were themselves participating in a transformative process.

Nevertheless, I would argue that the methods described here have *proved* to work for a sufficient number of group participants to be worth trying more widely within higher education.

Evaluation forms were received from 350 staff and feedback was obtained from over 700 students across twelve institutions. Most of the feedback was positive, suggesting that what we set out to achieve was feasible and worked well for participants. Where respondents supplied suggestions for improvements or alternatives, these were fed back to the team and acted upon. The suggestions were usually about how the tasks could be made clearer or how we might offer more precise guidance for 'first time' users of the materials and methods. Nowhere did we encounter real opposition to the proposition that students need to learn about group dynamics in order to take control of their own group learning environment. Where we received comments about difficulty finding time within the already crowded curriculum to address group dynamics, participants were reassured and sometimes surprised how feasible this could be once they had experienced a workshop demonstrating flexible methods and approaches.

Qualitative data such as module evaluation by module tutors and Annual Subject Monitoring Reports within the six consortium institutions, indicated that there has been a perceived improvement in the quality of student group work. We would argue this is due, at least in part, to project interventions. It is, of course, impossible to 'prove' this since there are no control groups and improvements might have occurred without any influence from the project. Similarly, we have anecdotal evidence in the form of positive feedback regarding peer assessment and learning about group dynamics from students within the six consortium institutions (and a few who attended workshops). By and large, this is not recorded in any formal evaluation sheets but has been commented upon in discussions and workshop debriefings.

What we have learned through working directly with colleagues at staff development sessions and at workshops, which has been gratifying to consortium members, is that many *are* changing their practice as a result of engaging with project methods and materials. Quite often this might be in the form of attempting new ways to involve students in their own assessment process, or by shifting the emphasis of their assessments to match more accurately the learning objectives. Two comments neatly illustrate this sort of shift in practice which is so difficult to quantify:

I thoroughly enjoyed the workshop [*Developing Effective Group Behaviour*] and want to try it on my students, not because I'm a fan of peer assessment but because the workshop raised so many other critical issues that have been bugging me lately.

Since the workshop over a year ago, a group of us have used various [*Assessing Group Practice*] materials to raise students' awareness of group dynamics. We are convinced that the standard of work has improved but also that group work seems to be more fun with participants appearing to feel safe to take more risks.

ACKNOWLEDGEMENTS

The author gratefully acknowledges the contribution of all members of the *Assessing Group Practice* consortium to the development of this chapter:

Bretton Hall College (University of Leeds): Paul Cowen, Wendy Johnson.
Central School of Speech and Drama: Linda Cookson (Chair), Cordelia Bryan (Project Director), Anthony Dean, Debbie Green.
Dartington College of Arts: John Hall, Simon Persighetti, Catriona Scott, Claire Donovan.
Goldsmiths College: Robert Gordon, Ajay Kumar, Gareth White.
University of Salford: Steve Dixon, Jackie Smart, Tracy Crossley.
University of Ulster: Tom Maguire.

I would like formally to thank all the staff and students who shared their experiences with consortium members and who took the time to explain what does or does not work for them.

NOTES

1. This paper is informed by field research and case studies conducted as part of a three-year consortium project, *Assessing Group Practice*, funded by HEFCE's Fund for the Development of Teaching and Learning. The consortium was formed in 2000 to research issues in the assessment of group work in HE performing arts and to identify, develop and share successful practice. The project was led by Central School of Speech and Drama and also involved the Universities of Leeds, Salford and Ulster, Dartington College of Arts, and Goldsmiths College, University of London. Further details are available from the consortium website, www.ulst. ac.uk/assessing groupwork/

2. In 2000–01 the *Assessing Group Practice* consortium interviewed a number of staff and students in our own institutions and conducted a questionnaire survey from 36 neighbouring institutions. In addition, 142 tutors in performance and creative arts departments in 61 UK institutions were contacted for information about courses in which group activity formed a major part. Although the response rate was lower than we had hoped (just under a third of the 142 tutors contacted responded), there was considerable congruence in a variety of themes, many of which accorded with the experience of consortium members (Bryan, 2001).

3. During the three-year project (2000–03) and six months (2003–04) additional consultancy with CADISE (Consortium of Art and Design Institutions in the Southeast of England) a total of over 700 staff and in excess of 1,000 students have engaged with *Assessing Group Practice* materials and approaches.

REFERENCES

Adkins, J. (2000). 'Editorial' *Contact Connection*, Issue 19, Winter, p.1.

Boud, D. (1995). 'Assessment and learning: Complementary or contradictory?' In P. Knight (ed.), *Assessment for learning in higher education*. London: Kogan Page in association with SEDA.

Bourner, J., Hughes, M. & Bourner, T. (2001). 'First year undergraduate experiences of group project work'. *Assessment and Evaluation in Higher Education*, Vol. 26, No. 1.

Brown, S. and Glasner, A. (eds). (2000). *Assessment matters in higher education: Choosing and using diverse approaches*. Buckingham, UK and Philadelphia, USA: Society for Research into Higher Education & Open University Press.

Bryan, C. (2001). 'Assessing group practice: Background and project summary'. *Palatine Newsletter*. No. 2. Winter.

Bryan, C. and Green, D. (2003). 'How guided reflection can enhance group work'. In C. Rust (ed.), *Improving student learning: Theory and practice – 10 years on* (pp.316–325). Oxford: Oxford Centre for Staff and Learning Development.

Bryan, C. and Maguire, T. (2004). 'Notes on implementing peer assessment'. In Bryan, C. (ed.), *Assessing group practice* (pp.33–35). SEDA paper 17, Birmingham.

Crossley, T. (forthcoming). 'Letting the drama into group work: Using conflict constructively in undergraduate performance projects'. Submitted for publication in *Arts and Humanities in Higher Education*.

De Bono, E. (1994). *Parallel thinking: From Socratic thinking to De Bono thinking*. London: Viking.

Gibbs, G. (1995). *Learning in teams: A tutor guide* (revised edition). Oxford: Oxford Centre for Staff Development.

Heathfield, M. & Bloxham, S. (1996). 'From theory to reality: Research in practice and in action'. In G. Gibbs (ed.), *Improving student learning: Using research to improve student learning*. Oxford: Oxford Centre for Staff Development.

Janis, I. (1972). *Victims of groupthink*. Boston: Houghton Mifflin.

Jaques, D. (2001). *Learning in groups* (3rd edition). London: Kogan Page.

Jennings, S. (1986). *Creative drama in groupwork*. Oxon: Winslow Press.

Johnson, D.W. & Johnson, F.P. (1994). *Joining together: Group theory and group skills*. London: Allyn & Bacon.

Knight, P. (ed.). (1995). *Assessment for learning in higher education*. London: Kogan Page in association with SEDA.

Lapham, A. & Webster, R. (2000). 'Peer assessment of undergraduate seminar presentations: Motivations, reflections and future directions'. In S. Brown & A. Glasner (eds), *Assessment matters in higher education: Choosing and using diverse approaches*. Philadelphia, USA and Buckingham, UK: Society for Research into Higher Education & Open University Press.

Quality Assurance Agency for Higher Education. (2002). *Subject benchmarking statement for dance, drama and performance, phase 2* (online). Available from www.qaa.ac.uk/crntwork/benchmark/phase2/dance.pdf (accessed 28 June 2002).

Rowntree, D. (1977). *Assessing students: How shall we know them?* London: Kogan Page.

Rust, C. (2003). *Assessing group practice*. External Evaluation Report, available at http://assessing-groupwork.ulst.ac.uk

Sherpa, C. (2000). *Principles that should underlie all group-work assessment*. From Internet http://learn.lincoln.ac.nz/groupwork/policy/principles.htm

Tuckman, B.W. & Jensen, M.A.C. (1977). 'Stages of small group development revisited'. *Group and Organizational Studies, 2*, 419–427.

Zuber-Skerritt, O. (1992). *Action research in higher education: Examples and reflections*. London: Kogan Page.

6
Empathetic Creativity:
The Product of Empathetic Attunement

Fred Seddon

INTRODUCTION

My involvement with collaborative creativity originates from an interest in how jazz musicians communicate when they play together. When improvising, communication between jazz musicians can occur at a profound level and this is often referred to as 'striking a groove' (Berliner, 1994). Descriptions of this phenomenon include extreme feelings of relaxation that increase powers of expression and imagination, of being able to handle instruments with athletic finesse and of being able to respond to every impulse. Musicians talk of altered states of mind when ideas are not blocked and of creative musical freedom. Individual musicians exhibit extraordinary receptiveness to each other, combining their talents to raise periods of communal creativity to a supreme level (Berliner, 1994). Much of the prior research into the practice of jazz and improvisation has been based on retrospective accounts of experience gathered in interview studies with professional American jazz musicians (Berliner, 1994; Monson, 1996; Sawyer, 1992). Some studies have attempted a cognitive modelling of perceptual or generative processes involved during playing (Kenny & Gellrich, 2002; Pressing, 1988; Sloboda, 1985). Relatively few studies, however, have attempted to explain the psychological processes involved in jazz musicians' collaborative communication (although see Sawyer, 2003). This chapter reports an exploratory study that investigated the communication between student jazz musicians during rehearsal and performance (see also Seddon & Bachelor, 2003). Based on the evidence of this study, the chapter will offer a description and interpretation of the processes involved in the communication between student jazz musicians, mapping these onto a theoretical framework addressing the notion of 'empathetic creativity'. This proposed concept of empathetic creativity is based on the concept of 'empathetic intelligence' developed by Roslyn Arnold (Arnold, 1998, 2003, 2004). Following a brief account of Arnold's work, the chapter will move to an explanation of how these ideas can be extended to apply to the ongoing musical communication between jazz musicians.

EMPATHETIC INTELLIGENCE:
THE PHENOMENON OF INTER-SUBJECTIVE ENGAGEMENT

Arnold argues a case for empathetic intelligence from a pedagogical perspective. She maintains that effective learning can take place when an educator creates a dynamic between thinking and feeling and that empathetic intelligence articulates aspects of the inter-subjective (i.e. between people) and intra-subjective (i.e. within the person) (Arnold, 1998, 2003, 2004). This pedagogical perspective resonates with descriptions of how jazz musicians acquire and develop their improvisation skills by combining personal performance histories with jazz's artistic traditions allowing them to mutually absorb and exchange ideas. Unique visions are cultivated that accommodate change from without and within in an ongoing learning process (Berliner, 1994). In order to understand the phenomenon of inter-subjective engagement it should be firstly understood that learning will be best achieved in a climate of care and mutual respect (Arnold, 2003). The learning environment should offer care through providing autonomy, self-determination and challenge in an environment of security and safety facilitating experimentation without fear of making mistakes. Within this type of environment, learning is democratic and dynamic and engages with both the past and the present, the felt and the known, the tacit, and the visible, kinetic and potential energy (Arnold, 2003, 2004). An empathetically intelligent person will understand and be able to create this environment, harnessing complex intellectual and interpersonal skills for the benefit of others whilst at the same time providing creative self-affirmation. This level of care transcends the feeling or attitude of warmth for an experience and is the embodiment of attention and engagement in that experience. Learning through experience is limited without such attention and engagement which positions inter-subjective and intra-subjective engagement as the foundation for transformative pedagogy (Arnold, 2003, 2004). Empathetic intelligence is the fluid and dynamic engagement between individuals who observe, feel, intuit, think, introspect, imagine and evaluate their own data gathering of phenomenological moments while being aware that their attitude influences their subjective-objectivity (Arnold, 2003, 2004). In order to achieve this dynamic state individuals need to be able to differentiate self-states from others' states, be able to reflect and understand the dynamic between thinking and feeling in both self and others and be committed to the development of self and others. This endeavour will require the cooperation of rationality and emotion in psychic, cognitive, affective, social and ethical functioning. Inter-subjective engagement through empathetic intelligence promotes cognitive and affective ways of interpreting experience in order to relate effectively and affectively with others. Empathetic intelligence is grounded in personal histories and how they play a formative role in the development of personal, interpersonal and professional life. It is a blend of theory, reflective practice and idiosyncratic experience (Arnold, 2003, 2004).

According to Arnold, empathy is achieved by understanding the thoughts and feelings of self and others through attunement, decentring and introspection engaging in an act of 'thoughtful, heartfelt imagination' (Arnold, 2003, p.15). Attunement prepares individuals for exploration, risk taking, concentration and rapport. In this context it goes beyond mere concentration and aesthetically pleasing self-absorption to include cognitive distancing or the awareness of self-engaging in the experience resulting in the phenomenon of aesthetic judgement.

Whenever we reveal or display ourselves there is a need for affirmation of self. Attunement is often conveyed through 'mirroring', during this process the 'other' is recognised and validated but the 'self' is also validated. Mirroring can be unconscious or deliberate, such as when people choose to dress alike. In pedagogy, mirroring can be verbal, for example echoing or elaborating words used in an exchange. Decentring serves to distinguish between sympathy and empathy because sympathy suggests we share common experiences but empathy encourages us to decentre and see things from another's point of view experiencing layers of thought and feeling beyond what might be immediately accessible. Introspection requires the capacity to reflect on past experience to guide future action by working through stored, embodied and often unconscious memories to select significant ones. This process requires analytical skills and emotional awareness, which can give perspective to experiences enabling one to distinguish between personal and public importance, temporal and lasting significance. The symbiotic or interdependent nature of affect and cognition is secured through introspection (Arnold, 2003, 2004). Empathy is a complex condition requiring objectivity, self-understanding and complex cognitive and affective functioning. Distinction should be drawn between sympathy and empathy. Sympathy suggests that we share common experiences with others but empathy involves decentring. Empathetic intelligence in teaching and learning requires collaborating individuals to interact empathetically through mirroring and attunement creating a preparedness for exploration, risk taking, concentration and rapport taking into account shifts in intra-subjective and inter-subjective experiences resulting in a creative act.

EMPATHETIC CREATIVITY:
THE PHENOMENON OF INTER-SUBJECTIVE CREATIVITY

Arnold's pedagogically orientated inter-subjective engagement resonates with jazz musicians' inter-subjective creativity if we consider the following. Jazz musicians engage in a mutual creative learning experience when they improvise together. They have to be able to trust the musical abilities of the other band members during performance especially if they are taking musical risks. Musicians rely on each other to orient and reorient themselves particularly when playing 'against the time' (Monson, 1996). Improvisers can only avoid predictable responses by risk taking and self-challenge during group improvisation where they constantly reassess their responses in relation to the creative contributions of other individuals in the group (Kenny & Gellrich, 2002). By relinquishing authoritarian control in favour of a more democratic engagement, jazz musicians produce more creative results. This can be exemplified in Miles Davis's creation of a 'ritualised performance space'. Davis refused to provide authoritarian certainty in his group creating a heightened form of group cohesion with democratic and dynamic exchanges. This meant that his musicians needed to listen and defer to one another's projections more closely than before (Kenny & Gellrich, 2002). By listening and responding to other musicians a collaborative, and inter-subjectively generated performance is produced. No-one acts as a leader directing the performance; instead the performance emerges out of the actions of everyone working together (Sawyer, 1999). Emotion in music can be viewed as a form of social action rather than an internal state. Music is a powerful constructor of emotion in interactive contexts that can produce a 'community of sentiment' binding performers into something larger than the individual (Appadurai, 1993). Musical conversations are not conducted in a solely abstract, semiotic sense; they are created through interactive activities that are more than just linguistic properties. Inter-musical associations are not merely in the head but also in the heart and the body (Monson, 1994).

Empathetic musicians are sensitive to 'attunement' in order to signal attention and 'mirroring' to affirm and modulate musical responses. Empathetic attunement between musicians goes beyond mere concentration and aesthetically pleasing self-absorption to cognitive distancing coupled with self-engagement and aesthetic judgement. Such empathetic attunement in jazz often evolves from 'mirroring' rooted in the 'call and response' of African American music. Musical exchanges often begin with the repetition of a passage or a complementary musical response that develops later into a highly idiosyncratic and innovative improvisation (Monson, 1994). This process musically recognises the 'other' and the musical response validates the 'self' and can echo the phrase or 'lick' but more often will involve elaboration. Musical attunement can occur at both a sympathetic and empathetic level. At a sympathetic level of attunement there can be musical cohesion but clashes of musical styles, interpretation of rhythms or accommodating a weaker player can prevent musicians reaching an empathetic level of attunement. In order to reach empathetic attunement musicians must decentre and see things from the other musician's musical point of view. During decentring, improvisers are not only concerned with their collective time-keeping role but they strive also to achieve a 'collective transparency of sound' where each part is discernible. This requires them to musically occupy a complementary space in horizontal and vertical planes. Horizontally, they seek complementary rhythmic activity of an appropriate density within the space made available to them by the other musicians. Vertically, they improvise melodies that will not obscure the performances of the others. The process of decentring facilitates empathetic attunement and can lead to improvisers hearing things from the other musicians' points of view and, as a consequence, thinking of and feeling phrases beyond what had been immediately accessible to them. Introspection plays a part in empathetic attunement as either consciously or sub-consciously improvisers draw upon past experience to negotiate the many possibilities from multiple associations of their ideas. By going over old ground in search of the new, improvisers constantly strive to put their thoughts together in different ways. During improvisation a distinction may be drawn between the interplay of 'stocks of musical knowledge' and truly 'spontaneous musical utterances' (Davidson & Good, 2002). For example, musicians describe how they listen to recordings they have made and hear themselves playing phrases they have never previously practised that have emerged as a result of what the other musicians were playing at the time. These spontaneous musical utterances rely upon the process of improvisation evolving to an empathetic mode of communication requiring empathetic attunement between the musicians, which although rooted in the sharing of stocks of musical knowledge evolves beyond this process. It is proposed that empathetic attunement is synonymous with 'striking a groove' and is a prerequisite for the emergence of spontaneous musical utterances which exemplify 'empathetic creativity'. Attunement can only occur through communication so in order to reveal attunement it is necessary to investigate the communication processes employed by musicians during rehearsal and performance.

Investigating communication processes employed by musicians when they are improvising is a complex activity. Controlled experimental conditions with post-event analysis would influence the creative impetus for improvisation, which often depends on volatile performance variables (Kenny & Gellrich, 2002). Improvisation is essentially a social process and should be investigated in a naturalistic environment (Monson, 1996). However, it is difficult to reveal what improvisers are thinking about at the precise moment of creation because at that time they do not have access to their own sub-conscious processes (Sloboda, 1985). In the past this has precluded the examination of concurrent think-aloud verbal protocols made by improvising musicians with research investigation relying on retrospective enquiry requiring musicians to relate prior experiences. The current study attempted to address these problems by employing a combination of videotaped observation techniques with retrospective verbal protocols stimulated by viewing videotaped rehearsal and performance sessions (see also Seddon & Bachelor, 2003). Videotaped observation and interview data are analysed and interpreted by the researchers and supported with participants' accounts of their perspectives on the sessions.

THE RESEARCH APPROACH

The participants were six second-year students (five male, one female) pursuing an undergraduate Jazz programme at a university situated in the south of England. All the students were in their second year of study and were used to playing together occasionally as part of their course evaluations. The jazz course at the university where the current study was conducted was designed to incorporate three major areas in learning to become a jazz musician. The first year is spent developing individual instrumental and improvisation skills. The second year is spent learning the standard jazz repertoire and performing together in impromptu and fluid bands with a minimum of prior notice. This is designed to train the students for the professional world of jazz where often bands are put together to perform at a gig with a minimum of prior rehearsal. The third year is spent developing shared personal and musical skills in more static ensembles.

The participants were asked to select a repertoire and rehearse together with the ultimate aim of performing at a 'Gig' for one evening in their student union bar. This meant that the task they were given was closely related to their everyday activities. Six, hour-long rehearsals and the performance gig were observed and videotape recorded. A Retrospective Verbal Protocol (RVP) (Richardson & Whitaker, 1996) was conducted with the group of musicians after the performance gig had taken place. During the RVP the participants collectively viewed the videotape of the performance gig as a prompt for discussion. The Retrospective Verbal Protocol itself was also videotaped for future analysis.

The analysis of the videotape data was adapted from the procedure used for the qualitative analysis of text. This method of analysis is based upon 'grounded theory' (Glaser & Strauss, 1967) where categories emerge through a process of inductive reasoning rather than being specified in advance with the data being allocated to predetermined categories. The researchers repeatedly viewed the videotapes of the rehearsals and performance gig to analyse and interpret communication emerging from the sessions. In order to identify and describe significant moments during the performance gig from the participants' viewpoint the researchers also viewed and analysed the videotape of the RVP.

Six modes of communication formed two main categories (verbal and non-verbal) each containing three distinct modes of communication that were subsequently interpreted as instruction, cooperation and collaboration (see Table 6.1). In this context 'mode' represents the communicative mode of interaction the participants are adopting during either verbal or non-verbal communication. These modes provide a framework that gives meaning to the participants' activities (Hoogsteder, Maier & Elbers, 1998). A hierarchical distinction is made between 'cooperative' modes and 'collaborative' modes with cooperative modes associated with lower level cohesive processes and collaborative modes associated with higher level creative processes (Underwood & Underwood, 1999).

Table 6.1 Modes of communication

	Verbal	*Non-verbal*
Instruction	Musicians are told what and when to play in pre-composed sections (the head)	Musicians learn pre-composed part by ear or read from music notation
Cooperation	Musicians discuss and plan the organisation of the piece prior to performance in order to achieve a cohesive performance	Musicians achieve sympathetic attunement and exchange stocks of musical knowledge producing cohesive performance employing: body language, facial expression, eye contact, musical cues and gesticulation
Collaboration	Musicians discuss and evaluate their performance of the music in order to develop the content and/or style of the piece	Musicians achieve empathetic attunement, take creative risks. This can result in spontaneous musical utterances signalling the achievement of empathetic creativity.

Verbal modes

Verbal instruction

A verbal communication was interpreted as an instruction when a member of the group gave the other members specific verbal instructions (without involving any discussion) on how a pre-composed section of the piece should be performed. For example, during a rehearsal Laura gives the rest of the band clear instructions on the structure of her piece.

Laura: Right, it's Pete and Chris playing what they just played...
Keith: Twice or...?
Laura: Just once.

Verbal instruction emerged mainly when the group were beginning rehearsal of a piece and provided an appropriate non-democratic mode of communication for initiating performance.

Verbal cooperation

A verbal communication was interpreted as cooperation when discussion between the musicians regarding possible organisational changes (e.g. the form, sequence of solos and possible endings) took place in a democratic way. These organisational changes to the form of the piece were agreed to enable the musicians to cooperate, in order to achieve a cohesive performance by agreeing the basic form of the piece beforehand. For example, during rehearsal after playing a piece through, the following group discussion evaluating the organisation of the piece took place:

Chris: It worked.
Pete: It wasn't too bad was it?
Anthony: So what does it do...you know, when it gets into the solos?
Pete: Yeah...in between each solo you nod when you get to the last one.
Anthony: Yeah, yeah, yeah but I mean it goes erm...der.der.der. der,der,der [sings phrase]...and you're straight in there aren't you?
Pete: That's on the top that der.der.der. is at the top of the solo, yeah.

Verbal cooperation was employed each time musical communication either broke down or was suspended. It provided a medium for the musicians to clarify, evaluate and adapt organisational issues, which did not involve creative issues. This evidenced the link between cooperation and organisation indicating a lower level mode of communication than collaboration, which was linked to creative issues.

Verbal collaboration

A verbal communication was interpreted as collaborative when discussion regarding possible creative changes took place in a democratic way. During verbal collaboration creative changes were discussed, developed and implemented following group evaluation of both the piece and the musician's individual and combined performances. For example, during rehearsal after playing a piece through, the following group discussion evaluating the 'feel' of the piece took place:

Paul:	I didn't think the feel worked for me in the solo...it doesn't really happen...
Chris:	The blow [improvised solo playing] over it?
Paul:	Well just the whole feel of it...the whole...
Laura:	I think maybe we could try it a bit quicker.
Chris:	Yeah.
Anthony:	Yeah.
Paul:	You didn't want to swing it...did you, or did you?
Keith:	I don't think you would be able to swing it anyway. It would sound like a completely different tune...

Verbal collaboration also took place when musical communication was suspended or broke down. It operated on a higher level than verbal cooperation and involved the expression of collectively agreed preferences, which gave a sense of the creative development of the piece belonging to the group rather than the individual who introduced the piece.

Non-verbal modes

Non-verbal instruction

Non-verbal communication was interpreted as instruction when there was a musical dialogue, which consisted mainly of one musician demonstrating how a pre-composed section of the piece should sound by playing it on an instrument or vocalising the tune. For example, during a rehearsal the group wanted to learn a new piece but they had no written copy of it so one of the musicians who knew the piece played it for the others to learn by ear.

Non-verbal instruction adopted the same role as verbal instruction in that it was used to initiate a piece and served as a means to communicate the pre-composed sections of the piece between the musicians.

Non-verbal cooperation

Non-verbal communication was interpreted as cooperation when the musicians became sympathetically attuned to one another, displaying non-verbal communication (e.g. body language, facial expression, eye contact, musical cues and gesticulations). This mode of communication facilitated a cohesive performance and at times contained sympathetically attuned musical cues, but focused on cohesive issues rather than creative issues.

Non-verbal cooperation was employed when the group was engaged in playing together and included musical and visual cues. These non-verbal cooperative communications were restricted to promoting cohesion and when they proved unsuccessful (in rehearsals) playing would often cease with verbal communication replacing it. Non-verbal cooperation, both musical and visual, requires sympathetic attunement between the musicians to occur even though it addresses lower level cohesive rather than higher level creative issues.

Non-verbal collaboration

Non-verbal communication was interpreted as collaboration when communication was conveyed exclusively through musical interaction and focused on creative exchanges. This non-verbal collaborative form of interactive creative musical communication requires empathetic attunement to occur and provides the potential vehicle for empathetic creativity to emerge.

Non-verbal collaboration took place when the musicians were playing together in an empathetically attuned condition. This facilitated creative musical development during the improvised solos and produced a perceptible 'atmosphere' between the musicians.

Researcher judgements of sympathetic vs. empathetic attunement were based upon comparisons of observed participant communication, both visual and musical, produced during videotaped observation sessions. When sympathetically attuned, the musicians were perceived to be drawing on their musical knowledge base, improvising without taking risks with cohesion or challenging their individual or collective creativity. Sympathetic attunement was visually evident in expressions of relative disinterest (e.g. no smiles, affirmative nods or energetic body movements). Sympathetic attunement was musically evident in comparatively predictable, complementary musical responses providing musical cohesion without creative risk through sharing stocks of musical knowledge. When empathetically attuned, the musicians seemed to respond to each other in an atmosphere of risk taking and challenge which extended their knowledge base. They took risks with musical phrases and timing and in so doing challenged each others' musical creativity. Empathetic attunement was visually evident in expressions of interest (e.g. smiles, collective affirmative nodding and animated body movements). Empathetic attunement was aurally evident in the production of unpredictable musical invitation or response when participants challenged each other to 'musical duels'. Researcher interpretation indicated that responses went beyond the mere sharing of stocks of musical knowledge and that empathetic attunement had occurred during these exchanges. However, the researchers perceived no spontaneous musical utterances being made in the taped sessions, therefore there were no examples of empathetic creativity.

Participants' perspectives: Retrospective Verbal Protocol (RVP)

The RVP offered the opportunity for the participants' perspectives to be heard. In the example below two of the participants discuss the importance of their personal shared history. These two participants (Pete, alto sax; and Anthony, guitar) had spent three or four summers together in Spain playing jazz and improvising. What they say here indicates they believe that this time playing together gave them special insight into each other's playing, resulting in a special musical rapport between them. This exemplifies and supports the notion of sympathetic attunement between the pair. In this example they are sharing personal stocks of musical knowledge acquired by playing together over time. The other band members are not included in this shared knowledge and as a result do not respond in the same way. This works positively on this occasion because if the whole band had reacted in the same way it would have destroyed their desired musical effect. Both musicians recognise their interaction as sympathetic attunement as evidenced by their comment: 'It wasn't a spontaneous improvisation thing.'

Pete: ...in that sort of circumstance you know...that sort of riff. From him hearing me play a lot he's bound to go up a semitone. If I play something like that, you know, so he jumps straight on it. Erm... and anybody who hears that knows exactly what I'm doing but it's just one of those things you make a decision. If the whole band went up it would sound really boring, you know but erm...The idea of the going up a semitone is for the crunch; it's completely out of key, every note is really, really crunchy you know. If somebody follows me; that's great. If the whole band follow me then it defeats the object of doing it in the first place.

Anthony: 'Cos I mean I...you know...I predicted it through...through prior knowledge. It wasn't like erm...It wasn't a spontaneous improvisation thing; it was just the fact that...I...we'd already shared this dialogue so I know...we understand each other's language.

Having some shared personal history can facilitate the exchange of stocks of musical knowledge that rely to some extent on anticipation of musical events as evidenced in the above example of sympathetic attunement. Shared personal history can also contribute to feelings of trust that can help to initiate risk taking when empathetically attuned, which can in turn lead to spontaneous musical utterances.

Participants were also shown video-clip examples from the performance gig of two solos identified by the researchers and by one participant (Chris, tenor sax) as being examples of the band in turn being 'empathetically attuned' and being 'not empathetically attuned'. After having viewed the video clips as often as they requested, participants were asked to comment on them in relation to how they felt about them being described as examples of the band 'empathetically attuned' and 'not empathetically attuned'.

'Empathetic attunement' video clip

I was enjoying what Chris was playing, he seemed to really like this piece. Overall I think we had a good energy here as a band I think, although not sure we were totally attuned at this point. It wasn't really flowing I don't think. (Laura, keyboard)

In the clip 'empathetic attunement' from the live gig, it is certainly true that something special seems to happen. Chris rises through several nice phrases before reaching a long and held note at the peak before descending through the horn and backing off the microphone. It is interesting that Chris felt this was a particularly creative moment, and I feel that it happened more or less by chance. From my experience it is possible to come away from a playing situation when one musician might feel that it was 'happening', or 'in the groove', and others may feel it was not for them. It's a very subjective thing, and I think it can be related to how one felt about one's own playing. One could hear a group, approach one of the members and say the music sounded great, only to find that it 'wasn't happening' for them. I think this can be related to people's personal perception at that time and can be influenced by all sorts of things such as mood, confidence and experience. I think the goal must be for everyone to feel the creative empathetic state before spontaneous musical utterances occur, which are to a large extent objective in nature as they can be identified. (Paul, bass)

'Not empathetic attunement' video clip

I thought the rhythm section were interacting better here than in Chris's solo ['empathetic attunement' video clip] actually, despite Pete getting lost in the form. It was a bit painful, I was trying to really make the chords clear in the hope Pete would be able to hear where he was. I was trying to mark the top, with my hand, but could have made it clearer for him. I think the rhythm section (Keith, Paul and me) were listening quite well to each other at this point, it actually heightened our ears because it was potentially a car crash and we wanted to avoid that! (Laura, keyboard)

Comment

There was not always unanimous agreement between the participants about whether or not they were 'empathetically attuned'. There was agreement between researchers and some participants on the occurrence of periods of empathetic attunement but neither the participants nor the researchers reported any spontaneous musical utterances. The lack of agreement between participants on whether or not they were empathetically attuned is problematic as the literature implies that professional jazz musicians perceive this unambiguously as a collective state. What must be remembered here is that although undoubtedly these student jazz musicians were highly musically competent they lacked the depth of experience one would associate with professional jazz musicians. One explanation for the sporadic nature of the students' empathetic attunement could be that they require more professional experience to be able to achieve wholly collective empathetic attunement at will.

DISCUSSION

The research reported in this chapter offers support for diverse modes of communication which characterise aspects of the musical communication between jazz musicians. The researchers observed a link between the activity engaged in and the mode of communication adopted. Instructional modes were adopted during initiation of the rehearsal of a piece. Cooperational modes were adopted when developing the cohesive nature of a piece. Collaborative modes were adopted for developing creative aspects of the piece. This supported the findings of Hoogsteder, Maier and Elbers (1998) who reported that modes of interaction had a typical dynamic that was linked to the overall activity of their participants.

The theoretical concept of 'empathetic creativity' was proposed in an attempt to clarify and explain psychological processes involved in the phenomenon 'empathetic attunement'. Much of the literature addressing this phenomenon is grounded in retrospective enquiry with experienced jazz musicians providing rich, recollected descriptions of psychological and physical states when 'striking a groove'. These descriptions indicate collaborative creative communication occurring while the musicians are in a collective 'altered state of mind', which results in extraordinary technical functioning, enhanced creative communication and the production of a creative product. Professional jazz musicians acquire the ability to reach this pinnacle of peak improvised performance by gaining mastery of their instrument, immersing themselves in the jazz community's traditional education system and by developing long term, collaborative musical and social relationships (Berliner, 1994; Kenny & Gellrich, 2002; Monson, 1996). It is proposed that during this process they learn to become collectively attuned when performing and improvising. At one level this attunement is sympathetic allowing for a cohesive performance revolving around sharing stocks of musical knowledge. At another level this attunement becomes empathetic, which is differentiated from sympathetic attunement by collaborating musicians either consciously or sub-consciously engaging in the psychological processes of decentring and introspection in order to become empathetically attuned. Once empathetically attuned an atmosphere of trust allows for creative risk taking, which can result in the production of spontaneous musical utterances that may be regarded as examples of empathetic creativity.

The current study indicated that, for the musicians performing in their educational environment during the data collection period, empathetic attunement was achievable for sub-groups of the band but was never achieved by all members of the band simultaneously. There are several possible explanations why the whole band was unable to become simultaneously empathetically attuned. Because the study focused on students in the second year of their studies, the participants may not have spent enough time playing together as a group to acquire enough shared personal and musical experience to become regularly empathetically attuned. This lack of shared personal and musical history may have inhibited decentring, introspection and the development of trust which are necessary precursors to empathetic attunement. The environment in which the students more typically performed could have had an indirect influence on the collaborative communication observed here. The students were usually continuously assessed during group performance and this can add pressure. This pressure can undermine congeniality and inhibit feelings of safety and security, which would not be conducive to collective risk taking. Thus it is possible that a lack of trust or feeling insecure in assessment situations (i.e. their usual sessions) may have had consequences for the collaborative interactions observed here – even though they were clearly not being assessed in these interactions (for a discussion of assessment issues in the context of collaborative creativity, see Bryan this volume).

There were examples of one member of the band experiencing what was believed to be empathetic attunement that was not experienced as such by fellow band members. In this case the individual could have been experiencing an individual optimal or 'flow' experience (Csikszentmihalyi & Csikszentmihalyi, 1988). As suggested earlier, this might indicate a lack of decentring, which may be related to longer periods of shared personal and musical history. The musician may be insufficiently experienced in jazz performance and may require more experience to be able to musically decentre. Empathetic attunement may be considered an optimal condition in collaborative creative music making or a form of collaborative 'flow' or 'optimal' experience (Csikszentmihalyi & Rich, 1997; O'Neill, 1999). This lack of agreement between participants highlights a major problem in investigating this phenomenon. Future research should conduct videotape stimulated RVP immediately after collaborative sessions with individual musicians followed by videotape stimulated RVP with the whole group to enable direct comparisons between responses to be made. This would highlight any individual or sub-group attunement not experienced by the group as a whole. The RVP example (see above) exemplified how shared previous musical experience facilitated sympathetic attunement between the two musicians. This supports the influence of shared previous experience regarded as important in the concept of empathetic intelligence (Arnold, 2003, 2004) and jazz improvisation (Berliner, 1994; Kenny & Gellrich, 2002; Monson, 1996).

Researching communication processes employed by musicians when they are improvising is also highly methodologically problematic because it can be over-reliant on researcher interpretation of observations of behaviour. The musicians may be employing sub-conscious cognitive and affective processes during improvisation that do not produce observable behaviours, or they may be insufficiently articulate to explain conscious processes. Empathetic creativity emerges during empathetic attunement which, like 'striking a groove', is an 'altered state of mind', that inhibits concurrent verbal protocols. Retrospective verbal protocols rely on memory and individuals can be influenced by collective, often exaggerated, 'folklore' influenced, accounts of previous musical events. The current study attempted to address the methodological problems discussed above. Videotape recorded observation allowed for participant interpretations to be explored during group RVP. Videotape stimulated group RVP also acted as an aid to participants' individual and group memory and allowed them to perceive their potentially 'altered state of mind' performances from more of a distance. Future studies could be improved by adopting a longitudinal design that would follow a group of music students from the beginning of their course through to the end and possibly beyond into their professional careers. A longitudinal study might reveal the progressive acquisition of skills and practices and their application to collective musical performance. This would enable further exploration of the proposed theoretical concept of empathetic creativity.

78 COLLABORATIVE CREATIVITY

REFERENCES

Appadurai, A. (1993). 'Topographies of the self: Praise and emotion in Hindu India'. In C.A. Lutz & L. Abu-Lughod (eds), *Language and the politics of emotion* (pp.92–112). Cambridge and Paris: Cambridge University Press and Editions de la Maison des Sciences de L'Homme.

Arnold, R. (1998). 'The role of empathy in teaching and learning'. *The Education Network*, No. 14, December.

Arnold, R. (2003). *Empathetic intelligence: The phenomenon of intersubjective engagement.* Paper presented at the First International Conference on Pedagogies and Learning, 1–4 October 2003, University of Southern Queensland.

Arnold R. (2004). *Empathic intelligence: Relating, educating, transforming.* Sydney: University of New South Wales Press.

Berliner, P.F. (1994). *Thinking in jazz: The infinite art of improvisation.* Chicago: The University of Chicago Press.

Csikszentmihalyi, M. & Csikszentmihalyi, I. (1988). *Optimal experience: Psychological studies of flow in consciousness.* Cambridge: Cambridge University Press.

Csikszentmihalyi, M. & Rich, G. (1997). 'Musical improvisation: A systems approach'. In R.K. Sawyer (ed.), *Creativity in performance* (pp.43–66). Greenwich, CT: Ablex.

Davidson, J.W. & Good, J.M.M. (2002). 'Social and musical co-ordination between members of a string quartet: An exploratory study'. *Psychology of Music*, Vol. 30, No. 2, 186–201.

Glaser, B.G. & Strauss, A.L. (1967). *The Discovery of Grounded Theory.* Chicago, Il: Aldine.

Hoogsteder, M., Maier, R. & Elbers, E. (1998). 'Adult-child interaction, joint problem solving and the structure of co-operation'. In M. Woodhead, D. Faulkner & K. Littleton (eds.), *Cultural worlds of early childhood* (pp.178–195). London: Routledge.

Kenny, B.J. & Gellrich, M. (2002). 'Improvisation'. In R. Parncutt & G.E. McPherson (eds), *The science & psychology of music performance: Creative strategies for teaching and learning* (pp.117–134). Oxford: Oxford University Press.

Monson, I. (1996). *Saying something: Jazz improvisation and interaction.* The University of Chicago Press: Chicago.

O'Neill, S.A. (1999). 'Flow Theory and the Development of Musical Performance Skills'. *Bulletin of the Council for Research in Music Education*, Vol. 141, 129–134.

Pressing, J. (1988). 'Improvisation Methods and Models'. In J.A. Sloboda (ed.), *Generative processes in music: The psychology of performance improvisation and composition* (pp.129–178). Oxford: Clarendon Press.

Richardson, C. & Whitaker, N. (1996). 'Thinking about think alouds in music education research'. *Research Studies in Music Education*, Vol. 6, 38–49.

Sawyer, R.K. (1992). 'Improvisational creativity: An analysis of jazz performance'. *Creativity Research Journal*, Vol. 5, No. 3, 253–263.

Sawyer, R.K. (1999). 'Improvised conversations: Music collaboration and development'. *Psychology of Music*, Vol. 27, No. 2, 192–204.

Sawyer, R.K. (2003). *Group creativity: Music, theater, collaboration.* Mahwah, NJ: Lawrence Erlbaum Associates.

Seddon, F.A. & Bachelor, C. (2003). *Modes of communication during collaborative, creative music making: An exploratory study.* Proceedings of The Third International Research in Music Education Conference, University of Exeter 8–12th April 2003, Exeter: University of Exeter.

Sloboda, J.A. (1985). *The musical mind: The cognitive psychology of music.* Oxford: Clarendon Press.

Underwood, J. & Underwood, G. (1999). 'Task effects on co-operative and collaborative learning with computers'. In K. Littleton & P. Light, *Learning with computers: Analysing productive interaction* (pp.10–23). London: Routledge.

7
Understanding Collaborative Creativity: Young Children's Classroom-Based Shared Creative Writing

Eva Vass

INTRODUCTION

Socio-cultural approaches to child development conceptualise human development as a culture-specific, context-bound, and inherently social process. This perspective is closely linked to the Vygotskian notion of social and cultural *mediation* (Crook, 1994). An overarching theme of socio-cultural research is the exploration of ways in which social interaction with adults or peers facilitates learning. Peer interaction has been the focus of growing attention in developmental psychology. Current socio-cultural theorising uses the term *collaboration* to describe ideal forms of peer interaction. This is seen as the *joint construction of knowledge*, requiring the shared understanding of the task and of the goals of the activity, and building on mutual commitment towards achieving these goals (Light & Littleton, 1998).

Research on children's collaborative work has mainly been concerned with problem-solving tasks in science, particularly physics and maths. Yet, there is a growing number of studies in the collaborative learning literature which shift the focus of enquiry to other subject domains, such as creative activities (see for example Dillon, this volume, examining collaborative music compositions). Such changes are especially timely in an era when education for creativity is gaining ground, yet teachers are reported to have difficulties regarding the teaching of creative techniques to be used in groupwork (Byrne, 1996 in MacDonald & Miell, 2000). Drawing on contemporary socio-cultural theory, this chapter contributes to this line of research, examining processes of shared creativity in the context of children's classroom-based collaborative creative writing. For the purposes of the current research, Marshall's definition of creative writing was adopted, which defines it as: 'the use of written language to conceptualise, explore and record experience in such a way as to create a unique symbolisation of it' (1974, p.10). The chapter also contributes to the collaborative learning literature by conceptualising peer work in this relatively under-researched context. In doing so, it aims to challenge existing conceptualisations which over-emphasise the role of externalised, reasoned argument in determining the productivity of peer collaboration. Building on discourse data of young children's shared creative writing, the necessity to move beyond the study of explicit reasoning and the need to consider the role of emotion-driven thinking is posited.

RESEARCH BACKGROUND

Models of writing

Classic cognitive models (e.g. Bereiter & Scardamalia, 1987; Flower & Hayes, 1980) define the process of writing as complex problem solving. In contrast, Sharples (1996, 1999) characterises writing as an unstructured activity with no fixed goals or clearly specified and ordered stages. Sharples argues that writing is comparable to creative design and, as such, can be defined as a fusion of synthetic (or productive) and analytic phases. It is seen as being based on two interlinking and interdependent processes, engagement – the generation of creative ideas – and reflection – the conscious breaking of the chain of association involving reviewing, contemplation and planning (Sharples, 1999).

In his model of writing as creative design Sharples incorporates existing conceptualisations. He builds on Bereiter and Scardamalia's (1987) coinage of knowledge telling – the creation of ideas through association, which can take the form of stream of consciousness or daydreaming or free association – and knowledge transforming – the exploration and transformation of conceptual spaces and reflection upon the writing process in order to monitor the text production and satisfy the constraints. Sharples links this dichotomy to the model of creativity offered by Gelernter (1994), comprising low focus thinking – a daydream-like mental state, in which 'whole episodes from memory are blended and linked together by a common flow of emotion' (Sharples, 1996, p.132) – and high focus thinking – the manipulation and construction of ideas or analytic thought. Sharples argues that when high and low focus thinking are mobilised towards text production, then they can be seen as knowledge telling and knowledge transforming.

However, existing models of creativity place the emphasis on different processes. While Boden (1990) links creativity primarily to deliberate explorations and transformations in the mind (high focus thinking or knowledge transforming), Gelernter (1994) argues that low focus thinking is the foundation of creativity, and unique analogies are formulated as emotion sparkles and binds thoughts in the dream-like associative process. Sharples (1996) joins these two arguments, and posits that the two types of thinking are both crucial to the writing process. They are combined by the mind's *conscious* effort to recreate an *emotional* experience, which prompts the composition of the written text. Thus emotion acts both as the trigger and the filter of thought at the same time (Sharples, 1996). Sharples' model emphasises the centrality of emotions instead of describing writing as a solely cognitive or solely emotive process. Also, by assimilating writing within creative design, his model reveals the complexity of the activity: it is not a linear process of problem solving but an unpredictable and seemingly serendipitous process of problem finding.

Research on children's creative writing

Research on collaborative creative writing is scarce. There is relatively little work exploring the role of peer collaboration in literacy development in the preschool and early primary school years (Pellegrini et al., 1997, 1998). The few studies which have been conducted comparing individual and collaborative writing have revealed that compositions written by pairs were more advanced than individually written ones, and the benefits of collaboration carried over into subsequent individual creative writing sessions (e.g. Hartup, 1996a). Other work on children's joint writing has examined the role of relationships (Hartup, 1996b; Jones, 1998) or the writing medium (Jones & Pellegrini, 1996) in mediating the collaborative activity. On the whole, there seem to be significant qualitative differences between collaborative and solitary text composition. However, with a few exceptions (e.g. Pellegrini et al., 1997, 1998), these studies measure the productivity of the writing activies in terms of the quality of the written product (mostly narratives). In accord with current socio-cultural work on peer collaboration, the study reported here shifted the focus to the analysis of the *processes* of paired writing, through the examination of children's paired discourse.

The analysis of collaborative discourse

As noted above, there is a strong interest in socio-cultural research on peer collaboration to examine collaborative processes through the analysis of paired talk. For example, studies by Mercer and colleagues (Mercer, 1995; Mercer & Wegerif, 1999; Wegerif, Mercer & Rojas-Drummond, 1999) have provided ample evidence that the quality of children's talk – their ability to coordinate the interaction and task-related action through verbal discourse, and their success in taking each other's perspective and negotiating – has a strong impact on the quality of learning. In the light of these findings, Mercer and colleagues developed a typology of productive talk, arguing that exploratory talk – the constructive and critical negotiation of views – leads to the highest cognitive gains in paired learning contexts in educational settings.

A further, highly influential, model describing productive forms of talk is presented by the line of research on transactive discussion (e.g. Azmitia, 1996; Azmitia & Montgomery, 1993; Kruger, 1992). The model for transactive analysis was developed for the systematic comparison of friendship and acquaintanceship talk. Although the framework was originally used to define productive talk in a problem-solving context – describing transactive discourse as reasoned argument – it has been modified (Kruger, 1992) and applied to collaborative music composition (Miell & MacDonald, 2000). In the modified description, transacts are utterances children use to refine, extend or elaborate on ideas that they or their partners introduced earlier in the activity.

However, the guiding principle of transactive analysis is to approach paired discourse as the sum of individual contributions, assuming linearity and turn-taking. Yet, working with the notion of joint construction of knowledge, peer collaboration can be seen as a less structured process by which children can 'put ideas together which would otherwise not have occurred to the person working alone' (Miell & MacDonald, 2000, p.350). Research needs to explore how such 'collective thinking' is reflected in paired discourse. For instance, in creative contexts, we need to explore what such sharedness means and how it is achieved at different stages of the creative process.

Also, building on Sharples' model of writing as creative design, discourse may be used differently to resource collaborative creative writing rather than problem solving activities. Since the two frameworks above were primarily geared towards effective ways of talking together and thinking together in problem-solving tasks, neither allows the study of paired writing in its full complexity. For example, neither framework informs us about the affective aspects of creative text composition, though the reviewed research indicated the salience of emotional engagement in writing (and in creative tasks).

To address these issues, this chapter presents a new analytic tool building on Sharples' model of writing as creative design. The model was developed to map features of paired talk to both cognitive and emotional processes associated with the joint composition of written texts. Therefore, it combines the study of language forms with the study of discourse functions associated with different phases in creative writing. Such a model is needed to understand how collaborative discourse supports the planning, composition and review of creative texts and to identify productive styles and collaborative strategies within this particular context.

RESEARCH APPROACH

Since the current research was concerned with the classroom-based creative writing of young children (i.e. aged 8 and 9), it focused on what *The National Literacy Strategy: Framework for Teaching* (DfEE, 1998) defines as Fiction and Poetry to be taught to this age-group: stories, poetry, radio advertisements, TV jingles and songs.

The reported research drew on naturalistic observations of collaborative creative writing sessions in Year 3 and Year 4 classrooms (children aged 7–9), over a period of two school terms. The study followed the collaborative activities of selected friendship and acquaintanceship pairs in two schools (10 friendship and 3 acquaintanceship dyads), whose collaborative work was observed and recorded by using video and audio equipment in the literacy classroom and in an ICT (information and communication technologies) suite. The observations involved a range of genres, including poem writing, story building and advertisement writing. Since the study focused on ongoing classroom activities with no intervention on the part of the researcher, the length and content of the recordings varied according to the teachers' lesson plan. The observed children were working together alongside the rest of the class and were not asked to do anything differently.

The 'literacy hour' teaching sessions followed the regular pattern of i) whole class teaching, ii) group activity (independent work) and iii) whole class activity (plenary), as defined by the *National Literacy Strategy for England and Wales:*

Framework for Teaching (DfEE, 1998). Some of the sessions were full writing sessions, whereas others involved editing and refining only. In the literacy classroom children worked in their literacy books and on draft sheets, whereas in ICT they were asked to share a computer and produce a joint copy.

The recordings were transcribed and the conversational turns were marked in each transcript (see p.95). Then each turn was marked for the writing-related function (or functions) it served. Discourse not linked to any of the functions in the model – for example off-task talk – was left unanalysed. The model was not intended to focus on individual turns. Rather, the analysis was extended to longer sequences, in which utterances were marked as centring around one or the other function. The following descriptions of the five central cognitive processes or functions were developed.

Content generation (1)

Creative content generation; the development of creative ideas through association, followed by the translation of these ideas into text. It largely draws on emotion-driven thinking – the retrieval of emotional experiences from the memory, or the exploration of emotions linked to events not experienced – which are used to stimulate the process of creative text composition. In joint content generation episodes discourse was used to pool ideas for the text, to engage in joint brainstorming and to extend and refine joint ideas. [Child A: 'S-A, S-A-I. I, What do we do for I? Ice-creams melting ((pause))' Child A&B: 'In the sand.']. Discourse involving musing, acting out and humour was also given the content generation function when aiding the joint development of creative ideas.

Planning of content (2)

Planning involves goal-setting regarding the text (theme, content, form or style). (Note that episodes focusing on the planning of procedure, collaborative strategies and working styles were assigned the process-oriented function.) Planning takes place at the macro level (general planning typically at the beginning of the writing session) and at the micro level (specific planning throughout the writing session, regarding the next line or idea). Episodes reflecting the joint planning of the composition were given this function [Child A: 'We do sailing.' Child B: 'Yeah, we do sailing.'].

Reviewing (3)

This involves re-reading and contemplation; the evaluation of the generated content and subsequent modification or redrafting if necessary. It requires the halting of the process of content generation. Evaluation can be carried out from two aspects, appropriateness – whether the writing fits the constraints of the task – and appeal – whether or not the composition pleases the writer. Discourse reflecting joint reviewing was given this function [Child A: 'Remember, you are not supposed to end with -ork, you are supposed to end with another sound.' Child B: 'I said the pork was so FAT, F-A-T!']. The joint reviewing process may focus either on written material or freshly generated ideas prior to transcription.

Thus, the analysis of shared reviewing was extended to the evaluation (and modification) of verbally shared ideas.

Transcription of generated content (4)

In this phase the writers focus on the spelling and formatting of the generated material while transcribing the text, or following the transcription. The function of joint transcribing was used to describe discourse centring around transcription, spelling, punctuation and formatting [Child A: 'What does it say? I don't understand your writing.'].

Process-oriented thinking (5)

Four out of the five phases were text-oriented. The fifth function was the process-oriented function. This function does not centre around the text, but on the ways in which it needs to be developed. The function of shared process-oriented thinking was used to label discussion about the step-by-step procedure, management issues, role division, sharing, strategies for collaboration, or the use of technical equipment [Child A: ((looking at their printed draft)) 'Let's use this to help us.'].

The analytic aim was to identify discourse strategies associated with (and characteristic of) these five discourse functions. The analytic process therefore involved the selection and examination of key episodes linked to these functions (e.g. joint content generation or reflection) and reflecting collaborative strategies associated with different phases in the writing process. Some of the key poem-writing episodes addressing two crucial aspects of the observed collaborative creative writing sessions are discussed below: the limited use of explicit argumentation on the one hand, and the centrality of emotions on the other.

ISSUES CONCERNING EXPLICIT ARGUMENTATION

The limited use of explicit argumentation in content generation

A key feature of the observed creative writing discourse was the apparent lack of explicit argumentation, especially in *content generation* phases. Instead, as the next two episodes elaborate, there was a heavy reliance on cumulative and sometimes disputational features of talk (Mercer, 1995), exchanges that build positively but uncritically on each other, including repetitions, confirmations and elaborations, or talk that is characterised by disagreement without reasons offered. Sequence 1 is an acrostics-writing[1] episode, where the first letters of each line spell out SAILING, the theme of the composition.

Sequence 1: Carina and Jenni

1 C: Right. We do sailing. There. How do you spell S. What can we do for S?
2 J: Sharks, swimming ((pause)) sssss-
3 C&J: ((overlapping, almost together)) Swish-swash ((pause))
4 J: ((happy, musing tone)) Swish-swash.
5 C: No, ((playful intonation, following it by shark-like gestures)) Sharks,

6   Swimming, Swish-Swash!
7   J: ((happy, musing tone)) Swish-swash!
8   C: ((overlapping, playful, giggly intonation)) Swashy. ((pause))
9   J: ((interrupting)) Right. What shall we, I tell you something. Right.
10   ((playful intonation)) Sharks ((pause))
11 C: ((musing tone)) eating ((contemplating silence))
12 J: ((with excitement)) Sh- I KNOW! Sharks
13 J&C: ((together)) Eating.
14 C: ((with excitement)) Scales of FISH! Yeah!
15 J: ((overlapping)) Yeah. Shall we put exclamation mark?
16 C: Yeah!

This episode reflects *collective thinking*, where ideas are not just shared, but jointly generated. Some of the ideas are articulated together (as in line 3), others are the source of inspiration for both partners, helping to set the scene and create the right atmosphere for the poem. For example, in line 3 the children expand on an idea – 'Sharks swimming' – with the same words – 'Swish-swash', which they verbalise together. The idea Jenni comes up with seems to trigger the same images for the two girls, and leads to a fully shared and sometimes simultaneous associative process. Thus, the children achieve sharedness in the core cognitive process which creative content generation builds on, and they form a chain of associations together. This type of talk is indicative of a very high level of sharedness in content generation phases, resourcing the collaborative generation of creative content.

The sequence consists of utterances which build on ideas uncritically, without challenging or evaluating them. (Note, that the 'No' in line 5 does not mark rejection, but indicates that the generated line needs to be recited with a different intonation.) The exchanges are short, and there are interruptions and overlaps. The sequence clearly demonstrates the educational advantages of cumulative talk in shared creative writing. Collaborative discourse with such features appears to be used to share new ideas, to link feelings and images and to start off a collective stream of consciousness.

One could also argue that it is the shared emotions – inspiring the jointly created images – which provide cohesion, and allow for the implicitness in the dialogue. The tone of the exchanges, and the exuberance of emotions highlight the centrality of affective aspects in the process of knowledge telling. The children display excitement (e.g. lines 12 and 14), they act out the images (lines 5–6), and mull over the lines they made up (lines 4 and 7). Their strong emotions with regard to the scene they have created are apparent. Both the content-generation phase and subsequent contemplation (musing and mulling over the words and ideas) are also strongly emotion-driven. Furthermore, the partners' acceptance of the created line is an emotion-based acceptance: no explicit reasoning is offered, only Carina's excited, immediate *Yeah*'s mark the end of the generating process. Thus, the shared generation of creative material (in this case the joint composition of a line in a poem) is a fundamentally emotion-driven and associative process, where explicit argumentation is superfluous.

Similarly, in the next sequence, two friends are writing a poem about hobbies, their theme being football. Through the slight modifications of an image (*running into post*), they come up with a new image (*sliding in mud*), linked to the original one through an intermediate product (*running in mud*).

Sequence 2: Mike and James

1 M: Hobbies. Football, football, running into post.
2 J: Running into mud.
3 M: Yeah.
4 J: Football, football, running
5 M: ((interrupting)) NO, sliding in mud. Football, football sliding in mud.
6 J: ((repeating)) Football, football, sliding in mud.

It is clear from Sequence 2 that both children are attentive to each other's ideas, and treat them as shared. It is Mike who starts the process, offering his suggestion for the first line of their poem. James modifies this idea (line 2), which is further refined by Mike (line 5). Once again, the collaborative discourse has cumulative features (lines 3 and 6), and is devoid of conflict regarding the modifications (lines 2 and 5), or the acceptance and rejection of those.

The collaborative content generation strategy the boys display – joint crafting – is very similar to the joint chain of associations, but the emphasis here is on shaping and fine-tuning. The metaphor of writing as creative design allows us to think of intermediate products as generators of new ideas (Sharples, 1996). This can be shown at the macro-level, via the study of how whole drafts serve as generators for something completely new, and at the micro-level, as above, through the analysis of how particular ideas are used as intermediate products. Joint crafting is a discourse strategy often found in the observed creative writing dialogues, which involves the extension and refinement of the other's ideas or its incorporation in one's own version. As noted above, the discourse is characterised by cumulative and disputational features, and frequent repetitions. The partners repeat each other's ideas for expansion, fine-tune them, and accept or reject the presented alternatives without explicit argumentation.

In collaborative content-generation episodes building on a joint chain of associations or joint crafting, ideas were used as shared property. The collaborative partners came up with a fully shared line, which they may not have thought of on their own. The examples used to describe these strategies demonstrate how paired talk resourced the sharing and joint composition of creative material, and underline the role of free accumulation and merging of ideas and the importance of emotion-driven thinking in this writing-phase.

Explicit argumentation and reviewing

The ability to reflect on one's own work was conceptualised as being fundamental to the writing process. This key role can be linked to the notion of constraint satisfaction. There are external constraints – for example a set topic, instructions or external guidelines – internal constraints – such as existing concepts and schemas constituting the writer's knowledge spaces – and the constraints set by the tools the writer uses. These constraints combine to both limit and resource the process of writing (Sharples, 1996). The analytic tool developed for the study contains two main discourse functions linked to reflective processes, joint planning and reviewing (evaluation and modification) of creative content.

During the observed writing activities, evaluative thoughts were often externalised by one or both partners. Evaluation was carried out using two criteria, one being appropriateness – whether the writing fitted the constraints of the task – and *appeal* – whether or not the writing pleased the writers.[2] In contrast to its limited use in shared content generation phases, explicit reasoning served an important role in the joint evaluation of appropriateness. To illuminate this distinction, the next poem-writing episode shows two boys generating a line that would rhyme with their previous one, *Your eyes would go blurry.*

Sequence 3: Martin and Alan

1 A: How about ((looking at the whiteboard)) it's so spooky,
2 M: So ( )
3 A: ((overlapping)) You would go skooky.
4 M: ( ) Yeah, but we've got blurry!
5 A: No. Oh, yeah, we need to get one to rhyme with this! Something that
6   has got an R and Y in. It is going to be hard.

Alan starts a short content generation process (lines 1–3), coming up with ideas for the next line. Martin rejects Alan's suggestion, noting that it would not rhyme with the previous line, which ends with *blurry* (line 4). This evaluative comment leads to the joint recognition that the generated line creates a constraint for the next line. Alan explicitly states this (line 5: 'Oh, yeah, we need to get one to rhyme with this'), listing the specific formal requirements ('Something that has got an R and a Y in'). This can be taken as a plan for the next line, which they will need to follow to satisfy the jointly recognised formal constraints. The plan is both content-related (what sort of a line is needed) and process-related (what needs to be done to come up with an appropriate line), revealing the difficulties with separating and distinguishing process-oriented talk and text-oriented talk. The partners take a general rule – every two lines need to rhyme – recognised and accepted at the beginning of the session, and apply it for the material they are working on. In the process, they build on exploratory talk, making reasoning explicit and available for each other. Thus, shared understanding regarding a small point of the task is achieved in the dialogue, through explicit argumentation. The episode reflects the children's attempts at joint reflection upon the creative content and upon the processess involved in creative text composition.

Such clear contrast between content generation and evaluation of appropriateness draws the attention to the complexity of the task of creative writing, and the need to study the function-specific affordances of particular discursive styles (e.g. the use and usefulness of explicit argumentation or the unconstrained accumulation of ideas). The next sequence further highlights this complexity, and the emerging skills of the observed young writers. The sequence is a long evaluation phase, in which the partners review the formal (syllabic) appropriateness of their first line.[3] In their attempts to count the syllables, they draw on the explanations of the teacher regarding a model poem, which was discussed in the whole group phase prior to the activity.

Sequence 4: Jenni and Carina

1 C: *There was a young girl from York.* So we have to ( ), I wonder, I want to
2   know if all that's one beat.
3 J: ((counting)) There was a young girl from- Yeah.
4 C: ((interrupting)) Young-e, young-e, young-e, young-e
5 J: Young.
6 C: Young-e, young-e young-e ((almost singing))
7 J: There was a young girl-
8 C: ((interrupting)) No-
9 J: ((interrupting)) There was a young girl-
10 C: ((interrupting)) There was a young-e
11 J: ((interrupting)) No, she ((teacher)) said young up on there ((whiteboard)).
12 C: girl
13 J: ((simultaneously)) She said up on there.
14 C: from York
15 J: Yeah but she said up there. Like it used to be young up there, and then
16   we said no because that's got one beat.
17 C: Oh, yeah, one beat. So we do one beat.
18 J: Yeah.

Carina starts the evaluative process by externalising her thoughts about the newly composed line (line 1: 'I wonder, I want to know if all that's one beat'). They both start to count out loud, comparing the beats they assign to words. The central issue is whether the word *young* has one or two syllables (*young* or *young-e*). First they try to convince each other just by sounding the word out repeatedly (lines 4–6). Then Jenni, who is convinced it is one syllable (or *one beat* as they put it), draws on previous classroom discussions to justify her argument (line 11: 'She said young up on there'). During the lead-in group discussion the teacher put a sample limerick on the whiteboard. In this limerick, she replaced the word *young* with a two-syllable word to show ways in which problems with syllables can be sorted out. This is a strong argument, one which Carina has no choice but to agree with ('Oh, yeah, one beat. So we do one beat').

There is a discrepancy in views between the partners, which they resolve by making reasoning transparent and available for each other. Jenni is employing the strategy of bridging from known to new – a term originally used to describe teaching strategies supporting learning in adult-led activities (Rogoff et al.,

1998). The partners draw on previous experiences to solve the problem of syllables, demonstrating the recursive nature of the process of creative design. The two episodes above show that joint reflection upon the creative content benefits from the children making their views explicit to each other, and underline the importance of explicit argumentation for collaborative evaluation (or in general, reviewing). The next section will examine the role of emotions in joint reviewing phases.

EMOTIONS AND REVIEWING

The reviewed literature indicated the centrality of the affective aspects in phases of creative content generation, where the emotion serves as the prime generator of thought, bringing up and linking ideas together. The analysis of young children's paired creative writing discourse supported this argument. Linked to the function of joint content generation, the study identified humour, acting out, musing and singing as the crucial facets of discourse carrying emotive content. (Although the discussion of these features is beyond the scope of this chapter, see the analysis of Sequence 1 on the use of musing and acting out.)

However, emotion-driven thinking was not restricted to content generation phases. While the evaluation of appropriateness was typically negotiated using explicit argumentation, leading to rejection or modification, appeal was simply *declared* in emotional terms without reasons offered. Evaluation of appeal was typically marked by short exclamations of 'Yeah, that's good'. Yet, it is the non-verbal message of such short utterances that made them marked. The short evaluative remarks were characteristically preceded, followed or substituted by grins, smiles, an excited tone, or playful, exaggerated intonation. Evaluation of *appeal* is therefore hard to represent with a tool focusing on the analysis of verbal discourse. To illustrate this, Sequence 5 shows such an evaluative episode within a poem-writing session, in which intonation and non-verbal communication play a very crucial role. So far the girls have written two lines: *Horses racing, pigs snorting.*

Sequence 5: Carina and Jenni

1 C: What shall we do? Cows rough, pigs buff. Arggggh.
2 J: We've already got pigs. Cows rough.
3 C: No.
4 J: Oooh. Look. Cows rough, crocodiles tough! ((They look at each other,
5   heads close, then Carina smiles and starts writing, Jenni giggles.))
6 J: That's good! ((both writing))
7 C: ((suddenly)) What is it? Crocodiles? ((looks over Jenni's shoulder))
8   Tough.
9 J: ((parallel)) Tough. ((Both continue writing, then look at each other.))
10 J: That's good! ((with a grin))
11 C: ((pen in mouth)) Yeah.
12 J: ((grinning)) I like that one.

13 C: Cows rough-
14 J: ((interrupting, reciting, head moving with the rhythm)) Horses racing,
15   pigs snorting,
16 J&C: ((together, Carina beating the rhythm on the table with her pen)) Cows
17   rough, crocodiles tough. ((they look at each other, Jenni grinning))

Carina comes up with an idea for the next line, 'Cows rough, pigs buff'. First
Jenni evaluates it in terms of appropriateness, and rejects part of the line (line
2: 'We've already got pigs'). Then she switches back to content generation, and
comes up with a modified line, 'Cows rough, crocodiles tough'. They look at
each other and start writing, without any verbalised acceptance. The decision
is made through the exchange of glances. This is followed by an emotional
appraisal by Jenni ('That's good', lines 6 and 10). During the transcription of
the line Jenni expands her appraisal, further highlighting its appeal (line 12: 'I
like that one'). In the end, they start to recite the poem, Jenni moving her head
with the rhythm, and Carina beating it with her pencil on the table.

   There is good verbal evidence in this episode of reviewing at an emotional
level (lines 6, 10 and 12). However, the children's non-verbal language (glances,
giggles and grins) carries the most direct and immediate evaluative message.
Note also that the use of recital in the appraisal of the work is a feature which
further demonstrates the fundamental role of emotions in the process of
creative writing. The children find great pleasure in repeating lines from the
poem they have just written, and by reciting they acknowledge their acceptance
and shared ownership of the work. This sequence clearly shows that emotion-
driven thinking is not restricted to joint content generation, highlighting its
all-pervasive role in creative writing. Note that, apart from these task-related
functions, emotive language also appeared to have social functions.

DISCUSSION

Explicit argumentation and emotion-driven thinking

This chapter examined how paired talk can support joint processes of creative
text composition. It was shown that patterns of paired talk associated with
different functions were qualitatively different. Joint processes of content
generation were shown to be supported by the uncritical accumulation and
sharing of ideas. Joint content generation was characterised by cumulative
and disputational features, intensity, and the lack of explicit argumentation
and reasoning. At the same time, reflective phases such as the evaluation of
appropriateness were shown to be resourced by detached perspective taking and
explicit argumentation. However, the differences found between the evaluation
of appeal and appropriateness indicate that the clear-cut separation between
content generation and reflection in terms of the use of explicit argumentation
does not hold. Rather, the use and usefulness of explicit reasoning for shared
creative writing was seen to be restricted to the evaluation of appropriateness.

This finding shows the unnecessary over-emphasis on explicit reasoning in models studying the productivity of peer collaboration through the analysis of paired talk. Equally, it supports arguments about the complexity of creative writing (e.g. Sharples, 1996). In particular, it provides evidence for the iterative, cyclical nature of creative writing, building on the qualitatively different cognitive processes described as high and low focus thinking (Gelernter, 1994) or knowledge telling and knowledge transforming (Bereiter & Scardamalia, 1987). This finding has both theoretical and methodological implications, informing research on collaborative creative writing, and on collaborative creative design in general.

Also, the discussion highlighted the centrality of emotions in the process of creative writing. It showed that reviewing was equally driven by emotion (evaluation of appeal) and reason (evaluation of appropriateness). Thus, different phases within the writing process may be associated with different levels of emotion-driven and intellect-driven thinking. Yet, the emerging model goes beyond the clear-cut dichotomy of engagement and reflection posited by Sharples. The centrality of emotions in this formulation is not restricted to the process of content generation, it permeates much of the activity.

Whilst the chapter discussed content generation and reflection as distinct phases, in the observed activities ideas were often immediately reflected upon, triggering the emergence of new thoughts and resulting in swift iterative cycles. This meant that clear-cut distinctions between functions proved difficult to make. Although this aspect is beyond the scope of the chapter, the iterative process of writing and the interlinking nature of its phases have been explored elsewhere (e.g. Vass, 2003), indicating the need for future research in this area.

Intensity of sharing

The analysis of discourse in different phases revealed young children's ability to achieve high levels of collectivity and sharedness. This, in turn, was seen as an indicator of collaborative productivity, leading to the joint composition and refinement of ideas which most probably would not have emerged in individual writing sessions. This conclusion – linking collectivity to productivity – is supported by Hartup (1996a), who provided empirical evidence for the strong interaction between mutual orientation (as opposed to individualism) and the quality of compositions.

However, the discussion was restricted to productive uses of collaborative discourse. Thus, what has been presented so far was one end of the collectivity–individualism continuum. Yet, the discourse of the observed pairs varied in terms of collectivity and individualism, and pairs did not necessarily exhibit the same level of sharedness for the whole duration of the research study, or for the duration of one writing episode. The analysis of the variations in the level of sharedness is beyond the scope of this chapter, however, it needs to be noted that the study of contextual features may help understand the reasons behind these variations. In particular, the role of the relationship between partners requires consideration (as discussed in Vass, 2003). Although the affective aspects of peer collaboration (e.g. the role of friendship) has been examined by research (e.g. Azmitia, 1996; Miell & MacDonald, 2000), it is not widely studied with younger children.

The analysis of collaborative talk

The work reported in this chapter contributes to the current methodological debate about how best to analyse collaborative discourse. It has shown that at different stages of the writing process the collaborative partners engaged in different types of talk. They exhibited a variety of discourse strategies clearly linked to processes central to creative writing: content generation (e.g. joint chain of associations or joint crafting) and reflection (e.g. the joint evaluation of appropriateness or appeal). Such a rich discursive and collaborative repertoire shows the complexity of the task of creative writing.

Different styles were successfully employed to support different task-specific functions within collaborative creative writing. Consequently, we need to recognise that the values we attach to discourse styles are not only context-specific or task-specific, but that they vary within this particular task. In the context of shared creative writing, the analysis of the productivity regarding these discourse styles needs to come from an in-depth study of both the forms and task-specific purposes of the language used. The analytic tool developed for this study proved useful in differentiating phases of the creative writing process, and in the identification of discourse styles and collaborative strategies characteristic of each phase, thus distinguishing different writing-related functions within the paired talk. The significance of this qualitative, functional model lies in its task-sensitivity and descriptive power in the specific context of paired creative writing. As such, it is a useful tool to examine processes of collaborative creative writing, and thus to describe and understand the process of shared creative writing better.

Young children's creative writing

In contrast to previous work focusing on the quality of the writing product (creative outcome), or using think-aloud protocols of individual writing sessions (e.g. Bereiter & Scardamalia, 1982), the current research studied ongoing cognitive processes through the analysis of paired discourse. Such a method is more effective for documenting emerging writing skills, which are not shown in the writing product, and may not be explicitly represented in a think-aloud-protocol. Indeed, the work reported in this chapter showed the young partners' ability to switch between different phases of the creative writing process. This finding contradicts existing research (Sharples, 1999), and shows the potential capacities of young writers at an early age. It is possible that this finding is attributed to the collaborative context, which enables the children to share the cognitive load. This interpretation supports the socio-cultural perspective of collaboration as a learning context where the coordination of individual efforts enables the partners to carry out a task which they may not necessarily be able to perform individually. In this way, the study further highlights the need to explore the role of peer collaboration in literacy development in the early primary school years, with special regard to the development of creative writing skills. It also offers a powerful tool to study the emerging creative writing skills and developing competencies of young writers.

CONCLUDING REMARKS

Following on from this discussion, one plausible conclusion would be that the limited use of explicit reasoning or the all-pervasive nature of emotions distinguish creative writing (or creative design in general) from scientific problem-solving and hypothesis-testing tasks as defined in existing research (Mercer, 1995, 2000). Instead, it could be argued that the two types of tasks differ in their emphasis on emotion-driven and intellect-driven thinking. Indeed, mathematical problem-solving tasks may benefit from shared associative brainstorming (similar to the content generation sequences discussed in this chapter), leading to unique connections and unexpected solutions. This interpretation underlines the necessity to reconsider the undervalued status of the affective aspects of cognition in general. It also underlines the need to move from models over-emphasising the role of intellect-driven thinking (the explicit expression of logical arguments) towards more complex models of productive and creative peer collaboration.

NOTES

1. Acrostics are poems in which the first letter of each line forms a meaningful word when read vertically, usually the title or the theme of the poem.
2. I use the word *appeal* to refer to the emotional response of the young writers to the material they have generated: the affective value of the emerging text (i.e. whether it sounds good or not, whether they like it or not, whether it is exciting, pleasing, entertaining for them or not).
3. They are writing a limerick, a humorous poem with a strict syllabic and rhythmic pattern.

REFERENCES

Azmitia, M. (1996). 'Peer interactive minds: developmental, theoretical, and methodological issues'. In P.B. Baltes & U.M. Staudinger (eds), *Interactive minds – Life-span perspectives on the social foundation of cognition* (pp.133–62). Cambridge: Cambridge University Press.

Azmitia, M. & Montgomery, R. (1993). 'Friendship, transactive dialogues, and the development of scientific reasoning'. *Social Development, 2* (3), 202–221.

Bereiter, C. & Scardamalia, M. (1982). 'From conversation to composition: The role of instruction in a developmental process'. In R. Glaser (ed.), *Advances in instructional psychology* (Vol. 2, pp.1–64). Hillsdale, NJ: Lawrence Erlbaum Associates.

Bereiter, C. & Scardamalia, M. (1987). *The psychology of written composition.* Hillsdale, NJ; London: Lawrence Erlbaum Associates.

Boden, M.A. (1990). *The creative mind: Myths and mechanisms.* London: Weidenfeld & Nicolson.

Crook, C. (1994). *Computers and the collaborative experience of learning.* London: Routledge.

DfEE (1998). *The National Literacy Strategy.* London: DfEE.

Flower, L.S. & Hayes, J.R. (1980). 'The dynamics of composing: Making plans, juggling constraints'. In L.W. Gregg & E.R. Steinberg (eds), *Cognitive processes in writing* (pp.31–50). Hillsdale, NJ: Lawrence Erlbaum.

Gelernter, D. (1994). *The muse in the machine: Computers and creative thought.* London: Fourth Estate.

Hartup, W.W. (1996a). 'Cooperation, close relationships, and cognitive development'. In W.M. Bukowski, A.F. Newcomb & W.W. Hartup (eds), *The company they keep – Friendship in childhood and adolescence* (pp.213–37). Cambridge: Cambridge University Press.

Hartup, W.W. (1996b). 'The company they keep: Friendships and their developmental significance'. *Child Development, 67* (1), 1–13.

Jones, I. (1998). 'Peer relationships and writing development: A microgenetic analysis'. *British Journal of Educational Psychology, 68*, 229–241.

Jones, I. & Pellegrini, A.D. (1996). 'The effects of social relationships, writing media and microgenetic development on first-grade students' written narratives'. *American Educational Research Journal, 33* (3), 691–718.

Kruger, A.C. (1992). 'The effect of peer and adult-child transactive discussions on moral reasoning'. *Merrill-Palmer Quarterly, 38* (2), 191–211.

Light, P. & Littleton, K. (1998). 'Cognitive approaches to group work'. In D. Faulkner, K. Littleton & M. Woodhead (eds), *Learning relationships in the classroom*. London: Routledge.

MacDonald, R. & Miell, D. (2000). 'Musical conversations: Collaborating with a friend on creative tasks'. In R. Joiner, K. Littleton, D. Faulkner & D. Miell (eds), *Rethinking collaborative learning*. London: Free Association Press.

Marshall, S. (1974). *Creative writing*. Basingstoke: Macmillan.

Mercer, N. (1995). *The guided construction of knowledge*. Clevedon, Avon: Multilingual Matters.

Mercer, N. (2000). *Words and minds: How we use language to think together.* London: Routledge.

Mercer, N. & Wegerif, R. (1999). 'Is "exploratory talk" productive talk?' In K. Littleton & P. Light (eds), *Learning with computers: Analysing productive interaction*. London: Routledge.

Miell, D. & MacDonald, R. (2000). 'Children's creative collaborations: The importance of friendship when working together on a musical composition'. *Social Development, 9* (3), 348–369.

Pellegrini, A.D., Galda, L., Bartini, M. & Charak, D. (1998). 'Oral language and literacy learning in context: The role of social relationships'. *Merrill-Palmer Quarterly, 44* (1), 38–54.

Pellegrini, A.D., Galda, L. & Flor, D. (1997). 'Relationships, individual differences, and children's use of literate language'. *British Journal of Educational Psychology, 67*, 139–152.

Rogoff, B., Mistry, J., Göncü, A. and Mosier, C. (1993). 'Guided participation in cultural activity by toddlers and caregivers'. *Monograph of the Society for Research in Child Development, 58* (8), no. 236.

Schegloff, E.A. (2000). 'Overlapping talk and the organisation of turn-taking for conversation'. *Language and Society, 29*, 1–63.

Sharples, M. (1996). 'An account of writing as creative design'. In C.M. Levy & S. Ransdell (eds), *The science of writing – theories, methods, individual differences and applications* (pp.9–28). Mahwah, NJ: Lawrence Erlbaum Associates.

Sharples, M. (1999). *How we write – writing as creative design*. London: Routledge.

Silverman, D. (1998). 'Analysing conversation'. In C. Seale (ed.), *Researching society and culture* (pp.261–274). London: Sage Publications.

Vass, E. *Understanding collaborative creativity: An observational study of the effects of the social and educational context on the processes of young children's joint creative writing*. PhD Thesis. September 2003. The Open University.

Vygotsky, L.S. (1978). *Mind in society: The development of higher psychological processes*. Cambridge, MA: Harvard University Press.

Wegerif, R., Mercer, N. & Rojas-Drummond, S. (1999). 'Language for the social construction of knowledge: Comparing classroom talk in Mexican preschools'. *Language and Education, 13*, 133–150.

TRANSCRIPT SYMBOLS USED IN CHAPTER 7

(adapted from Silverman, 1998 and Schegloff, 2000)

Symbol	Example		Explanation
(( ))	M:	Ok, my go. We'll go down one. Let me think.	Double parentheses contain author's descriptions rather than
	A:	((pointing at the screen)) Oh, it says that that's wrong!	transcriptions
(word)	J:	Ermmm big and small	Parenthesised words are possible
	C:	No, big (corks)!	hearings
( )	A:	I wanted to ( ) ship, ship, ship.	Empty parentheses indicate the
	M:	I think.	transcriber's inability to hear what was said
WORD	J:	Sharks	Capitals, except at the beginnings
	C:	((musing tone)) eating	of lines, are used for words/syllables
	J:	((with excitement)) Sh- I KNOW!	uttered with emphasis
-	M:	I, I, I was going to say, s-	A hyphen indicates an incomplete
	A:	((interrupting)) Sailing away	word or utterance

8

The Social Consequences of Classroom Art: Collaboration, Social Identities and Social Representations

Gabrielle Ivinson

This chapter will argue that collaboration is central to the achievement of most social acts, even those that initially appear to be solitary. For example, the art student sitting silently in the still life art examination is in collaboration with: the community of artists who developed the conventions of still life drawing in the past; with the school through her recognition of what counts as legitimate subject practice and with her family as she tries to fulfil their expectations through her performance. Art, the subject of this chapter, like all school subjects, can be seen as a fundamentally collaborative activity. Collaboration can take place on individual, interpersonal and socio-cultural planes as individuals draw upon traditions and conventions in their everyday practices. Viewed from a subjective position this process is creative if it takes individuals beyond what they knew previously. Ideas from the past are drawn into the present as people take inspiration from role models, traditional skills and cultural systems that are captured in language, texts and tools. From a sociological perspective, the triumph of the past over the present is characterised as cultural restoration. When new ideas enter society and the previously unimagined becomes thinkable sociogenesis is creative. The two processes, ontogenesis, individual creativity and sociogenesis, social creativity, cannot be treated as independent (cf., Rogoff, 1995) and the place of contact between the two is the interaction plane of microgenesis 'where individuals meet, talk, discuss and resolve conflicts' (Duveen & Lloyd, 1990, p.8). This chapter is concerned with the ways in which social representations identifiable at the sociogenetic plane impose limits and possibilities on individual creativity. It explores how the past, in the form of dominant social representations about art, exert an ubiquitous influence over the development of adolescents' 'artistic' identities.

Within socio-cultural literature the influence of the past on the present is often examined through social 'tool' use (Hutchins, 1996; Rogoff & Lave, 1984; Vygotsky, 1978; Wertsch, 1995). For example, one of the tools used in modern navigation, the Mercator projection chart, dates back many years (Hutchins, 1996). Through ethnographic studies of sailors navigating large ships Hutchins showed that the mastery of technically difficult procedures relies less on the expertise of individuals and more on what is achieved through the coordinated efforts of many people acting together with social-cultural tools. For example, in order to navigate with Mercator charts, three bearing-takers standing at different positions of the ship's deck have to send bearings of landmarks to the chart room where they are logged by the bearing time-recorder so that the plotter can draw lines on the chart. Distributed cognition relates to thinking that takes place between people and between people and tools. Wertsch's (1995) description of the influence of materials used in the manufacture of poles, from wood to fibreglass, on the achievements of pole-vaulters in the Olympic games, provides an example of the way tools call into question the boundary between the individual and the rest of the world. These studies highlight the importance of collaboration in which tools as mediating means draw ideas, know-how and representations that belong to the social plane of analysis into cognitive processes that are irreducible to individual cognition.

A different yet complementary approach to social thinking can be found in Moscovici's theory of social representations. This approach highlights ideas, or social representations, as socially distributed. Social representations provide the material for social interaction and for thinking. Moscovici makes a strong distinction between ideas that are shared equally among interlocutors and ideas that are imposed on the individual as if from outside. When people speak and act with an authority equal to others, collaboration is reciprocal and creative. When collaboration is governed by the rules of institution, creativity is often constrained. Moscovici captures this distinction by dividing the world into two universes, the consensual and the scientific. The consensual universe refers to the commonly held ideas and beliefs that circulate in everyday conversations as opposed to abstract or formal systems of ideas such as mathematics and logic. Moscovici explained the distinction as follows:

> In the consensual universe society is a visible, continuous creation, permeated with meaning and purpose, possessing a human voice, in accord with human existence and both acting and reacting like a human being. In other words, man is, here, the measure of all things. In the reified universe, society is transformed into a system of solid, basic unvarying entities which are indifferent to individuality and lack identity. The society ignores itself and its creations and which it sees only as isolated objects, such as persons, ideas, environments and activities. The various sciences that are concerned with such objects, can, as it were, impose their authority on the thought and experience of each individual and decide, in each case, what it true and what is not. All things are the measure of man. (Moscovici, 1984, p.20)

The distinction between the consensual and the scientific universe has historical roots in that between the sacred and the profane, and religious versus mundane life (Bernstein, 1996; Douglas, 1966; Lévy Bruhl, 1925/1929 cited in Moscovici, 2001; Moscovici, 1984). Moscovici suggests that science has replaced religion as the field in which the as yet un-thought becomes thinkable. Science represents an alien world of abstract, objectified concepts that people cannot understand. It is only when ideas that originate in science are absorbed into the consensual universe that people can connect with them and make sense. As new ideas are incorporated into everyday life they are endowed with communities' fears, desires and values. As the external, alien objects of science are brought into the realm of the familiar, simultaneously the past is drawn into the present. The disciplines that make up the curriculum belong to the scientific universe and initially they confront adolescents as unfamiliar concepts. In order to grasp these concepts adolescents have to develop social representations of school subjects and to achieve success, align them with those of their teachers.

The curriculum as a whole can be viewed as a social representation in its own right. At the core of this social representation is an opposition between the interior, that which belongs to the individual, and exteriority, that which belongs to society (Ivinson, 1998a, 1998b, 2000). Art is associated with knowledge that flows outward from the individual into society. Common sense notions such as 'talent' and 'innate ability' are often used to describe an internal competence associated with art, music and drama. Art is also associated with autonomy and creativity. Science is associated with knowledge that is external to the person and which needs to be internalised. For example, students are expected to display knowledge in science examinations that is uncontaminated by subjective opinion. The curriculum is made up of elements which, taken as a whole, function symbolically to calibrate the balance between external social control and internal, individual autonomy. The line drawn between the internal and external worlds, between autonomy and control varies across cultures and across different moments in history. For example the 'back to basics' reaction against child-centred pedagogies in the 1990s in the UK shifted the balance away from autonomy towards control. This was intensified in the mid-1990s through a shift towards central government controlled pedagogies in literacy and numeracy which teachers experienced as constraint. In schools, as in society, art fulfils a symbolic function to counteract social constraint.

THE ART STUDENT'S DILEMMA

This dominant social representation of art ensures that more than in other subjects, the objects produced in art are interpreted as the outward manifestation of interiority. Corresponding to this is a sense that art cannot be taught; either it is in you or it is not, and this sense of art as a 'natural, innate' property places art at the limits of pedagogic intervention. Adolescents are therefore confronted with what appears to be an intractable dilemma – how to learn art when art is represented as inborn talent? This problem frames the development of social identities within art and presents a different set of problems for adolescents than those found, for example, in mathematics (Abreu, 1995; Lave, 1988; Walkerdine, 1988). Art, like other subjects, is an uneven and socially distributed field. Communities anchor different social representations of art according to their own networks of meaning. Anchoring refers to the way abstract notions such as 'art' are endowed with meaning and value according to what is familiar and useful within specific communities. For example, one family may talk about art as something that belongs to museums and galleries and another may talk about art as artefacts that they seek out to adorn the home. Even so, viewed from a macro plane of analysis, a dominant social representation of art sets limits and possibilities on social collaboration, participation and social identities. In schools in the UK art is a compulsory subject up until Year 9 (13/14 years of age). In order to opt into school art after age 14 adolescents have to overcome these limits. Either they have to be recognised by others as 'talented' or they have to find social recognition that defies the naturalist association.

DEVELOPMENT IN ART

The symbolic function that art is expected to fulfil in the curriculum becomes increasingly strained due to the pedagogic necessities of preparing students for art examinations in secondary schools. As Dewey (1934) pointed out, there is a common misperception of art as spontaneous and instinctive. Dewey's point alerts us to the presence of a dominant social representation of art in Western societies. Yet, in order to achieve mastery in art, practice and thought must come together as intelligent action characterised by reflection:

'Overemphasis on activity as an end, instead of upon *intelligent* activity, leads to identification of freedom with immediate execution of impulses and desires. This identification is justified by a confusion of impulse with purpose'. Purpose requires a sense of a forward trajectory – foresight of the consequence of carrying the impulse into execution – a foresight that is impossible without observation, information, and judgement...the intellectual anticipation, the idea of consequences must blend with desire and impulse to acquire moving force. An idea then becomes a plan in and for an activity to be carried out. (Dewey, 1934, p.69)

The developmental process related to Art has been described as a 'journey to becoming more reflexive' (Steven, 1998). However, becoming reflexive involves acquiring ways of thinking from which to reflect back on practice. The process of becoming a social actor in the field of art requires learning concepts and vocabulary as well as skills and techniques. Some of the symbolic resources that students have available to make sense of art objects derive from the legacy of a Western European Renaissance tradition of 'high art'. It has been claimed that art lessons themselves have relatively little influence over children's developing representations of art compared to the effects of parental capital and cultural participation at least up to the age of 12 (Aschaffenburg & Maas, 1997).

RESEARCH STANCE

The study reported here focused on the objects produced by adolescents in art classes. Art objects can be understood in a number of different ways. First, the production of school knowledge in the form of texts, speech and art objects can be understood as extensions of the self outward into material and verbal forms. Second, the extension of the self outward into objects such as lino-prints, clay models and paintings can be seen as an *objectification* of a students' artistic know-how. Indeed the functional necessities of school institutions demand that knowledge is assessed and in art it is the object that is inspected, judged and marked. However, for the adolescent who produces the art object the way it will be received, recognised and judged is initially unknown. Therefore the moment when the object emerges from the hands of the adolescent can be characterised as a rupture. A gap opens up between the creator and the object and for a while the taken-for-granted meanings that ensure the smooth running of the everyday are disrupted. In these moments representational labour is required so that new adjustments can be made and the problem can be solved. We have identified such situations as moments of developmental transition (Zittoun, Duveen, Gillespie, Ivinson, & Psaltis, 2003) and this is the third sense in which the object can be understood. In order to resolve the situation the object needs to be recognised and named in some way. Once the object is named it is anchored back into a system of meaning and order is restored. The way the object is named will reflect the systems of meaning that belong to a group or individual who names the object. The students may of course themselves name the object initially. However, in the study reported here that was rarely the case, students relied strongly on the commentaries of others. The commentaries that were applied to objects extended a social identity to the artist that they then had to reject or accommodate. Commentaries given by others provided symbolic resources that were used to effect developmental transitions, to reaffirm or displace social identities, to restore order or to set up further tensions. The empirical study of school art therefore placed objects, and students' relationship to their art objects, at the centre of investigation.

THE STUDY

A series of three consecutive art lessons in two parallel Year 9 classes were observed. This methods has been used in a number of classroom studies (cf., Ivinson and Murphy, 2003). The school, which was a comprehensive school on the outskirts of a city in Wales, was chosen because it had an excellent reputation for art in the locale. Three consecutive lessons in each class were observed, in which students were instructed in the techniques of lino-printing. By the end of the third lesson students had produced a number of prints with abstract face designs. The lessons observed formed part of a wider series in which the topic 'The Face' was used to introduce a range of techniques such as clay modelling, designing wrapping paper and pencil drawing of self-portraits. Interviews were carried out with twelve students (six boys and six girls) from the two parallel co-educational art classes. In each classroom teachers were asked to identify students who were considered to be highly involved, mid-way and on the periphery of classroom practice (Lave & Wenger, 1991). Photographs of all students' lino-prints were taken and presented to students in individual interviews. The semi-structured interview schedule asked for students' views on the following:

- What is art?
- What did the teacher want students to do in the observed art lessons?
- What did the teacher want you to do in those art lessons?
- What was the teacher looking for?
- What did the teacher think was good/successful?
- What did the teacher think was not good/successful?
- What did you think of your own lino-print(s)?
- Are there things that boys are particularly good at in art?
- Are there things that girls are particularly good at in art?
- Do you ever take your artwork home?

Photographs of lino-prints were used to prompt students to answer the questions about what were considered to be successful and unsuccessful lino-prints. They were asked to find a photograph of their own lino-print from the pile when they were talking about good and bad lino-prints. After questions students were prompted with phrases such as 'tell me more about that?', 'why do you think that happened?'

CLASSROOM PRACTICE

At the beginning of one of the first lessons observed, the teacher presented the class with a range of prints by famous artists such as Picasso. In her commentary she reminded them of the German woodcuts of the twentieth century and spoke about the political unrest and religious symbolism depicted in various prints. Her commentary provided a conceptual language that linked the tradition and practice of print making to the social issues depicted in the symbolic representations of images. Following the presentation she told the students to gather round the 'Printing Station' (a group of tables covered with newspaper) where she demonstrated how to 'ink up'. This involved applying ink with special rollers to designs cut out of lino. In her commentary she stressed the need to achieve a consistent texture and a 'clean', 'strong' image. The teacher's discourse and practice provided a conceptual language as well as visible models of print techniques. An identifiable 'art' discourse referred to colours, texture, shading, shapes, techniques and how to use equipment.

During the lesson students talked about the combinations of colours they were using, aspects of the design of the image and the general effectiveness of the finished product. Specialist art concepts were anchored in peer group chat as conversations about texture, design and the use of colour were interspersed with speculations about romance, fashion and football. Some students spoke about aspects that had 'gone wrong', and experiments that they were not happy with. Sometimes prints were ripped up and put in the bin. For example William threw away a print and explained he had done so because 'it's smudged'. The experience of art was dominated by the need to master techniques and produce various effects. During the one-to-one interviews that took place after the classroom observations, no mention was made of the social issues that the teacher had referred to in her commentary about the history of woodcuts. However, across all twelve interviews students referred to art as a creative process that involved 'expression' usually described as inner feelings and emotions depicted in images. The following interview extracts illustrate how students in one class spoke about art as 'expression'.

ART AS THE EXPRESSION OF INNER FEELINGS

During interviews a pile of photographs of the lino-prints produced during the lessons was laid out on a table and students were free to search for examples to illustrate their points.

Hayley associated art with inner feelings and emotions. She chose a photograph to represent good art that was not her own:

> …looks like a really angry face, really sad, depressed, everything like that, it just…or embarrassed because like that then and the cheeks makes it look like he's embarrassed. Afraid.

She particularly liked the print because it depicted sadness and when asked why, she said because, 'I'm usually in that mood – annoyed basically.' Val, who was described by her teacher as good at art said that you were expected to know what you want to do. She described a series of techniques such as achieving clear lines and incorporating different shapes, wavy lines and lots of colour. Although hesitant, she described art as 'drawing out your feelings'. When asked what art was about she replied: 'Just like expressions…inner feelings and stuff like that.' She related the expression of ideas to the use of colour: 'Yeah, because like feeling sad you tend to do dark colours and mood stuff but if you're in a good mood you do bright colours and everything like that.'

One of the most elaborate explanations of the use of colour in art came from William who described art as:

W: How to draw, how to shade, how to express feelings as well. And how different colours mean emotions.
R: (Prompt) take me through that a little more.
W: Well, red is sort of like passion, love. Blue is cold. Black and grey is dark and dull. White is bright. Green is cheerful.

Students drew on examples from the immediate context of classroom life and spoke about their own and their peers' lino-prints to illustrate a dominant social representation, that art is the expression of inner feelings.

Scott also described colour as a means of expression. He liked the lino-print that he had produced in the lesson and searched for it in the pack of photographs until he found it and then said: 'Well, I've put a lot of colour into it, and I've like…expressed it.' He related expression to faint and strong colours when comparing various prints:

...it's like faded like, faint and haven't got much expression and it doesn't express itself. And that one's even worse again...Because that one you can see it's pressed on the ink like properly like. Pressed it hard down. With that one it's soft, soft touch.

Scott stressed the way ideas could be formed through physical action such as pressing hard or soft. His use of a concrete and physical language may still indicate an awareness of expression as inner feelings because he linked his own ability to 'express it' with colours.

None of the examples given to illustrate art as 'expression' referred to those given by teachers in their introductory commentaries, for example of German woodcuts. A possible reason is that these historically rooted illustrations refer to a remote and alien world, analogous to Moscovici's scientific universe. Some students, such as Scott and Val, thought they were good at art while others such as Hayley and William had decided not to continue with art. Although students shared the dominant social representation of art they took up different positions with respect to it and this often depended on the social identities extended to them by others. The transformation of identity lies at the centre of how learning is understood from a socio-cultural perspective. Social validation came from many sources and not just the classroom. The intentional instruction that takes place in classrooms is not necessarily the source or cause of learning (Aschaffenburg & Maas, 1997; Lave & Wenger, 1991). Adolescents encounter art in social contexts beyond the classroom and they bring these ideas and social identities with them into classrooms. Art departments are often more open and tolerant of adolescents' out-of-school identities than other subject departments are. Art classrooms can be viewed as 'interstitial communities of practice' that may or may not 'truncate possibilities for identities of mastery' (Lave & Wenger, 1991, p.42). As they move between communities, young people struggle for identity achievement. The following examples illustrate the different barriers to achieving a positive social identity with respect to art. Some students found their art object validated across communities of practice, such as Gemma who was extended an identity of mastery by her family, her peer group and her teacher (see below). Others encountered tensions between competing social representations of art encountered across communities of practice. In order to opt to continue with art after the years of compulsory schooling adolescents have to find enough validation to imagine a forward trajectory (Dewey, 1934). One of the tensions that had to be resolved was the conflict between the dominant social representation of art as the expression of inner feelings outward and students' subjective experience of the classroom as dominated by the struggle to master techniques and materials. The following section considers the way five students in the same class encountered and resolved these tensions.

RESOLVING THE TENSIONS

Gemma explained her position by saying, 'all my family think I'm good at art'. She had been to Florence with her family and visited art galleries where she saw pictures that 'took your breath away'. At home she had completed an oil painting that hangs on her bedroom wall. Her sister had chosen art as one of three specialist examination subjects at 'A' level (age 18). Gemma had experienced art in many social contexts. She distinguished school art that was generally recognised by students in this study as 'modern art' from art encountered outside school that was variously referred to as 'fine art' or 'real art'. Gemma as follows:

> Fine art is something you have to be really good at to be able to achieve, obviously the school knows that everyone can't be brilliant at art so they do something that's more [within] everyone's reach really.

Scott, who had been excluded from many subjects as a result of behaviour problems, was just returning to mainstream lessons after a period of special tuition.[1] He was struggling to adjust to classroom life especially in science and mathematics, which he found too restrictive (cf., McDermott, 1996). He enjoyed being able to move around the classroom freely and had opted to continue with art. One of the incidents that he recalled with pleasure was using Batik methods:

S: Ever heard of Batik?
R: Yes, Batik, Yes, yes.
S: I've done those in primary school. I done a pillow, made a pillow, I made pockets, made those for my bed at the end of my bed.

He talked with great enthusiasm about his pillow and revealed that his little brother still used the pockets on his bed. His good experience of art in the past and the tolerance with which the teacher accepted his behaviour, the validations by his family and a recent good mark allowed Scott to imagine a forward trajectory. During the interview he made no mention of art galleries or visits to places where art featured. He had a representation of art that included an awareness of the physical engagement required to work with different media such as clay and ink. His choice to continue with art was partially influenced by the difficulty he encountered in other subjects.

Val had also chosen to continue with art although unlike Gemma and Scott she encountered tensions between home and school. She liked art and said that her teacher thought she was good at it, yet when she took art objects home her mother received them with suspicion. She said that her family considered her school artwork to be 'weird':

R: So what do they think is weird about it?
Val: I don't know really it's just erm…because we did this tin foil thing last year and we had to scratch out the colour and things, and they thought that was weird. It looked a bit weird though, I think it did.
R: So do you think they would think your lino-print would be weird if you took it home?

Val: Probably, yeah.
R: Why?
Val: Because I don't really know, it's just different. Because like my mum likes
       pictures of like you know paintings where it's not just stuff, like that
       really.

She explained that her mum liked pictures of flowers in pots and her Nan
(grandmother) had framed photographs of family members on her walls and
mantelpiece. Given that most of the art used for instruction and displayed
on the walls of the classroom was modern and abstract, Val encountered a
dislocation between the kind of art that was recognised and legitimated at home
and in school. However, the encouragement received from her teacher and the
good marks that she had received provided Val with a way to imagine herself
continuing with school art despite her mother's lack of comprehension of the
objects produced there.

William was considered by his art teacher to be one of the best students.
He had an ambivalent relationship to art that was expressed in the interview
as regret for having decided not to continue with art on the one hand and
satisfaction on the other with his choice to take food studies instead as an
examination subject. He had a fear that he would be mocked by his younger
brother for taking art objects home that were 'not very good' although he said
that his parents probably would not mock him. He cooked for his family at least
once a week and at the weekends for his Gran (grandmother) and he reported
receiving a great deal of encouragement. He had an identity of mastery that
was more strongly anchored by his family in relation to cooking than art and
this seems to have overruled the identity of mastery extended to him by his
art teacher.

Hayley had thoroughly rejected school art and yet was the student who
articulated the difference between 'school art' and 'real art' in the most elaborate
way. Her rejection of school art was based on a disappointment at her own
inability to express strong emotions in her own artwork. She had a clear sense
of which lino-prints were 'artistic' and which were not and particularly liked
one of her peer groups' prints because it depicted sadness. She said in the
interview, 'I'm usually in that mood – annoyed basically.' She related her general
feeling of annoyance to her family and especially her mother. When talking
about her unsatisfactory art objects she described messing up the design (on
the lino-print) because the knife, 'went right through to the stuff'. She spoke
about a pot that she had made in Year 8 that she liked, yet when she tried
to take it home to show her mother it had been accidentally smashed. She
explained that normally she did not take art objects home because 'there's not
enough room in my house' and 'my mum just doesn't keep stuff', and 'it just
gets smashed anyway'. She said that her brother had spent four months on a
piece of examination artwork which 'the teacher just lost'. She had decided not
to continue with art and her main reason repeated the theme of loss – 'work
gets lost'. During the interview she spoke about 'real art' as opposed to 'school

art' as idealised representation of worthy subjects, such as famous people and historical buildings. 'Real art' was:

Like drawing, like landscapes and everything. Like going to like see the Castle and drawing the castle and actually, like, having a look at the texture of the stone before you actually draw them, so you look at the shape.

She described how artists might choose to draw because they felt attracted to the model, suggesting a strong understanding of art as the outward manifestation of 'inner feeling':

H: People doing pictures of other people because either person needs romance.

R: Prompt – Say that again.

H: Like people draw pictures of other people because either they fancy them, and they kind of like get to them, or they just show their feelings.

R: Prompt – Explain that to me a bit more. Give me an example maybe.

H: Well, a girl draws a picture of a boy, and she makes him out to be everything, and then, when she sees him and she's like he's not as good as I put him on the picture but like, there you go.

Hayley's social representation of art incorporated aspects of the Western European legacy of 'high art'. In comparison, she described her own lino-print as 'wonky':

'Cause mine just looked…wasn't that good like, it was just wonky. That one there doesn't look so wonky. And it looks, eyes and nose and mouth look in the right place. 'Cause mine is just the top half of my face, it looked a bit odd.

Hayley struggled to locate herself as successful with respect to art. She expressed disappointment in her own lack of mastery of lino-printing techniques and an inability to create objects that captured feelings, especially feelings of anger and annoyance that she said she experienced often. In order to preserve her representation of 'real' art she created a strong boundary between school art and non-school art and decided to opt out of school art, abandoning an unsatisfactory social identity anchored in classroom practice.

SOCIAL CONSEQUENCES

Within the curriculum the symbolic burden placed on art, as a counter-balance to pedagogic control that suppresses individual expression, ensures that the dominant social representation of art is actively maintained in schools. However, the symbolic burden carried by art as 'individual creativity' becomes increasingly strained due to the pedagogic necessities of preparing students for public examinations. A fault line opens up between the social representation of art as the expression of inner feelings and situated classroom practice dominated by the need to master techniques and materials. By focusing on art objects as transitional objects and asking students to comment, evaluate and justify their productions, the research probed around the fault line inherent in school art.

Firstly, it was found that all students in one way or another represented the dominant social representation of art as 'expression', and were able to give limited descriptions of art as the translation of interiority into external forms. Second, all of the students interviewed in this small sample had created a boundary between 'school art' and 'real art' and this strong distinction can be seen as the first step in resolving the tension between a dominant social representation of art and classroom practice. Third, although students shared a dominant social representation of art they took up different positions depending on whether or not they could imagine a forward trajectory for themselves in art.

Because art productions are visible and are socially marked as objects that require appreciation, attention and evaluation, students are particularly vulnerable to the 'gaze of the other' (see Zittoun et al., 2003). In order to resolve tensions between school art objects and the various social contexts in which these were received, acknowledged, and evaluated, adolescents had to take up positions with respect to art. Taking up a position entails the expression of a social identity (Duveen, 1997), and interviews revealed the ways in which students aligned themselves with or distanced themselves from school art. One of the social consequences of resolving these tensions is that some students rejected school art because they could not find sufficient symbolic resources to sustain a positive social identity for legitimate reasons.

Gemma's 'artistic identity' was strongly anchored with her family who valued art and encouraged her artistic activities. Her interview suggests that her family recognised a range of art that included 'high culture'. To resolve the tension between home and school art she excused school art as a simplified version accessible to all. Scott's interview revealed little about his family's social representation of art, except that they valued the functional use of the pillow-case and pockets that he had made. In contrast, Val's mother received her daughter's 'abstract' art objects with suspicion. The social representation of art anchored within her family was in conflict with school art. William's art productions were appreciated by his parents but not his brother and Hayley failed to make a connection between school art and her own objects. Taking up a position with respect to art requires a resolution of the competing social representations of art encountered in various communities of practice. By this stage in their school careers we can see adolescents finding ways to resolve tensions between competing systems of meaning, notably between home and school, through autonomous thinking.

Art, as with other symbolic fields is contested, uneven and valued differently by various communities of practice. Even so, like other social representations, art has a core that has deep historical roots and which is reinvigorated through institutional practices because it has a useful symbolic role to play within Western societies. At the core of the social representation of art is the notion of individual creativity and autonomy as a counter-balance to social and indeed pedagogic constraint. Classroom observations revealed that students anchored teachers' formal, instructional art concepts in informal chat with classmates, bringing the unfamiliar 'scientific' discourse of art into the 'consensual universe' of peer culture. This micro-genetic collaboration served also to reinvigorate dominant social representations of art that played a role in framing the construction of social identities with subsequent social consequences either to recommit to or opt out of school art. It was through collaborative processes that students found the symbolic resources needed to make sense of art and to resolve conflicting social representations of art.

ACKNOWLEDGEMENTS

Grateful thanks to Judith Marshall, School of Social Sciences, Cardiff University for help with fieldwork and data analysis.

NOTE

1. Many secondary schools in the UK have special departments that provide extra support and tuition for students who struggle to keep up in class. Students may be withdrawn from mainstream lessons for a specific period of time and be given intensive, often one-to-one tuition to develop their skills and knowledge. When they are considered to have caught up sufficiently they return to mainstream classes.

REFERENCES

Abreu, G. (1995). 'Understanding how children experience the relation between home and school mathematics'. *Mind, Culture and Activity, 2*, 119–142.
Aschaffenburg, K. & Maas, I. (1997). 'Culture and educational careers: The dynamics of social reproduction'. *American Sociological Review, 62* (4), 573–587.
Bernstein, B. (1996). *Pedagogy symbolic control and identity: Theory, research, critique*. London and Bristol: Taylor and Francis.
Dewey, J. (1934). *Art as experience*. London: Allen and Unwin.
Douglas, M. (1966). *Purity and danger*. London: Routledge and Kegan Paul.
Duveen, G. (1997). 'Psychological development as a social process'. In L. Smith, J. Dockrell & P. Tomlinson (eds), *Piaget, Vygotsky and beyond*. London: Routledge.
Duveen, G. & Lloyd, B. (1990). 'Introduction'. In G. Duveen & B. Lloyd (eds), *Social representations and the development of knowledge*. Cambridge: Cambridge University Press.
Hutchins, E. (1996). 'Learning to navigate'. In S. Chaiklin & J. Lave (eds), *Understanding practice: Perspectives on activity and context*. Cambridge: Cambridge University Press.
Ivinson, G. (1998a). *The construction of the curriculum*. Unpublished PhD, Cambridge University, UK.
Ivinson, G. (1998b). 'The child's construction of the curriculum'. *Papers on social representations: Threads and discussions. Special Issue: The development of knowledge*, Vol. 7, Nos 1–2, 21–40.
Ivinson, G. (2000). 'The child's construction of the primary school curriculum'. In H. Cowie & D. Van der Aalsvoort (eds), *Social interaction in learning and instruction: The meaning of discourse for the construction of knowledge*. Amsterdam: Pergamon Press and EARLI
Ivinson, G. & Murphy, P. (2003). 'Boys don't do romance'. *Pedagogy, Culture and Society, 1* (11), 89–111.
Lave, J. (1988). *Cognition in practice: Mind, mathematics and culture in everyday life*. Cambridge: Cambridge University Press.

Lave, J. & Wenger, E. (1991). *Situated learning: Legitimate peripheral participation*. Cambridge: Cambridge University Press.

McDermott, R.P. (1996). 'The acquisition of a child by a learning disability'. In S. Chaiklin and J. Lave (eds), *Understanding practice: Perspectives on activity and context*. Cambridge: Cambridge University Press.

Moscovici, S. (1984). 'The phenomenon of social representations'. In R.M. Farr and S. Moscovici (eds), *Social representations*. Cambridge: Cambridge University Press.

Moscovici, S. (2001). *Social representations: Explorations in social psychology* (edited by G. Duveen). New York: New York University Press.

Rogoff, B. (1995). 'Observing sociocultural activity on three planes: Participatory appropriation, guided participation and apprenticeship'. In J.V. Wertsch, P. Del Rio & A. Alvarez (eds), *Sociocultural studies of mind*. Cambridge: Cambridge University Press.

Rogoff, B. & Lave, J. (eds). (1984). *Everyday cognition: Its development in social contexts*. Cambridge, Mass.; London: Harvard University Press.

Steven, K.A. (1998). 'A study of the thought and perceptions of selected adolescent art students, their teacher and the researcher during the process of creating art'. *Dissertation Abstracts International Section A: Humanities and Social Sciences Vol. 58* (7-A), 2498.

Vygotsky, L. (1978). *Mind in society: The development of higher psychological processes* (edited by M. Cole, V. John-Steiner, S. Scribner & E. Souberman). Cambridge, Mass.: Harvard University Press.

Walkerdine, V. (1988). *The mastery of reason*. London; New York: Routledge.

Wenger, E. (1998). *Communities of practice: Learning, meaning and identity*. Cambridge: Cambridge University Press.

Wertsch, J.V. (1995). 'The need for action in sociocultural research'. In J.V. Wertsch, P. Del Rio & A. Alvarez (eds), *Sociocultural studies of mind*. Cambridge: Cambridge University Press.

Zittoun, T., Duveen, G., Gillespie, A., Ivinson, G. & Psaltis, C. (2003). 'The Use of Symbolic Resources in Developmental Transitions'. *Culture and Psychology, 9* (4), 415–448.

Part II
Enabling Creative Collaborations

9
Creative 'Communities':
How Technology Mediates Social Worlds

Stephen O'Hear and Julian Sefton-Green

INTRODUCTION

Ostensibly this chapter describes a young man's use of an online forum dedicated to the band, 'Interpol'. We will describe Tom's online interactions on this forum or bulletin board and, in particular, describe how he and others used the forum to exchange and comment upon artwork devoted to the band. We are really interested in how the structural features of the forum (both social and technological) supported Tom's growth as a young artist and how communities like these offer a different model of a 'learning community' – a model, we suggest, which has profound implications for education and the creative industries.

The forum, and Tom's use of it, are of course leisure activities and in as much as the forum is dedicated to a band, it and associated activity could generally be said to form part of youth culture. We shall return to questions of a distinction between formal educational interactions and leisure/cultural activities, but right at the beginning we want to signal that the forum's 'voluntary' status, its subject matter and its use,would customarily be investigated as youth culture phenomenon and it is here that the first of our theoretical interests can best be raised.

Studies of Youth over the past 40 years have consistently located forms of creativity and, of course collaboration, within aspects of the youth cultures which have developed over this period. An emblematic study might be Hebdige's (1979) study of Punk. This study analysed the ways in which a whole culture (dress, music, style values, etc.) were created out of a kind of *bricolage* where young people adopted representations and significations through symbolic activity to create Punk. How individuals actually worked together in any precise kind of collaboration is not explored empirically. Later studies like Willis (1990) argued that youth cultures offered a kind of 'symbolic creativity' and that there was a dialectic between young peoples' creative uses of youth culture and the developing commercialisation of youth cultures. Again though, the specifics of individual or group collaboration are not explored. Thornton (1995) argues that studies of youth culture have traditionally sought refuge in a romantic view of youth cultures, and that it is naive to suggest that as young people adopt, mediate and consume mass culture, they are in some ways re-writing or resisting the meaning produced for them by the market place. Our study will show how a young fan – highly emotionally involved in his world – uses its symbols and values for his own purposes. However, Tom's engagement was highly motivated and he was participating in the forum 'as an artist' – a position of some difference from the 'innately creative' youth of Hebdige and Willis who by the very act of participating in peer culture, were deemed creative. Thornton also developed Bourdieu's (1984) concept of cultural capital to explore what she called 'taste cultures', that is, groups of sub-cultural affiliation formed by self-defining what groups did and did not like. We will return to this idea as participating in Tom's forum is based on the same key principle of membership and exclusion based on taste. The opposition between authentic (romantic) youth cultures and those promoted by commercial interests may be a bit of a false dichotomy and again, in the context of a forum (used by fans but developed as the band's official site) may need rethinking in the digital era.

The second theoretical lens we need to apply to our study relates to discussion around the meaning of community in atomised, post-industrial societies. Intriguingly some of the key tropes from the proceeding debate crop up here. On the one hand, it is suggested that we are witnessing a decline in authentic face-to-face social interactions (Putnam, 2000), whilst other commentators (e.g. Turkle, 1995) suggest that the virtual world is offering complementary and supplementary forms of social engagement. Questions around the digital divide and exclusion from the online world (Schon et al., 1999) raise a series of concerns about how commercial interests are driving participation online and echo a pattern of debate revolving around the authentic, the real, the commercial and the excluded. Again, we will show that Tom is relatively privileged in his engagement with the Interpol forum. However, the host of recent literature exploring the ethnography of life online (e.g. Hine, 2000), argue that the features of online communities (including, for example, anonymity, asynchronous chats, different systems of validation) (see Rheingold, 2002) make the very nature of social engagement qualitatively different to 'real life'. We will seek to show how this impacts on Tom's artwork though unusual kinds of virtual collaboration.

This emphasis on community in the virtual domain is mirrored by an attention to the role of community in recent educational studies. Here the work of Lave and Wenger (1991) emphasises the social 'situated' nature of learning, which explores the transactions between individuals in specific social settings. This approach has been most radically investigated in studies of workplace learning (e.g. Seeley Brown & Duguid, 2000), which have 'replaced' psychologistic notions of learning with a concept of 'knowledge production' – emphasising the collaborative inherently social nature of learning at the expense of an attention to the individual actor within the field. Again we will want to position Tom within a specific social nexus of community participants to show how he develops within this context.

Our final set of issues relates to the tools of digital production (software such as Photoshop and Flash) used by Tom and his peers. We will be showing not only how the forum provides a space and a 'discipline' for Tom but how the social world and its exchanges fostered his creative and aesthetic education. The fact that his work is digital adds another dimension to the online world as a medium of exchange but there has been very little discussion of how software itself supports contemporary aesthetics (see Manovich, 2001, 2002). The common use of such tools promotes its own community, which we suggest functions in a cultural way and this too impacts on how Tom is enabled to develop. We will develop this theme further in reference to other kinds of 'open'[1] products as the shared nature of software skills and formats establishes its own agenda for collaboration and media production.

As the next section will describe, we found out about Tom's 'work' in this forum semi-accidentally. How and why we found out is as much part of the story of Tom's education as the activities he described to us in interview and casual conversation. He, or at least his participation in the forum, seems to represent to us an example (and clearly we are suggesting such a case is indicative rather than representative) of a new kind of *ad hoc* creativity where participation in a 'local community' sustains, develops and supports individuals in explicit and more hidden ways. Tom's engagement in this forum was 'necessary' for him at this stage in his life – whether he found the forum or it found him is one of those puzzles we have to disentangle as we seek to explain how groups learn the way they do. Our discussion of Tom's participation will show not only how the forum functions as a learning community, and therefore what structural implication it might have for both youth cultures and education systems, but also how such collaborative communities might encourage and be encouraged by the 'new' economics of open-source style developments in the creative industries (Howkins, 2001).

INTRODUCING TOM

We first met Tom in 2001 when he walked through the doors of WAC Performing Arts and Media College, an informal education centre in London (www.wac.co.uk). The college runs a programme on Sundays offering performing arts and media production classes for young people aged between 14 and 24. Tom (then only 14) had come along to sign up for 'Digital Design'. It was clear from his admission interview that he was serious about developing himself as an artist and that he had an interest in the Internet as a potential platform on which he might publish his work. Whilst his digital design skills were underdeveloped what struck us at the time was Tom's ability to reference and name-drop other new media design companies and artists in the same way that aspiring film-makers will comment on favourite directors. The positioning of himself as a young digital art student within the context of the 'grown up' new media industry, showed that even at 14 Tom was thinking about how he might develop a career as a digital artist. At school, Tom's favourite and strongest subject was Art and Graphics, and after completing his GCSEs (now at 16 years of age) he has been accepted onto a full-time Graphic Design course at a well-known London art college. Besides graphic and multimedia design, Tom's interest in the creative industries (both as a producer and consumer) includes film, television, computer games, animation and music.

Tom has developed a range of web design and multimedia skills – becoming competent in the use of an array of software from 2D design tools, video editing software, to interactive-content authoring packages. However, his real love is the industry standard photo-editing program Photoshop in which he has, over the last two years, become an expert user. We'd suggest the skill level that Tom has reached appears to be of a higher standard than that which he would have been taught at school or college, and that he has produced an enormous quantity of work. In this way Tom is to some extent 'self taught' and 'self motivated'. In 2003 he found an online community, which would support and encourage his self-directed learning. However this wasn't a website intended for e-learning or even digital artists, but instead was a forum on the message board for the official website of indie rock band 'Interpol'. He discussed his interest and participation on this forum with us during a series of 'taped' conversations in late 2003, during time he dedicated to a student production company, New Forms (www.nforms.co.uk).

THE 'INTERPOL' MESSAGE BOARD

This 'Interpol' message board is a place where fans can express their interest in the band and discuss such things as the band's music, lyrics, TV and radio appearances, as well as write their own reviews. The message board is divided into a number of forums (each with its own moderator) of which some are simply used for 'official' band announcements and competitions etc. However, most of these forums encourage the growth of an online community, providing a tool to facilitate asynchronous text-based discussions (although users can add hyperlinks to other websites or media e.g. images). Posting to any of the forums requires that the user creates a membership account – which involves choosing a username (usually an alias) with an option of providing a few details about themselves, for example e-mail address and homepage URL. This gives each contributor an online identity and promotes a sense of community, even if that identity retains a liberal dose of anonymity.

The forum that concerns us here is dedicated to the sharing of 'Interpol artwork and photos'. Within that forum users have hijacked the message board as a place to post up original digital artwork for other Interpol fans to critique, and share production tips: 'that wasn't there in the beginning – we just nagged a lot until it got there'. Here users publish their self-produced alternative album covers, posters, desktop wallpaper and flyers.

It is clear that first and foremost the message board as a whole offers a place in cyberspace for Interpol fans to socialise – exchanging thoughts about the band, jokes, musical tastes and recommendations – and in a sense the sharing of digital artwork within a dedicated forum grew out of this. According to Tom, this particular forum was developed because of pressure by fans, who began to post up artwork, and requested that a dedicated forum for their work be set up. The site administrators obliged and the 'Interpol artwork and photos' forum was born.

FINDING AN AUDIENCE

I've even had a thread dedicated to me...set up by someone who appreciated my work.

From talking to Tom and reading the exchanges it is immediately apparent that the 'Interpol artwork and photos' forum offers him (and the other contributors) an audience for their work. If nothing else, this sense of audience has provided Tom with increased confidence and motivation: 'it's a good way to get your ego up and so you do more work', although at the same time he is adamant that he does not produce work 'for' the forum but for himself. Posting to the forum is perceived as an afterthought:

None of the work I do – I think. hmm. I'll do it for the Interpol board – I do it if I like the picture and think 'oh I can do something to this picture...if I like it, I might post it'.

There exists a slight paradox here. On the one hand the audience is viewed as providing an ego boost 'so you do more work' and yet work is not specifically produced for this audience. However, the audience that Tom has found (despite being made up of 'virtual identities'), is acutely responsive and acts as a source of encouragement, criticism and even collaboration.

PRACTICAL ADVICE AND COLLABORATION

Within the 'Interpol artwork and photos' forum, messages can be broadly put into three categories. Many exchanges consist of playful banter and 'in jokes' of the type that we suggest take place within most informal social spaces. As researchers looking in from the outside, this makes much of the dialogue hard to follow. A second category consists of comments expressing taste and offering encouragement; for example, 'I really enjoy your Interpol art. That would look great on a t-shirt.' A third (and perhaps the most interesting) category exists which we describe as practical advice. These are exchanges that directly offer specific suggestions about how to improve or develop a work in progress. This can be anything from how to make better use of the software used or detailed aesthetic suggestions such as 'add text or put in a background image'. Tom told us of one important instance (that is, important to him) where the forum moderator 'Chavo' made several key suggestions resulting in the re-working of one of his creations:

People like Chavo usually tell people how to improve their stuff...like with me...some of my work is actually better than it was.

Tom had started with some 'raw' source material, a picture of Interpol's lead singer: 'it was a nice picture I found so I decided to trace[2] it…so it looks like a comic or something…' After Tom had published it on the forum 'Chavo' offered some suggestions as it 'looked a bit odd':

> …he told me to add some sort of background with buildings, which I did… with a I picture I'd done already where I'd 'traced' a picture of the twin towers. So I just added that in the background…and the work actually looked much better.

Sometimes practical suggestions lead to collaboration. Users request that they are sent an editable version of the work – in the native Photoshop file format (.psd) – so that they can re-work or 're-mix' it into something new:

> He said it was good at first but then he told me how to improve it and then he wants me to send him the .psd so he can re-mix it.

In this example, it is not just the distribution and communication function of the message board that supports creative collaboration but the digital authoring tools used by the members. Digital authoring software often allows users to save their creations in a file format that is 'open' to further editing and changes. In Photoshop for example, artistic creations can be made up of a number of separate layers such as text, a background image, and various visual elements. Each of these layers can be edited separately and can have various 'filters' or effects applied to them. By saving the file 'native', these layers remain as a separate editable entity, and this maximises the creative options that will be available at a future date – either to the original author or to a collaborator. Tom refers to the process of re-working a piece of digital art which is supported by having access to the native Photoshop file, as *re-mixing*, a term borrowed from electronic music production.

LEARNING COMMUNITY MEMBERS AND LEADERS

…everybody kind of loves Chavo and his work.

Technically 'Chavo' is the 'Interpol artwork and photos' forum moderator. Moderators are designated members of a message board who have been given additional 'privileges' by the message board administrator. Moderators are allowed to edit or delete posts within their allocated forum and are typically chosen because they are seen as active participants and are experienced or expert in the subject for which the forum is set up. Chavo's own web presence suggests he is a 'professional' graphic artist and he is obviously a dedicated fan of the band. Partly because he is such an active member of the forum and because his artwork is of a professional standard he has come to have an influence on the work and progress of forum members, and in particular Tom (as shown in the quote above).

Over time, Tom has come to trust the critique offered by Chavo, mainly we think, on account of the quality of Chavo's own artwork. Despite receiving praise from various members of the forum ('great work') a recent creation that Tom posted did not receive approval. Chavo told him:

> take it down and redo it. You have done much better and this isn't the quality we have come to expect from you. C'mon you know you can do better. Rework and resubmit. (post by Chavo 22 October 2003)

Here Chavo has clearly taken on the role of teacher or mentor. The final comment is perhaps most telling. To us, the words 'Rework and resubmit' echo an examiner's red pen! Yet, for Tom this is as far from formal education as it gets:

> it's completely different from college…college is learning and stuff like that. This is just a board of people just doing whatever.

Tom's refusal to describe the learning that takes place within the forum as 'educational' is of course consistent with his previous comments about how he does not create artwork for the forum. However, we would suggest that the forum is indeed a learning community – but that defining it as such is at odds with the forum's cultural meaning for participants:

> with college they will be really descriptive 'cos they know how you're gonna get good marks. This, you're not marked, this they'll say if the image looks a bit odd, a bit bland, they'll say 'try adding this'. Then when you add it, it might look good or not.

The exchanges of advice are very practical – and knowledge or suggestions can be acted upon and made use of straight away. There is no scheme of work or curriculum (this is 'people just doing whatever') and so learning is exchanged on an *ad hoc* basis and delivered in a 'just in time' fashion. We would suggest that the asynchronous and networked nature of the message board makes it able to support and to encourage this kind of teaching and learning as collaboration.

TEACHING AND LEARNING – TECHNOLOGIES OF COLLABORATION

Our description of Tom's development has focused on the unique quality of the collaboration fostered by his use of the forum. Our discussion now attempts to identify the technological features of the forum, which underpin this learning process. We have shown how Tom's use of the forum concentrated on extremely practical advice, almost resembling 'technical support' and this is an area of collaboration for which the Internet and in particular the 'message board' functions well. One of us (O'Hear) has substantial experience as a web developer and has inhabited many message boards offering and seeking support. We suggest that many Internet message boards create a healthy climate for sharing technical knowledge and collaboratively solving practical problems.

Unlike live or 'real time' chat rooms, communication on a message board is 'asynchronous'. This allows an idea or problem to be posted at the moment of discovery – and for it to be read and replied to by a wide range of participants because they don't have to be online at that moment in time. It could be minutes, days or months after the original post. Discussions are threaded and organised in such a way that allows 'late comers' to track back and see what has been said already – so that any insight or advice offered usually contributes something new to the solution creating a sense of an ongoing narrative.

Message boards set up to facilitate the exchange of practical knowledge tend not to discriminate between temporary and sustained collaboration. First-time or infrequent contributors are welcomed and supported in just the same way as regular users. It is not uncommon to hit a programming problem and, unable to solve it alone, to dive into a well-populated forum and ask for ideas and solutions from the wider development community. Often this will involve a number of exchanges – where a specific solution is not always given but is sufficient to point the user in the right direction or to kick start another round of creativity – only for that user to never frequent the board again. This kind of 'no strings attached', 'just in time' creative collaboration is uniquely facilitated by the message board. However as a tool it does not limit users. Features such as the ability to create dedicated topic forums and send private messages to individual users, allow *ad hoc* collaborations to develop into sustained and more formal relationships. We will suggest below that this is common in the incubation of 'open' projects, which go on to be supported by a community of developers.

As Turkle (1995) and others have argued, the identity of users in or on message boards is crucial to their success. Some message boards allow users to post anonymously, but most require that each user join the board after creating a user account, thereby creating an online identity whose sole purpose is to provide a voice for the contributions that they make. This usually takes the form of an alias, some personal trivia, an avatar, and if credibility or verifiable authority is required, a link to a homepage. An online identity can remain as anonymous as the user chooses. This, we suggest removes many of the inhibitions associated with asking for help and from those perceived to be at a higher skill level. Whilst this may make it easier to ask for assistance or to ask 'beginner' questions it would follow that it should be easier for users to criticise or 'put down' other members of the community. However in our experience this is rarely the case and, as Raymond (1999) argues, this kind of generous information exchange represents a 'gift culture' which is based around the positive aspects of sharing practical knowledge quite dissimilar from any competitive or negative exchanges familiar to the assessed school environment.

The 'Interpol artwork and photos' forum exhibits a strong sense of ownership by regular contributors. This is very much due to the way in which the forum was created (from the ground up) and the fact that the designated forum moderator

'Chavo' was one of the original contributors who lobbied for it to be set up. Most message board software allows levels of control to be allocated to its users. Where this regulation is relaxed and allows for users to create new designated forums around particular topics, and where moderators use their powers for administrative purposes rather than to censor what has been posted, the best conditions for collaborative communities are created. It is true that these kinds of communities do function exclusively over a period of time but we suggest that it would be possible to observe generational growth as peer cohorts graduate through these kinds of forums and communities.

TEACHING AND LEARNING – THE COLLABORATIVE MODEL

We have shown how Tom was resistant to the suggestion that his participation in the forum was in any way a form of 'work' or 'education'. Our first response was to discount these objections because we felt that he only possessed relatively limited views about learning and education (on the basis of his restricted experiences), but his resistance to our suggestions is also instructive. Given how he made and refined work for the forum and given the clear sense of audience it provided, we found it difficult to see why Tom didn't see his activity as a kind of work – a sort of graphics club. Of course, from his point of view, participation in the forum was very much of a leisure time or 'social' activity, so the idea that this was 'work' and that it could in some way be recuperated into a narrative of his artistic education seemed to work against the spirit of such identification. This perfectly sensible 'refusal' has interesting implications for the ways in which discourses of lifelong leaning often seem to permeate every aspect of modern social lives, blurring the distinctions between work and play which are so important to our sense of self (see debates in Coffield, 2000).

Part of Tom's reluctance to identify the forum as in any way important to his development lay in his conceptualisation of it as 'fun' or 'jokey', as a place to 'have a laugh'. We realised in discussion that this was an important classification for Tom; for example, when we pushed him to compare his participation online to his (serious) work at college. Recently, considerable attention has been paid to how important a learner's concept of themselves (as learners) as well as the complementary role that the activity of learning plays in identity construction, is to our understanding of the learning process (Davis et al., 2000; Gee, 2003). We have already suggested how the use of a persona or role in the forum is important but here, we would also argue that we need to frame Tom's participation very much in terms of a subcultural or youth culture activity. From that perspective the role of identity is foregrounded in ways that don't surprise us. Tom's enthusiasm, his commitment, his emotional investment, all make much more sense to us because of the way he approaches participation in the forum in terms of a self-defining membership of a taste-culture. We must not underestimate this seeming paradox when we try to adapt such technologies or social structures for formal education.

It seems to us crucial that Tom felt confident to participate in this forum quite soon after he joined. He doesn't seem to have hung around waiting to get involved, but quickly introduced himself and his interests to the forum. Here, the role of anonymity is crucial. Again and again, Tom emphasised how the forum didn't matter, that for all his work, for all the praise and feedback he received, it was fun and therefore not to be overvalued. We obviously didn't take this at face value, but what it shows us is how being able to put yourself in situations where you can take risks, where not so much hangs on each action or event and where trust in friendly camaraderie is almost part of the implicit contract you sign on joining up to such a forum (and we'd suggest that anyone in this community who broke such rules would have been excluded), is a rich and necessary creative environment.

Two other features of the social interaction fostered by the forum are important in this mix. First is the role of Chavo – the allegedly experienced, 'professional' graphic artist – who seems to us to play a mentoring role for Tom in particular and possibly for the forum in general. Secondly, we were interested in the discourses of criticism, which seemed very important to us in specifically developing Tom's creative work. Chavo is important because he represents some sort of authority. We are sure he really is a professional artist, and his integrity is confirmed by his own website (hyperlinked from the forum). This gives him authority and authenticity and possibly gave Tom and the other younger members of the community a direction to which they could aspire. As we have already implied, the actual critical commentary used by Chavo and the other members of the group is also quite different from that used in education – even art schools. Like Tobin's (1998) study of a young web designer and his online mentor in an 'otaku' community, the language used here was very practical and very direct. Phrases, like 'use up the dead space', 'change fonts' etc. were used directly. Tom found this discourse helpful and clearly didn't find its brevity or directness off-putting. Again the half anonymity of the remarks coupled with a sense of fun and consequence-less adventure (in the sense that it didn't matter and he could try out or experiment without worrying about formal feedback) is instructive. Whilst Tom's tutors at Art School we are sure would like to think they can create the same kind of trusting environment, Tom told us how much more worried he was by their comments on his work whereas this medium allowed for a 'freer' kind of exchange and development. The fact that this criticism was extremely practical and direct again seems to be more useful than the discourse of evaluation used in more formal educational settings. However, we would be cautious about this conclusion because it seems to us that the fact the forum is different and unlike Art School is important in itself. We aren't suggesting that Art School should become like the forum, more that a properly creative environment for young people like Tom requires exposure to both kinds of experiences, that the forum and Art School together, provide the right kind of learning infrastructure.

OPEN COLLABORATION – BUSINESS IMPLICATIONS

The band Interpol were quick to recognise the interest their fans had in using the Interpol message board as a place to share and comment upon original digital artwork based on images of the band. After setting up a dedicated 'Interpol artwork and photos' forum, they have gone even further by turning a blind eye to copyright infringements by fans who have downloaded and doctored band photos from the website. The encouragement of consumers to become 'half-producers' by opening up all or parts of a product offers a new business model only made possible through the capacity of digital technology (via editable or 'open' formats) and by the Internet functioning as a distribution and communication platform.

Computer game developers were early adopters of the 'consumer to producer' concept. If game players could be given the tools to create their own extra levels and use the Internet to share these creations as well as discuss aspects of the game – then a whole community and culture could be created to support the brand. In 1993 id Software created a 'first-person shooter' computer game that featured huge advances in game play and 3D graphics compared with its predecessors. But what made DOOM even more of a breakthrough was that it was distributed on the Internet as a nine-level playable demo with parts of the game's architecture left 'open'. DOOM's popularity soon grew rapidly as did the online community surrounding it. Using DOOM editors (based upon the open 'WAD' format) thousands of modifications and add-ons have been created by members of the DOOM Community. Based on DOOM's success it has now become common practice for games developers to build community and production tools into their game concepts (http://www.popsci.com/popsci/computers/article/0,12543,281377-1,00.html).

A second example concerns software called ReBirth, released in 1997 by the Swedish company Propellerhead Software. The music application emulates two analogue bass-line synthesisers and a classic drum machine. Using the software users can produce original music productions that can be saved either in the editable ReBirth file format or as an audio file ready to be made into an audio CD. ReBirth also allows for the sound and appearance of the program to be altered by installing additional 'mods'. A 'mod' is a user modification of the program, which adds new sound sets and changes the look of the user interface ('skin'). In addition, Propellerhead Software's website has a very lively user community forum and a space where users can share their own 'mod' creations and musical compositions. As Tage Widsell (Marketing Manager for Propellerhead Software) described, this wasn't the plan from day one:

The interest that ReBirth generated caught us (and our ISP) a little off guard…ReBirth users started sending us songs, so we opened a song archive where users could share music. Other users started hacking the application to exchange the graphics and drum sounds. We got hold of some of the hacked versions [and] decided they were cool and put them up for download. Later, we added support for user modifications in the program itself. (http://www.ohear.net/full_publication.php?publicationID=12)

The user community of ReBirth collaborated to hack the application in order to improve upon its functionality and to support increased creativity, by adding a broader set of sounds, and sharing compositions in an editable format. This demonstrates how the Internet creates what Lessig (2002) calls an 'innovation commons' – a place or space where original creativity is held in common ownership yet commercial exploitation by the few is acceptable and is tolerated.

In exploiting the opportunities that 'open' technology creates, companies inevitably leave parts of their brand 'open' (or in fact make this openness part of the brand). The 'openness' of Interpol's website meant the band took a relaxed stance to copyright enforcement in respect of the band's images – after users starting using the board to exchange digital re-workings of those images. The same is true in our other two examples: the game level design architecture of DOOM was left 'open' letting users design additional levels and characters, thereby altering the look and feel of the game (brand); the 'mods' that can be created for ReBirth change the software's appearance and sound-set, altering the image of the product from being an emulation of 'classic' instruments.

LEARNING AND COLLABORATION – EDUCATIONAL IMPLICATIONS

Our interest in this chapter has been to explore how a causal, culturally motivated online interaction might function as a new kind of learning community. We were interested in looking at the structural features of the message board and its use to see how various kinds of collaboration can act as kind of creative infrastructure. We have suggested that a number of features in the message board technology interact productively with cultural uses and subjective investment. Together this creates a striking learning environment. One way of summing up Tom's online education is to suggest that learning is collaboration and collaboration is learning. It is impossible to distinguish between the processes of participation, interaction and response and creative activity and learning. They are indissolubly structured through very specific cultural and technological mechanisms.

So what might be the point of such an analysis? There are clearly advantages to be gained for educators to understand how young people might be learning in different ways and in different arenas to traditional schools – even state-of-the-art Art colleges. However, whilst we'd like to acknowledge the learning that went on in Tom's education, we don't think that it is simple to extrapolate elements of this process. Our understanding of how identity might work in these environments, shows just how much we need to continue to pay attention to the role of identity in conventional learning situations, and how much we need to acknowledge how collaboration might play a significant part in developing our learning. Structures of both the cultural and technological variety will play an increasing role in our learning experiences and we will need to allow for them in new forms of evaluation and assessment. We are excited by the ways in which these new kinds of collaborative structures offer promises of certain kinds of business and creative developments but we recognise that these will not offer models for all areas of human endeavour. We would suggest that, where possible, students might be encouraged to participate in different kinds and varieties of challenging environments because they are stretching and important, as Tom himself would be the first to acknowledge. However, these kinds of collaboration are best practised by 'experts' in an extra-curricular domain and we suggest that many creative developments in education will emerge from similar out-of-school experiences. This may be Tom's most enduring lesson.

NOTES

1. We struggled to find the right term for this concept and ended up with the term 'open'. We use it to refer to a product where some or all parts of its architecture are left open to user modification and that these products (either in or not in a modified form) can be exchanged between users. This might be something as simple as a file format that remains editable or where modifications can be made to the functionality of the software itself.
2. Tracing refers to a technique in Photoshop whereby an original photo is digitally traced to create a new image which has a hand-drawn 'graphic' quality and no longer resembles a photograph.

REFERENCES

Bourdieu, P. (1984). Distinction: *A social critique of the judgement of taste* (trans. Nice). London: Routledge.

Coffield, F. (ed.). (2000). *Differing visions of a learning society: Research findings* Vols 1 and 2. Bristol: The Policy Press.

Davis, B., Sumara, D. & Luce-Kapler, R. (2000). *Engaging minds: Learning and teaching in a complex world.* Mahwah, NJ: Lawrence Erlbaum Associates.

Gee, J. (2003). *What video games have to teach us about literacy and learning.* New York: Palgrave Macmillan.

Hebdige, D. (1979). *Subculture: The meaning of style.* London: Methuen.

Hine, C. (2000). *Virtual ethnography.* London: Sage.

Howkins, J. (2001). *The creative economy.* London: Penguin.

Lave, J. & Wenger, E. (1991). *Situated learning.* Cambridge: Cambridge University Press.

Lessig. L. (2002). *The future of ideas.* New York: Random House.

Manovich, L. (2001). *The language of new media.* Cambridge, Mass.: MIT Press.

Manovich, L. (2002). 'Generation Flash'. www.manovich.net

Putnam, R. (2000). *Bowling alone. The collapse and revival of american community.* New York: Simon and Schuster.

Raymond, E. (1999). *The cathedral and the bazaar: Musings on Linux and Open Source by an accidental revolutionary.* Sebastopol: O'Reilly.

Rheingold, H. (2002). *Smart mobs: The next social revolution.* Cambridge, MA: Perseus.

Schon, D., Sanyal, B. & Mitchell, W. (1999). *High technology and low-income communities: Prospects for the positive use of advanced information technology.* Cambridge, Mass.: MIT.

Seeley-Brown, J. and Duguid, P. (2000). *The social life of information.* Boston, MA: Harvard Business School Press.

Thornton, S. (1995). *Club cultures.* Cambridge: Polity.

Tobin, J. (1998). 'An American Otaku' (or, a boy's virtual life on the Net). In J. Sefton-Green (ed.), *Digital diversion: Youth culture in the age of multimedia.* London: UCL Press.

Turkle, S. (1995). *Life on the screen: Identity in the age of the internet.* New York: Simon and Schuster.

Willis, P. (1990). *Common culture: Symbolic work at play in the everyday cultures of the young.* Milton Keynes: Open University Press.

http://www.ohear.net/full_publication.php?publicationID=12

http://www.popsci.com/popsci/computers/article/0,12543,281377-1,00.html

http://www.nforms.co.uk

http://www.wac.co.uk

10
Creativity and the Net:
How Do Researchers Collaborate
Creatively Using the Internet?

Maarten De Laat and Vic Lally

INTRODUCTION

Distributed research communities necessarily rely upon the use of a range of technologies to pursue their creative endeavours. In this chapter we aim to explore how the technologies now at hand may shape creative processes, and may also generate new ways in which members of a community might collaborate together. In order to pursue this aim we will explore a first-hand account of an academic collaboration in order to attempt to understand the creative processes through which the present authors, both academic researchers, worked to produce a research paper using computer-mediated communication and other information and communication technologies (ICTs), as well as bibliographic and writing technologies, digitisation and access technologies.

Contemporary literature on learning has suggested a move away from an individualistic conception of learning, locating it within a wider socio-cultural context (Creamer, 2003a; Dillenbourg, 1999; Engeström, 1987; John-Steiner, 2000; Koschmann, 1996). Increasingly, knowledge is believed to be constructed in settings of joint activity (Brown & Campione, 1994; Scardamalia & Bereiter, 1994), where people are dedicated to learn and collaborate around shared tasks and issues that matter to them. Learning does not take place in isolation, but is acknowledged to be situated in the context in which actions take place (Brown et al., 1989; Lave & Wenger, 1991). Knowledge is now more commonly viewed as being socially distributed amongst participants (Salomon, 1993). This means that learning is often seen as a form of participation in cultural practices (Wenger, 1998). As a consequence, people learn in these practices not only which knowledge is historically and culturally accepted and used in the context of the particular community of practice, but by engaging in these activities, they are actively (re)negotiating and constructing new meanings and therefore transforming the knowledge of the community by developing culturally accepted creative solutions in order to interact with their changing environment. Creativity may be viewed as a distinct form of collaborative learning in which the participants develop an original contribution to their area of activity. The capacity to identify and solve problems, making use of prior knowledge and

126

experiences both individually as well as collaboratively has been acknowledged to be part of the creative process (Craft, 2000; Feldman et al., 1994). In this way creativity is placed in a social context where the activity is situated in both a historical and cultural setting (Boden, 1991). For the purpose of this chapter creativity has been defined as innovative collaborations aimed at contributing something new to a domain of expertise (John-Steiner, 2000).

Current ICTs, and the increasing availability of broadband connections, have the potential to stimulate and support creative collaborations at a distance. Much of the early driving force for the development of what has now become the Internet came from research groups wishing to extend their collaborations at a distance. With the use of e-mail and asynchronous discussion boards it has now also become commonplace to learn and work together at a distance using these technologies. In higher education, for instance, more and more courses are offered online and students and tutors can form networked learning communities (NLCs). In this way it is possible to create an active learning context to enable the participants to interact and collaborate with each other online to fulfil and coordinate their learning needs. By 'networked learning' we mean the use of Internet-based ICTs to promote collaborative and cooperative connections at a distance (see Banks et al., 2003). Distributed research communities in higher education may operate in similar ways. However, at the moment, so much is still unclear about the nature of creative collaborative processes (Creamer, 2003b) in general, and it is even less clear how ICTs assist creative processes and shape distance collaborations. More empirical research is needed to provide an evidence base for understanding creativity in these emerging distance collaborations.

As we explained above, we take a socio-cultural perspective on creativity. By this we mean that learning and creative processes (a special form of learning) take place in social contexts (between individuals and groups) that are historically and culturally situated, but also constantly challenged by new developments and practices such as the use of ICTs. This view points us in the direction of investigating the interactions occurring between creative collaborators in order to address the central question of what these creative collaborations actually look like. John-Steiner suggests that creative collaborations can be roughly typified into four categories: distributed, complementary, family and integrated (John-Steiner, 1997). In a distributed collaboration the participants are loosely connected. Their involvement, commitment and ownership of a shared project may vary. Participants exchange information necessary for the particular project but their values and outlook may go only as far as similar interests. She describes the second type of collaboration as having clear divisions of labour. The participants are disciplined and they have complementary skills. The family type of collaboration is characterised by shared common values. The participant roles are less rigidly defined. Here, according to John-Steiner, expertise is integrated instead of being divided. These collaborations often go beyond a working relationship alone and might transform into a form of friendship. The participants are more integrated and synthesised, even though they retain their unique individuality. The last category that John-Steiner describes is the most intense form of collaboration. These collaborations involve long-term, intimate partnerships in which participants have strong shared ideologies and drive a vision to transform their particular domains, as well as the collaborators themselves. In essence these collaborative groupings might be viewed as being on a kind of continuum from loosely connected to well integrated. The continuum describes the nature of the relations between collaborators.

In other words, these categories help us to understand, to some extent, how creative collaborations function in terms of how the members are related to each other. Here they are presented on a scale from being loosely connected to having a very intimate relation. This is an important first step in understanding creativity in collaborative partnerships, but it does not provide us with a description of the collaborative processes themselves and how groups work together. Creamer (2003a, 2003b), who has been studying academic collaborative processes, is interested in the way participants work together and how they negotiate differences of opinion that emerge during their collaborations. In her research on academic collaborations Creamer (forthcoming) makes a distinction between three groups of collaborators: the first group she calls the 'like-minded', the second group work like 'triangulators' and the last group are 'multiplists'. The like-minded tend to have a shared or similar perspectives or points of view on matters central to their work and respect each others' expertise, they are willing to listen attentively when a new idea is advanced. In triangular collaborations, Creamer found that the participants tend to have different theoretical perspectives or look at a problem from different angles. These differences are not interpreted as a problem; rather they are seen as an enrichment to their collaboration. They try to understand each others' backgrounds as they reconcile their different perspectives. The multiplists, on the other hand, try not to reconcile their differences. During their collaboration they want to make use of these different backgrounds and perspectives to elevate their thinking into something new. The participants agree on some core or basic assumptions but see their differences as instrumental to creating something new by crossing their 'personal' boundaries (Creamer, forthcoming).

These distinctions enable us to understand collaborative processes and how they contribute to the creation of new products and ideas. To further study these collaborative processes Creamer (forthcoming) provides a model that describes four key steps during the collaborative process. The steps in the collaborative process begin with dialogue and move to familiarity, then to collective consciousness, and finally to engaging differences. The intensity of these processes in any particular collaboration will depend on the extent to which the particular group has a previous history of collaboration. If the participants have previously worked together on related tasks these stages may be less extended and intense, and will build upon their existing shared understanding.

Creamer (forthcoming) describes the steps as follows:

Step 1 – Dialogue: In this first step collaborators become immersed in dialogue with each other. The primary features of this process are interaction, and exchange of ideas. Creamer reports that these are features common to all of the collaborative narratives she investigated. A high level of interaction is required for collective interpretation to occur. While the emphasis is on dialogue in this step, collaborators also achieve some familiarity with each other as they acquire an understanding of each others' work.

Step 2 – Familiarity: This step refers to the part of the interpretive process in which collaborators gain more than a nodding acquaintance with their team mates' worldview and subject matter expertise. A great deal of mutual education and learning occurs as familiarity is acquired, even if it does not necessarily lead to conceptual change at this point. As an example of this process, one manifestation of familiarity is when a collaborator accurately anticipates another's point of view.

Step 3 – Collective consciousness: The third step in the interpretive process is when collaborators internalise the concerns or issues considered to be of central importance by other members of the team. This produces an expanded or more nuanced and complex vision of the phenomenon under study. This is the point in the interpretive process when collaborators do begin to undergo conceptual change.

Step 4 – Engaging differences in perspectives: The fourth step she describes as a point in the interpretive process where collaborators explore the implications of the differences in their perspectives. Not all collaborators achieve this step. Collaborators can learn about each others' point of view (familiarity) without incorporating new elements in their own way of seeing and thinking to develop a more complex understanding (collective consciousness) or mining differences to unearth new insight that may ultimately lead to the creation of new knowledge (synthesis).

The study reported in this chapter was inspired by these four collaborative steps, which are used to reflect on our own distributed academic creative collaboration and to identify ICT tools used during this creative collaboration, as we strive to write an academic paper about the learning and tutoring behaviour of participants engaged in a networked learning community. The John-Steiner model helps us to locate the nature of our relationship (integrated). However, Creamer's collaborative steps help us to focus on our particular concern in this paper: the collaborative processes. We are both researchers in education, interested in the use of computer (network) technology to support collaborative learning. Making a contribution to our own academic community is a creative activity, because in this process academics contribute something new to the knowledge domain of a research community by extending and critically addressing its existing shared knowledge and leading questions, in a dialectical process with peers (members).

Since our own working relationship is itself distributed, we have to rely on computer technology to mediate and conduct our creative academic collaboration. In this chapter, we will focus on how we made use of several ICT tools to shape and mediate our collaborative processes towards the creation of an academic paper. By focusing on our own collaboration we are able to access a very rich case study in which we are both participants with interpretive insight. Our data set is also very extensive, and includes detailed conversational transcripts from synchronous communication, because the ICT tools enabled automated archiving of this communication. Through analysis of these archives we are able to uncover some of the otherwise hidden processes of our creative collaboration. The use of this personal case study has also allowed us – as called for by Moran and John-Steiner elsewhere in this book – to access the real-time, ongoing dynamics of our collaboration that would not otherwise be possible.

CONTEXT AND METHOD

Firstly we will describe our type of collaboration and then we will describe the technologies used and relate this to the four key steps as identified by Creamer (above). To further understand our collaborative process we will draw upon our own research practice, in which we use a descriptive system of analysis for investigating the creative collaborations between members of networked learning communities (NLCs). The coding schemes we use to conduct our research are aimed at extracting and describing learning and tutoring processes that are present in NLCs (De Laat & Lally, 2003). Creating a research paper together might be understood as a form of collaborative learning because the researchers are engaged in a dialogical process; with each other, with the new text they are creating, and with the existing knowledge of the domain. In this engagement process they themselves learn about the domain, as they probe its boundaries with new questions, and articulate this learning in their writing. Therefore we thought that viewing our creative collaboration as learning would give us an analytic approach which would enable us to build a framework for analysing the data associated with our own academic collaboration. We use these coding schemes as a lens to identify and describe how we used several ICT tools and the Internet to mediate these processes. However, we are aware that this framing does not take account of significant aspects of creative collaboration as an academic practice. For example, making judgements about academic creativity based upon our knowledge of the existing academic literature to which we are contributing. This will require further research entailing the development of more refined coding categories.

The coding scheme (see Table 10.1) we use can be subdivided into three main categories. One deals with the activities supporting learning, used to process the learning content and to attain and monitor learning goals. For example, discussion enables participants to articulate what they know and don't know and how they will structure their learning. The second deals with regulations activities, used to process the organisation and facilitation of collaborative work. The third category deals with affective activities, used to socialise and stimulate the collaboration. These three categories form the initial analytical framework used when trying to describe our own collaboration throughout the identified key steps of creating a research paper (see Table 10.1).

Table 10.1   An analytical framework of activities for creative collaborations

Category	Code	Description of activity
Learning activities:		
Discussion	Dis	Negotiating or discussing the collaborative project
Producing the work	Pro	Working or referring to work done on the collaborative project
Questioning	Que	Questioning or critiquing the collaborative project
Regulative activities:		
Organisation	Org	Creating a way of working together and initiate a topic
Coordination	Coo	Managing the collaboration
Affective:		
Socialising	Soc	Keep in touch
Stimulating	Sti	Supporting each others' contributions
Technological	Tec	Messages concerning the use of the tools involved

The data available to us comprises recordings of our chat sessions, short messages, e-mail messages, and word documents, and span more then three years of academic collaboration between us. In this chapter we will provide a broad overview of the nature of our collaboration and explore the ways in which we used ICT tools to create our academic products. We will then present selections, based on the four steps of the collaborative interpretive process, as we work on an article for a research journal. To follow the progress made on this article we analysed data that was drawn from the ICQ program history, because this is the tool we used most extensively to stay in touch and discuss our progress. Although our academic collaboration is distributed by nature, since we work and live in separate countries, we think our type of collaboration can be characterised as more intense than the distributed category described by John-Steiner (1997). Instead of being loosely connected we managed, especially because of the use of ICT tools, to maintain frequent and constructive interactions. Tools that allow synchronous communication proved to be of high value for us to interact, and with the aid of these tools we managed to create a sense of continuous virtual presence and availability whenever needed. Over time these interactions have grown from being purely work-related towards a collaboration that is characterised by friendship, in which both work and personal interests are being transformed and integrated. Our collaboration started when we met at the Euro-CSCL conference in 2001 (held in Maastricht, The Netherlands) when we realised that we came from a similar academic background in education and that we shared not only a similar interest in the research domain but also had each independently developed a similar approach to researching it. This discovery led into the idea of starting our academic collaboration by trying to further inform and familiarise ourselves with the interests and research questions we shared and tried to create a paper together to underline and support our shared perspective. In terms of Creamer's (forthcoming) descriptive continuum our academic collaboration could be identified as 'like-minded'.

FINDINGS

At the end of 2001 we began using e-mail to learn about each other's expertise and background. This was followed by a face-to-face meeting to create a grounding layer for our academic collaboration. During this meeting we also discussed how to keep in contact over time and we decided to use ICQ as our main tool for this purpose (see Table 10.2 below for a brief description of ICQ). The tools and forms of communication we have used over the past three years to maintain our collaboration are summarised in Table 10.2.

Table 10.2   CMC and other computer technologies used to support our creative processes

Type of meeting or tool of technology	Description of the communication mode or technology tool	Role of the mode or tool in the creative process
Face-to-face meetings	Meetings in Utrecht and Sheffield	Clarification and review of progress; social engagement of collaborators
Telephone	Standard real-time voice communication	Decision-making; social engagement of collaborators
Short Message Service (SMS / Text)	Instant computer-to-phone and phone-to-phone short messaging system	Making rapid and instantaneous contact, and providing reminders and prompts
ICQ messaging and chat	Instant computer-to-computer messaging and chatting	Discussion of ideas, writing, results and analysis
ICQ File Transfer / FTP	Moving data-files and text from computer to computer	Instant exchange of work completed by one collaborator to the other
E-mail	Text based extensive messaging system	Updating on progress, asking questions and providing reminders, general scheduling and ongoing discussion
Word 'track changes'	Editing tool allowing changes to be viewed	Both collaborators can work on the same document and review changes made by the other
Musicmatch	Digitisation of audio files from interviews	Allows transfer of audio interview files from one collaborator to the other using ICQ file transfer
VPN (virtual private network) Client Technology	Security features protecting collaborators' networks	Client allows each collaborator to access the secure network
VNC (virtual network computing) Client	Enables remote visualisation of one computer's desktop from another	Enables collaborators to navigate easily around each other's computer, remotely
EndNote	Bibliographic database system	Allows collaborators to share and manage the references for their shared writing
NVivo	Content analysis software	Enables semi-automated content analysis of textual data and sharing between collaborators
Discuss	Asynchronous discussion tool	Share and discuss relevant articles used for our research

Over the course of our distance collaboration we have conducted several studies together and at various stages we have needed different kinds of software tools to assist us in conducting the work. Tools like Musicmatch and NVivo were crucial in that they enabled us to digitise, prepare and analyse our data and allowed these data to be shared via the Internet easily and quickly by providing remote access to each other's computer using a VPN-connection and FTP-software. However, working intensively together at a distance was not possible without being able to communicate in different ways. Synchronous communication (like face-to-face conversation, telephone and chat) was found to be important when discussing project aims, and to establish a working agenda, and for managing unexpected incidents during the project. But, at times when a project is progressing according to plan, asynchronous communication was in most cases enough to keep each other updated, or to share new versions of the written document.

Since our collaboration began to develop into a productive and more integrated one, we tried to have face-to-face meetings every other month. However, due to other commitments this was not always possible. Because of this we found that it was very important to keep in regular contact using ICQ and e-mail, mainly to keep in touch and discuss and regulate the progress we made on our work. It is our experience that regular contact is important for establishing trust and creating a sense of presence. Maintaining contact helps to build up a profile of the other person and therefore you know what to expect at different stages of the collaboration and how to tune in to each other's way of working. Over the past three years we have sent 622 e-mails, which is almost an average of four per week. On top of that we have also exchanged 1,699 ICQ messages, which comes to an average of a little more than 1.5 messages a day. Of course these are only averages, but it indicates some of the intensity of our partnership and the importance of using ICT tools as our main means of communication.

After this general overview of the nature of our academic creative collaboration, we would like to look more deeply into a particular period (2003) of our academic collaboration, in which we worked on a specific research project. In this section we will present several examples to illustrate how we used various ICT tools to collaborate as we conducted and reported a research project.

1. Dialogue

This phase of our creative collaboration was characterised by extending and building on our previous work and planning our new study. In this phase a lot of dialogue was needed to build and negotiate a shared perspective and a common set of goals to develop the research project and to set up the conditions for the work to be carried out.

The first sequence (Extract 1) represents an early stage of setting up a new design for this research project and is a record of our ICQ messages. The utterances are mainly coded as discussion (Dis), with a smaller number representing organisation, management (Org), and coordination (Coo) of our collaboration, as well as some production (Pro). Here we were in the process of creating a paper for the Ed-Media conference of 2003. Later we used this to create an article for submission to the journal *Information Systems Frontiers* (*ISF*). Our aim in the *ISF* paper was to research collaborative learning and tutoring processes in three networked learning communities using different models to facilitate students' learning. In the sequence presented below (Extract 1) we were trying to create a shared understanding of how we were going to set up the research project (indicated by * in the extract). At the same time we were discussing the collaborative task the participants would have to carry out and we were setting up the software environment in which the research would take place. All of these actions are part of the processes in which we are engaged as we begin to form our research for the paper, and in this sense can be seen as creative processes.

Extract 1   Setting up a new research project

Participant	Date	Message / Utterance	Code
Vic	4-3-2003 13:52	so, the ed-media paper and ISF article	Org
Maarten	4-3-2003 13:53	Yep	Org
Vic	4-3-2003 13:55	How many groups do you want?	Dis
Maarten	4-3-2003 13:55	i think we should create a small collaborative task that the groups have to work on*	Dis
Maarten	4-3-2003 13:55	if we make three groups of 4, would that work*	Dis
Vic	4-3-2003 13:55	It would be good if it could be a subset of what they are doing already...*	Dis
Maarten	4-3-2003 13:55	one group with PI and one with Roles	Dis
Maarten	4-3-2003 13:56	And the last one as a 'control' group with nothing actually	Dis
Vic	4-3-2003 13:56	Ok, so three groups PI; Roles and 'control'	Dis
Maarten	4-3-2003 13:57	yes these three groups will do. I will prepare the environment for it	Org
Maarten	4-3-2003 13:57	What are the students doing at the moment?	Dis
Vic	4-3-2003 13:57	They are...doing an investigation of an aspect of networked learning that interests them	Dis
Vic	4-3-2003 13:59	we could set up three groups with the same research paper*	Dis
Maarten	4-3-2003 13:59	but will there be a collective shared learning goal within these groups? Something to work towards*	Dis
Maarten	4-3-2003 13:59	i mean working towards a shared collective outcome...?	Dis
Vic	4-3-2003 14:00	well, I don't see why not; maybe to produce an assessment of the paper according to some criteria	Dis
Maarten	4-3-2003 14:00	aha excellent then.	Dis
Vic	4-3-2003 14:00	OKeedokeeeeee	Dis

Maarten	4-3-2003 14:00	could you give me the names of the students per group and what the name of their database/paper project would be?	Coo
Vic	4-3-2003 14:01	you are going to set up three spaces in your Discuss software?	Pro
Maarten	4-3-2003 14:01	Yes i will	Pro
Maarten	4-3-2003 14:06	vic go to www.discuss.nl username: vXXXXXXX password: pXXXXXXX	Org
Vic	4-3-2003 14:09	Ok, the list of students is in my ICQ shared FTP folder	Tec
Maarten	4-3-2003 14:10	will try to download it.	Tec
Vic	4-3-2003 14:11	I'm into Discuss now.	Coo
Maarten	4-3-2003 14:11	you will see three databases	Coo
Vic	4-3-2003 14:13	yep!! roles, wheel and reference	Coo
Maarten	4-3-2003 14:14	yes those are the 3 discussions i have made for you	Coo
Vic	4-3-2003 14:14	great, yes I see them	Coo
Maarten	4-3-2003 14:15	could you maybe phone me?	Org
Vic	4-3-2003 14:15	yep, where are you?	Org
Maarten	4-3-2003 14:16	home +31 30 2XXXXX	Org
Vic	4-3-2003 14:17	right, calling now	Org

We started off using ICQ to discuss our issues but later on (as we were, at the same time, exploring the new Discuss software environment) it seemed more appropriate to pick up the phone. ICQ is a useful tool to explicitly create a shared understanding because you talk in synchronous mode and you have to be very clear and concise in what you are trying to say. At the same time the other participant has to respond to make clear that the previous comment has been understood in some way because there are no visual clues to rely on. The conversation can seem a bit repetitive, but our experience is that this is really useful (especially at an early stage of a new project) and important when trying to create something collaboratively. In the presented sequence this is illustrated by the regulative codes (Org) assigned to some of the utterances. At the end of Extract 1 the amount of regulative talk can be seen to increase considerably and we realise it seemed better to use the phone because navigating through a new software interface while writing was very confusing and took up a lot of time.

Essentially we were creating the design for our research at this point in the creative process (indicated by * in the extract). At this point, the intensity of our interactions was best supported by highly interactive, instant technologies such as messaging and telephone. The ICT tools used during the dialogue phase were dominated by ICQ discussions and some phone calls. There is a need for direct and vivid contact because a new strategy is being developed and agreed upon. In this context, asynchronous tools like e-mail or a discussion board were found to be too 'slow' to make instant decisions and practical agreements about who was doing what.

2. Familiarity

In Extract 2 below, we have moved on with our project. Again, the dominant type of utterance was discussion. However, this is now supplemented by new utterance types (such as questioning) as we became familiar with the data set and exchanged our creative ideas about coding. At this stage of the project it was crucial to establish that we had developed a shared understanding and way of working in order to extend our understanding in new ways, and be able to contribute creatively to this research domain (indicated by * in the extract). The research study had ended and we were at the stage of coding and analysing the data we had collected. At this point we needed to have some coding conversations to fine-tune our method of analysis and to check if we had the data set correctly in NVivo. Again, a lot of organisational talk was needed to make sure we were keeping track of each other. Once we were both logged on to the NVivo file we could start discussing and comparing some of the codings that had been done.

Extract 2   Establishing a similar approach to coding the data (extract from ICQ messages)

Participant	Date	Message / Utterance	Code
Maarten	26-3-2003 14:05	Shall we discuss a bit of the codings I have done?	Org
Vic	26-3-2003 14:06	let's talk about the codings, yes	Org
Vic	26-3-2003 14:06	you set up a file...	Pro
Vic	26-3-2003 14:06	in NVivo?	Pro
Maarten	26-3-2003 14:06	yes have you opened it	Org
Vic	26-3-2003 14:07	computer crashed about 15 mins ago. will open it now	Tec
Maarten	26-3-2003 14:07	Okeedokee	Soc
Vic	26-3-2003 14:07	hang on....	Soc
Vic	26-3-2003 14:12	what's the name you used?	Pro
Maarten	26-3-2003 14:13	isf experiments	Pro
Maarten	26-3-2003 14:13	i have emailed it to you about an 45 minutes ago	Coo
Vic	26-3-2003 14:13	nope, login failed on that!	Tec

Maarten	26-3-2003 14:13	Try: mXXXXXX	Tec
Vic	26-3-2003 14:14	Okeeedokeeeeee	Soc
Maarten	26-3-2003 14:14	nice one	Sti
Maarten	26-3-2003 14:14	i have coded the messages called CM 1 – CM 5*	Org
Maarten	26-3-2003 14:14	shall we look at them ?	Org
Vic	26-3-2003 14:14	yes, lets do that	Org
Maarten	26-3-2003 14:15	Cm 1. I have coded this whole message as Instructional design*	Dis
Vic	26-3-2003 14:19	Right and you coded it Instr des?*	Que
Maarten	26-3-2003 14:19	yes if you browse to that message and select view - codings stripes in NVIVO, you can easily see what i have done	Org
Vic	26-3-2003 14:19	yes, right, thanks	Soc
Maarten	26-3-2003 14:20	this message was easy to code because it discussed only one thing. If we move on to cm 2 it becomes more blurred*	Dis
Maarten	26-3-2003 14:22	so my question is how would you code this message?*	Que
Maarten	26-3-2003 14:25	basically how i see it is that i read a unit. decide if it is Learning or Tutoring and then choose a code.*	Dis
Maarten	26-3-2003 14:26	to me:Are we working towards our goal? Are we happy with our progress? these are 2 separate units of meaning. Do you think that too ?*	Que
Vic	26-3-2003 14:28	Yes Yes, I think we are....*	Dis

The sequence in Extract 2 illustrates the use of ICQ to discuss and establish a shared view on coding our collected data. Prior to this presented extract, the NVivo file had been prepared and sent by e-mail. In NVivo it is possible to create two similar coding files within a shared coding project. Each coder can log-in his/her own file and start coding. When both researchers were finished coding, the two files could be merged and the coding results compared easily at a distance. In this sequence we had both opened the NVivo file to start our conversation in order to create a shared understanding of how to code our data. These coding conversations characterised the focus of our collaboration at this stage and were carried out frequently. At this point in our research, it was of great importance to be sure that we interpreted our work and understood the coding scheme (and the underlying theoretical perspectives) in a similar way (indicated by * in the extract). Because the results of the coding interpretations are the very basis of our data for the paper this is a central, creative task in the development of new understandings about the research topic in which we are engaged. As the utterances indicate, it is clear that we had moved on from a general dialogue to a deeper, more focused discussion, exploring each other's view as the mixture of discussion (Dis) and questioning codes (Que) indicate at the end of Extract 2.

3. Collective consciousness

During this step in our collaborative process, the questioning (Que) code emerges more frequently as the type of utterance used in our ICQ messages. At this point (see Extract 3) we had started to write the *ISF* article arising from our analysis and the Ed-Media conference paper. We were working on version 5 of the manuscript and we were trying to organise (Org) and coordinate (Coo) an efficient way of working together. Therefore both of these codings also appeared in the utterances at this stage. We were trying to avoid doing things twice or working on the same things at the same time. While we were managing our work we also discussed the results of the current version. This was the central creative task at this stage, as we built a new understanding from our shared view of the results (indicated by * in the extract). Vic had some questions related to the content of a certain section in the document and wanted to clarify them and make sure we were still working on the same level. During this conversation we anticipated some connection problems and thought that a reboot would solve it. As soon as this was done we picked up our conversation where we had left it.

Extract 3   Developing a shared understanding and discussing the progress of the document

Participant	Date	Message / Utterance	Code
Maarten	1-4-2003 17:33	shall we talk a bit about the ISF article	Org
Vic	1-4-2003 17:33	yes that's a good idea	Org
Vic	1-4-2003 17:39	How do you think it is going?	Que
Maarten	1-4-2003 17:39	Well i think we are making some progress	Que
Vic	1-4-2003 17:49	I'll get ISF5 on screen	Org
Maarten	1-4-2003 17:49	what would you like to talk about first?	Org
Vic	1-4-2003 17:52	well, there's this article to add in the reference list	Que
Maarten	1-4-2003 17:52	yep will take care of that, its in my endnote something must have gone wrong.	Pro
Vic	1-4-2003 17:52	there's a section on: Computer support for collaborative learning: theory and system development I didn't understand that bit*	Que
Maarten	1-4-2003 17:53	which bit ? only the beginning or the whole purpose of this section*	Que
Vic	1-4-2003 17:53	the bit in blue, see my comments by the track changes in the document*	Que
Maarten	1-4-2003 17:55	okay do you understand its content?*	Que
Vic	1-4-2003 17:56	well, I thought it was making a distinction between individual and group learning outcomes*	Que
Maarten	1-4-2003 17:58	well that but it also says something about the collaborative process. I thought it might be handy in relation to the stuff on co-construction*	Que

Vic	1-4-2003 17:58	Ok, that's really useful. I'll think about that*	Que
Vic	1-4-2003 17:58	Maarten, I'm going to restart my machine	Tec
Maarten	1-4-2003 17:59	see you sooooooooon	Soc
Vic	1-4-2003 17:59	it's really slowwwwwwww	Soc
Vic	1-4-2003 18:03	see if this is better	Tec
Maarten	1-4-2003 18:03	heeelllooo	Soc
Vic	1-4-2003 18:03	hiya	Soc
Vic	1-4-2003 18:03	seems faster now	Tec
Vic	1-4-2003 18:04	righteeho, shall we go back to the paper?	Org
Vic	1-4-2003 18:04	well, if you can, it would be great!!!	Org
Maarten	1-4-2003 18:04	i only wonder if it would be a bit to much also regarding the scope on social presence	Que
Maarten	1-4-2003 18:05	I will do it tomorrow and then we 'll see.	Coo
Vic	1-4-2003 18:28	ok, so if you finish the section on coding procedure till tomorrow lunchtime, and send the whole to me as ISF6	Coo
Maarten	1-4-2003 18:28	i will write tomorrow morning	Coo
Vic	1-4-2003 18:28	I'll do some and send it back later in the afternoon	Coo

During this phase most of our collaborative work was mediated via e-mail through sending new versions of our Word document. A particularly helpful feature assisting this process was the facility to keep track of how the document was developing between the two of us, using the 'track changes' tool within Word. Most of our asynchronous discussion related to how to report this project within the document we were currently putting together. Only when certain issues emerged and things needed further clarification would we start an ICQ-session or a phone call to have a direct discussion to talk things through. In Extract 3 Vic felt he needed to express some concerns or questions he had with a certain section in the article. He wanted some explanation to stimulate his thinking and develop his understanding of the content of that particular section. This was part of the creative dialogue that forged shared understanding of the written document as it emerged from our collaboration (indicated by * in the extract).

4. Engaging differences in perspectives

We were now approaching a final stage of the writing process. We were sending back and forth versions of our article and discussing what needed to be done to sharpen the text. Later on in Extract 4 (see below) Maarten tries to explain some of his comments made using 'track changes' on the document so that Vic can have a last look at it before deciding to submit it. It is clear that much of the actual engagement was taking place within the text of the paper itself, as we continued to modify it, read the changes, and respond to each other using ICQ. Most of the utterances presented here are examples of how we negotiated and agreed (Dis) the final changes that were made in the document, the central creative process in this sequence (indicated by * in the extract).

Extract 4   Wrapping up and submitting the article

Participant	Date	Message	Code
Vic	9-9-2003 12:04	The file should be with you now	Tec
Maarten	9-9-2003 12:04	okay will check	Tec
Maarten	9-9-2003 12:05	i have received it.	Tec
Maarten	9-9-2003 12:06	My word count is 7600 something. Keep in mind that the reference list counts as well!!!! Will get back to you when i have read it	Pro
Vic	9-9-2003 12:06	yep, with refs and conclusions it is 8489	Pro
Maarten	9-9-2003 12:07	nice	Sti
Vic	9-9-2003 12:45	how's it going M?	Pro
Maarten	9-9-2003 12:45	i am sending a comment back just now, used track changes	Pro
Vic	9-9-2003 12:46	Ok, is it OK -ish?	Que
Maarten	9-9-2003 12:46	yep it is good but the recall need more attention i think*	Sti
Vic	9-9-2003 12:47	right...I'll go with your comments*	Dis
Maarten	9-9-2003 12:48	I have summed up some comments as bullets*	Dis
Vic	9-9-2003 12:48	yes; I know. I've tried to integrate those key bullets into my selection*	Dis
Vic	9-9-2003 12:49	and revised the header to the results to make that clear, just now*	Dis
Maarten	9-9-2003 12:50	i think 'Bill' for instance is a good example of how the others could be done as well*	Dis
Vic	9-9-2003 13:40	I've incorporated all your comments and gone back to the conclusion*	Dis
Maarten	9-9-2003 13:40	oh i agree with that.* What do you think, do you feel confident about submitting it?	Que
Vic	9-9-2003 13:41	Yep, I feel ok about it	Dis

In the four phases described above we have attempted to indicate key sequences of discussion where the creative process of each phase is actually occurring between us as we collaborate on the task. In an analysis such as this, these 'creative' sequences are brief traces. A significant part of the creative process is also represented in the developing product of our collaboration: the journal article. More detailed analyses of this product, and other modes of communication, are needed in order to further develop our understanding of the process. However, we would like to argue that enough evidence of the creative process is present in our analysis to justify this exciting line of enquiry.

DISCUSSION AND CONCLUSIONS

In this chapter we have attempted to focus on the actual processes of collaborative creativity and the use of technologies that supported the distributed nature of the particular collaboration. The central question that we have posed ourselves is: What does a creative collaboration actually look like? We have attempted to answer this question by investigating some of the processes of an academic collaboration that we (the authors) engaged in creating a new academic journal paper. This investigation was facilitated by the archive of our conversations that was automatically stored in the chat software ICQ as we discussed the development of our work. In the pursuit of our academic goal we utilised several different ICT tools, including ICQ, and these served a range of purposes, depending on our needs at different stages of the work.

Our theoretical basis for understanding creativity as a complex of communicative, cognitive and socio-emotional processes occurring between collaborators as well as within an individual. In other words, creativity is viewed here as a socio-cultural phenomenon occurring in a particular context as members of a group strive to create a new understanding, idea or artefact that they contribute to a domain of expertise. This leads us in particular directions, in research terms. One of these is to focus on analysis of the processes of communication between collaborators as they work together in a creative endeavour.

In order to probe these communicative processes we adopted Creamer's model (Creamer, forthcoming) as a way of understanding and conceptualising various stages in creative collaborations. In the Dialogue stage of our work, a lot of organisation, coordination and discussion was involved in our conversations. This was the stage in which we were setting up the research project and the details of how we would proceed. We were exploring the range of possibilities for the work we were contemplating. In the Familiarity stage, as we began to analyse the results of our research activity, new types of utterance emerged. We were also exploring the meaning of our results and using NVivo to assist us in this task. Social exchanges now occurred, and a number of technical utterances also emerged. Organisation, discussion, and coordination all continued over from the Dialogue stage. As we progressed into the Collective Consciousness stage, a further new type of utterance appeared in the form of questioning. However, we were also working on the paper itself by this point. Much of our communication shifted from ICQ utterances into e-mail and the changes we made in the paper itself as the document was exchanged between us. This process continued into the Engaging Differences in Perspective stage. Again, a significant part of the creative process was also occurring within the document itself as we developed it to completion. The ICQ conversations we have presented in this chapter represent the creative 'wrapping' around our textual engagement, rather than the textual engagement itself. In this sense some of the creative processes are not visible within the ICQ extracts presented here. However, they do represent the processes that led to the text's development. These are almost always invisible in a finished product and hence represent a rare opportunity to view the creative 'history' of the document.

In conclusion, it is increasingly clear to us that creative distance collaborations between members of a group can be effectively supported by a wide range of software tools, including communicative tools that support dialogue in real time such as ICQ. No single tool can support all aspects of the creative process. Indeed, we used twelve different software tools and technologies, in addition to face-to-face communication, to produce the academic paper that is the focus of the creative efforts presented here. The varieties of tools we used at different stages were necessary to provide a way of working together at a distance.

Researching creative processes, in the way that we have attempted here, offers the possibility of beginning to open up to scrutiny the cognitive, social and communicative acts that are central to our understanding of creativity. In this chapter we have focused on only one aspect of this complex set of interacting processes: our real-time communication as recorded in the archive of one of our software tools (ICQ). It seems that through careful sampling of the dialogue we can begin to understand and characterise these processes in detail. Furthermore, we can begin to relate the developmental stages in this process to published schemas, such as the four-stage process of Creamer (forthcoming). However, it is also clear that a detailed understanding will require much more extensive scrutiny and analysis of multiple sources, including the product itself. This is feasible in the case of a written product, where several evolving and corrected versions may be stored by the participants as they work. It may be more difficult with other types of creative product. In research terms, the study of the central processes of creative endeavours through the analysis of software archives is an exciting new direction that may help us in developing a deeper understanding of the nature of such collaborative creativity.

REFERENCES

Banks, S., Goodyear, P., Hodgson, V. & McConnell, D. (2003). Introduction to the Special Issue on 'Advances in research on networked learning'. *Instructional Science, 31* (1–2), 1–6.

Boden, M. (1991). *The creative mind, myths and mechanics*. Weidenfeld and Nicolson. London.

Brown, A. & Campione, J. (1994). 'Guided discovery in a community of learners'. In K. McGilly (ed.), *Classroom lessons: Integral cognitive theory and classroom practice* (pp.229–270). Cambridge: MIT Press.

Brown, J., Collins, A. & Duguid, P. (1989). 'Situated cognition and the culture of learning'. *Educational Researcher, 18* (1), 32–42.

Craft, A. (2000). *Creativity across the primary curriculum: Framing and developing practice*. London: Routledge.

Creamer, E.G. (2003a). 'Exploring the link between inquiry paradigm and the process of collaboration'. *Review of Higher Education, 26* (4), 447–465.

Creamer, E.G. (2003b). 'Interpretive processes in collaborative research in educational settings'. *American Exchange Quarterly, 7* (3), 179–188.

Creamer, E.G. (forthcoming). 'Collaborators' attitudes about differences of opinion'. *Journal of Higher Education*.

De Laat, M. & Lally, V. (2003). 'Complexity, theory and praxis: Researching collaborative learning and tutoring processes in a networked learning community'. *Instructional Science, 31* (1–2), 7–39.

Dillenbourg, P. (1999). 'What do you mean by collaborative learning?' In P. Dillenbourg (ed.), *Collaborative learning: Cognition and computational approaches*. Amsterdam: Pergamon.

Engeström, Y. (1987). *Learning by expanding: An activity theoretical approach to developmental research*. Helsinki: Orienta-Konsultit Oy.

Feldman, D.H., Csikszentmihalyi, M. & Gardner, H. (1994). *Changing the world: A framework for the study of creativity*. Westport, CT: Praeger.

John-Steiner, V. (1997). *Notebooks of the mind: Explorations of thinking* (Revised edition). New York: Oxford University Press.

John-Steiner, V. (2000). *Creative collaboration*. Oxford: Oxford University Press.

Koschmann, T. (1996). 'Paradigm shifts and instructional technology: An introduction'. In T. Koschmann (ed.), *CSCL: Theory and practice of an emerging paradigm* (pp.1–23). New Jersey: Lawrence Erlbaum.

Lave, J. & Wenger, E. (1991). *Situated learning: Legitimate peripheral participation*. Cambridge: Cambridge University Press.

Salomon, G. (ed.). (1993). *Distributed cognitions: Psychological and educational considerations*. Cambridge: Cambridge University Press.

Scardamalia, M. & Bereiter, C. (1994). 'Computer support for knowledge-building communities'. *The Journal of the Learning Sciences, 3* (3), 265–283.

Wenger, E. (1998). *Communities of practice: Learning, meaning, and identity*. Cambridge: Cambridge University Press.

11
'It's in the Mix Baby': Exploring How Meaning is Created within Music Technology Collaborations

Teresa Dillon

INTRODUCTION

Across all UK secondary school subject areas, the proliferation of information and communication technologies (ICTs) has changed the nature of learning. Music education now includes the use of technological and digital tools, such as programmable keyboards and computers, as key learning and music making instruments. Despite such usage there is relatively little understanding of the kinds of musical experiences and interactions such instruments might support.

Recently, researchers (Dillon et al., 2001; Mills & Murray, 2000; Pitts & Kwami, 2002) have focused on investigating teachers' experience and researchers' or inspectors' observations of classroom-based music technology practices. These studies have mainly been descriptive, highlighting the advantages and disadvantages of such technologies for music education. One of the key findings to emerge from these studies is that keyboards and computer-based music technologies are most commonly used in group settings (Dillon et al., 2001). Although this finding has provided some indication of the kinds of interactions engaged in during school music lessons using music technologies, the nature of the complex process of creating music in these collaborative group settings has yet to be fully understood. As a result, little is known about the kinds of musical skills and competencies young people are developing through interacting with computer-based music technologies in formal school settings.

Outside of formal school settings, young people interact with a growing range of multimedia-based technologies from television to computer games, from the Internet to mobile telephony (for further discussion see Facer & Furlong, 2001; Prensky, 2001). In using such technologies, young people simultaneously use various modalities (visual, musical, written etc.), becoming both the consumers and producers of multi-literate texts. The popularisation and commercial availability of computer-based music editing and sampling software means that anyone who is interested and has the finance can record and manipulate their own musical and audio material. Such access has meant that young people have greater opportunities to become producers of their own musical compositions, styles and innovations out of school settings. A second question that therefore arises from investigating computer-based musical collaborations is the need to examine how young people use music technologies outside of school.

In addressing these issues, this chapter examines young people's collaborative creative music activities in two different settings, formal and non-formal. In exploring this, how meaning was created in the moment-to-moment interactions during the collaboration, within each setting was examined. Analysing the young people's verbal dialogues has led to a greater understanding of computer-based collaborative music making and the role of software in the creative process.

CREATING SHARED MEANING AND UNDERSTANDING

Within this chapter a socio-cultural perspective on understanding collaboration is taken. Socio-cultural theorists attempt to go beyond the individualistic analysis of cognition, emphasising the importance of participation in social interactions and culturally organised activities for development. From this perspective, collaboration is defined as 'the construction of meaning through interaction with others and can be characterised by joint commitment to a shared goal' (Littleton & Häkkinen, 1999, p.21). Ireson and Blay (1999) note that the context in which tasks are performed has begun to form a significant aspect of the analysis of collaborative learning. Socio-cultural perspectives emphasise the embeddedness of meaning and how it is created in a particular setting (Cole, 1997; Goodnow & Warton, 1992; Rogoff, 1990). As the performance of most activities offers a variety of potential meanings and interpretations, it is through the processes of negotiation that shared meaning and understanding is created and negotiated.

Considering this body of work, then, this chapter considers meaning not as a static entity but as constantly being created and re-created by the participants. In both the formal and non-formal settings, the work reported in this chapter aims to understand what references and meanings the young people draw on, share and negotiate in order to create music together.

DEFINING FORMAL AND NON-FORMAL LEARNING SETTINGS

In this study, formal settings were considered as hierarchically structured and chronologically graded learning situations, where prescribed learning frameworks, organised learning events and the presence of a designated teacher or trainer is the norm (Eraut, 2000; Smith & Jeffs, 1990). In comparison, non-formal settings were deemed as learning situations that take place outside dedicated learning environments and arise from the activities and interests of individuals or groups (Marsick & Watson, 1990; McGivney, 1999). Despite this helpful distinction, Sefton-Green (2003; also this volume) notes how difficult it is to distil what constitutes 'learning' in non-formal settings, particularly as it raises a provocative set of questions about what might be learnt outside the formal curriculum. Taking a similar view to others in the area (Marsick & Watson, 1990; McGivney, 1999), Sefton-Green sees formal and non-formal as lying on continua – explicitly contrasting the *learning setting* from the *learning organisation*. For example, on the continuum between formal and informal *settings* is learning that occurs in formal (e.g. school) settings, semi-formal (e.g. museum) settings, and non-formal settings, such as families and friendship groups. While on the continuum between formal and non-formally *organised* learning lies, at one end, learning that occurs explicitly, through for example formally organised lessons and, at the other end, implicit (or accidental) learning that can occur while playing a computer game. In contrasting the setting with the organisation, Sefton-Green attempts to articulate what others have also noted (Marsick & Watson, 1990; McGivney, 1999) that both formal and non-formal learning can occur in the same space and that defining the differences between them can be extremely complex.

In sum, much work has been carried out on the learning processes involved in formal settings and through formally organised means of learning. In particular, classroom settings where the computer has been central to the learning process (Crook, 1994; Littleton & Light, 1999; Wegerif & Mercer, 1996). However, there is a distinct lack of research on the kinds of interactions and processes that occur when working or playing in semi-formal and non-formal learning settings using computer-mediated music technologies.

CREATIVE THINKING:
HOW CONTEXT INFLUENCES THE CREATIVE PROCESS

In considering the kinds of interactions that might occur when making music, Webster's (2001) definition of creative thinking in music is useful. His definition encapsulates the open-ended nature of creativity but also accounts for critical and creative thinking skills, which are necessary for it to occur, and the ways in which both individual and social processes enable this. According to Webster, creative thinking in music is:

> …a dynamic mental process, alternating between divergent (imaginative) and convergent (factual) thinking, that moves in stages over time and is enabled by internal musical skills and outside conditions, which result in a final musical product, which is new for the creator. (2001, p.1)

Webster's understanding of musical creative thinking mirrors developments in the general understanding of the nature of creativity and the creative process. Since the late 1970s various researchers (Amabile, 1983, 1985; Csikszentmihalyi, 1990; Csikszentmihalyi & Getzels, 1971) have investigated how the 'qualities of the environment' or situational factors that arise though social, cultural, institutional and environmental discourses are interpreted and in turn influence our definition of creativity and the creative process. A number of music researchers (Barrett, 1995; Folkestad, 1998; MacDonald et al., 2002) also stress the need for a greater understanding of the complex socio-cultural underpinnings of musical creativity in collaborative settings. Despite this recognition, there remains a lack of understanding about how meaning and context are created when composing collaboratively.

AIMS AND RESEARCH PROCESS

Despite a growing emphasis on creativity within music and education (Craft et al., 2001; NACCE, 1999), and the finding that young people most commonly work in group settings when composing music in schools (Dillon et al., 2001), within this domain, the collaborative creative process is not yet fully understood. In addition, within semi- and non-formal learning settings and organisations, this process has also yet to be fully investigated. In attempting to explore this, the notion of context as a constantly changing entity, within and through which participants co-create meaning was used as a lens through which to understand creative collaborative processes, as young people composed music using sampling software in a formal and non-formal setting. To examine this, participants' verbal dialogues were analysed, as it was considered that these could lead to an understanding of what cultural references the young people drew on and considered relevant to making sense of the task.

The study in the formal setting was carried out in a comprehensive secondary school (with participants aged 13–14 years) in Milton Keynes, UK. The task given by the teacher was to put into practice: 'what the participants had learnt in previous lessons about riffs, hooks and repetitive motifs using *Dance eJay*'.[1] Within the school a total of 4 triads and 1 dyad (14 participants; 11 males and 3 females; mean age 13.7 years) were involved. The average task session lasted 42.09 minutes. The informal study was also carried out in Milton Keynes, UK during Brigade[2] meetings in a community centre setting. The researcher gave the task to young people who were attending a youth group. The task was 'to jointly compose a piece of music using the *eJay* samples as you wish', after demonstrating how to use *eJay*. There were a total of 9 dyads (aged 11–17 years) involved in the non-formal setting (18 participants; 10 boys and 8 girls; mean age 13.7 years) with the average time spent on the task 26.17 minutes.

In both settings, *eJay* sampling software was used. *eJay* is a CD ROM that contains pre-recorded, colour coded, vocal and instrumental samples. It allows users to turn their PC into a mini-editing suite, where they can compose, arrange, edit and record music in dance, rave and hip-hop music styles.

DATA COLLECTION AND ANALYSIS

During each session, participants' interactions were recorded on video and observational notes were also made. From the videotapes, all participants' verbal dialogues were transcribed verbatim. Transcripts included all talk and relevant non-verbal action. Analysis of the dialogues was carried out on both a quantitative and qualitative level using a coding scheme developed by the author focusing on both content and affect (see Table 11.1 for a summary of the coding scheme).

The coding scheme was seen as a means of capturing the complex and multi-faceted communication which occurred in the two settings. It focused on the *functions* of the students' verbal interactions, particularly on the processes involved in the generation of ideas and the purposes and uses of the utterances in the setting. Individual utterances were coded and the total number of utterances in each category was calculated as a proportion of the total talk in each session, using a dialogical software tool, MEPA (Multiple Episodic Protocol Analysis)[3] and statistical package SPSS 10.[4]

Table 11.1 Coding scheme

Category of talk	Description
(i) Content categories of talk	
S1 Musical Suggestions	The first introduction of new musical ideas related to the selection, arrangement and editing of composition.
S2 Technological Suggestions	The first introduction of new ideas regarding functions and manipulation of the technology, such as, listening, playing, saving, recording or programming the sample and effects bank.
i1 Descriptive Suggestions	The first introduction of new ideas based on descriptions of the quality of sounds.
i2 Cultural Suggestions	The first introduction of new ideas based on wider cultural experiences – such as from, television, film, pop charts and so forth.
E1a Musical Extensions	Utterances that extended musical suggestions (S1) and built on the first introduction of new musical ideas.
E1b Descriptive Extensions	Utterances that extended descriptive suggestions (i1) and built on the first introduction of descriptions of the quality of sounds.
E1c Cultural Extensions	Utterances that extended cultural suggestions (i2) and built on the first introduction references made to wider cultural experiences.
E2 Technological Extensions	Utterances that extended technological suggestions (S2) and built on the first introduction of new ideas on technological functions.
Q Questions	Utterances that began with question words and utterances that were question phrases.
A Answers	Utterances that are direct answers to direct questions, (Q) and did not provide any further detailed information.
(ii) Affective categories of talk	
H Humour	Non-verbal communication such as laughter and verbal such as jokes.
P Personal	Talk that was not related to the task, for example, about exams, personal lives.
SUP Non-verbal support	Non-verbal support such as 'ums', 'ahs', and so forth. Also included when participants hum and sing.
SUP1 Agreement	Utterances that expressed participant's agreement.
SUP2 Disagreement	Utterances that expressed participant's disagreement.
EM1 Positive emotive support	Utterances that expressed participant positive emotive reactions.
EM2 Negative emotive	Utterances that expressed negative emotive reactions.
X Miscellaneous	Miscellaneous utterances, which were not clear enough to transcribe.

RESULTS

Quantitative analysis

Quantitative analysis of the relative proportions of the various categories of talk indicated that musical suggestions (S1), musical extensions (E1a), questions (Q) and agreements (SUP1) were the most frequently occurring types of talk (see Tables 11.2 and 11.3). The frequency of these types of talk

Table 11.2 Descriptive statistics based on proportions of categories of talk in the school setting (n= 5 groups)

	N	Minimum	Maximum	Mean	Std. deviation
S1	5	10.66	19.27	15.4920	4.06314
S2	5	2.95	3.86	3.4380	.34032
i1	5	.32	.87	.5000	.22170
i2	5	.00	.46	.2400	.17132
E1a	5	17.01	26.73	22.9620	3.65555
E1b	5	1.03	3.02	1.6960	.81261
E1c	5	.00	.51	.1840	.21149
E2	5	2.28	5.83	4.3060	1.37729
Q	5	8.51	17.51	12.0200	3.34733
A	5	1.91	5.58	3.9780	1.55945
H	5	.16	1.74	.8960	.71423
P	5	.00	9.39	3.1200	3.78255
Sup	5	.81	4.46	2.9300	1.53524
Sup1	5	10.94	16.75	14.4340	2.46660
Sup2	5	2.03	5.57	3.8640	1.57364
Em1	5	1.62	3.82	2.7840	.90412
Em2	5	.70	8.33	3.3240	3.13959
X	5	1.16	5.32	3.8300	1.56721

Table 11.3 Descriptive statistics based on proportions of categories of talk in the non-formal, Brigade setting (n= 9 dyads)

	N	Minimum	Maximum	Mean	Std. deviation
S1	9	13.19	27.21	19.5711	5.2140
S2	9	.24	2.13	.8644	.6694
I1	9	.00	2.99	.5811	1.0247
I2	9	.00	1.80	.4678	.5553
E1A	9	13.95	34.07	20.2767	5.7904
E1B	9	.00	1.17	.5689	.4597
E1C	9	.00	1.10	.3111	.4351
E2	9	.00	2.04	.7378	.6842
Q	9	10.68	16.48	13.4022	2.1106
ANS	9	2.47	7.87	5.0744	1.7979
H	9	.00	1.70	.4889	.5923
P	9	.00	.93	.2311	.3323
SUP	9	1.33	5.09	3.3289	1.2296
SUP1	9	14.52	24.47	20.0378	3.3974
SUP2	9	.47	5.33	2.5789	1.7243
EM1	9	1.47	9.32	5.1278	2.5323
EM2	9	.00	1.60	.8911	.5091
MISCELL	9	2.56	8.77	5.4633	1.6369

showed that the partners were co-constructing new musical ideas, building on and extending them and supporting each other in this process. This finding was interesting as it had been expected that due to the differences in the task settings and instructions there would be different types of talk engaged in in the two settings. However the similarities between the talk in the two settings led to the conclusion that, within these music technology collaborations, the task setting and instruction did *not* have a major influence on the types of dialogue engaged in. However to shed further light on this situation, a deeper level of analysis was needed.

Qualitative analysis

Drawing on analyses of sequences of dialogue the aim was to provide further insight into more specific aspects of the setting and cultural contexts that partners were drawing on and negotiating in order to creatively collaborate together. The following sections use extracts of dialogue from both settings to illustrate the kinds of talk and creative processes participants engaged in and the role of *eJay* in scaffolding these interactions.

Formal, school setting – the creative and collaborative process

Sequence 1 from the formal context illustrates how the individual title names of the samples as they appeared in the software, such as 'my life' (line 80), 'Mikey' (line 86) and 'waterdance' (line 101) were used as a means of generating ideas. The first introduction of new samples often highlighted the beginning of a period of exploration and new idea generation. Such periods of open exploration were characterised by participants' actively searching, listening and choosing samples as they began to construct their arrangements. From this, more refined phases of reflection and editing developed (where participants' critically considered what they had constructed), which in turn provided further constraints as partners had discussed and refined their ideas by negotiating and agreeing what kinds of sounds and compositional structure they wanted to achieve. For example, after listening to many samples, participants' consciously searched for 'shorter' samples (line 91), deciding they could not keep the 'Mikey' sample as it did not sound 'good enough' (line 92). Decisions about whether or not to keep a sample were based on various criteria, such as whether the sample sounded good or fitted into the existing structure or was appropriate to the overall feeling of the piece. For example in lines 104 and 105, participants' collective 'mmmm' reflected their response to listening to the complete arrangement with the new samples added in. This in turn led to the debate about where to put the 'water dance' sample, for example (line 110) 'I reckon we should take it out and stick it there' (as the participant said this, she moved the samples closer together). Periods of critical listening also led to the generation of further ideas and evaluations. For example, when the group decided on the sample's final position, they listened to the piece from the beginning. Participant J1's final 'yeah' response reflects that she was satisfied with what they had done.

Sequence 1   Formal school context, Group 3 (Triad)

No.	Turn	Participant	Code	Transcribed discourse
80	1	T	S1	My life (s.n.), try my life
81	1	J2	Q	That one, where?
82	1	T	SUP1	Yeah
83	1	J2	E1a	Put it a bit further across, like, good. xxx (referring to spaces, placing samples up, J2 directing J1 where to put it)
84	1	J1	SUP1	There…yeah
85	1	J2	E1a	I knew you'd do that (they then listen to this new bit, laugh and take sample they just put in, out as they were testing it)
86	1	T	S1	Try Mikey (s.n.)
87	2	T	Q	What's that?
88	1	J1	Q	A far one, yeah? (s.t.)
89	1	T	S1	Hello (s.n.)
90	1	J2	Q	Where? About there? (J2 puts it up beside other vocal samples, then they all listen to it and burst out laughing a the Mickey vocal)
91	1	T	E1a	Eh, a shorter one (referring to get the a shorter Mikey vocal sample, pointing, J2 takes the above longer Mikey vocal off)
92	1	J1	E1a	You cannot keep Mikey, it's so pants
93	1	J2	Q	Where? There? (getting the shorter Mikey)
94	1	T	SUP1	Yeah (they listen to shorter Mikey, laugh, take it off)
95	2	T	E1a	We're not having that
96	1	J1	SUP	Here, here, we are (miming the Mikey sample in a high squeaky voice)
97	1	T	S1	More, down (that is, scroll down more through the vocal samples to get another sample)
98	1	J1	S1	Boom xxx (s.n.)
99	2	J1	S1	Go to sequence (J2 goes),
100	3	J1	S1	Whirlpool reveres (s.n.),
101	4	J1	S1	Water dance
102	1	T	SUP1	Yeah, water dance (pointing)
103	1	J2	Q	Here, here, where about? (that is, shall I put it here, J1 points to where it could go, they listen to sample)
104	2	J2	SUP	mmmm (t.t., refers to where they have placed the sample)
105	1	T	SUP	mmmm (t.t.)
106	1	J2	E1a	At the beginning (that is place it at the beginning, to where J1 pointed)
107	1	T	SUP2	No, not at the beginning
108	1	J1	SUP2	No
109	1	J2	Q	Where about, there? (leave it at about bar 2, listen to the sample)
110	2	J2	E1a	I reckon we should take it out and stick it there (moving samples closer together)
111	1	J1	SUP1	Yeah (in response J2 then plays comp from the beginning, they all listen to what they have done)

Note: s.n. = sample name; s.t. = sample type; t.t. = talk together; comp = composition

Non-formal setting – the creative and collaborative process

Similar cyclical creative processes of exploration, discovery, reflection and editing were also evident in the non-formal setting. For example, in Sequence 2 participant N suggested that they 'add something new' (line 206), while participant T suggested that it was necessary to edit the existing structure 'you might need to take one of the clicks off' (line 207) before they added any new samples. The process of editing allowed for discussions to develop about the rearranging of existing samples, which was dependent on keeping the sounds 'going' (line 210) and the choice of what sounds they should carry on (line 212). These kinds of discussions indicated that participants were considering how to construct the main beats which would form the basis of their composition, which also indicated that participants were drawing on the techniques used within this style of music, such as creating repeated motifs, interspersed with contrasting beats and sounds. In creating a shared understanding of what they wanted to achieve, open-ended phases of exploration (such as 'try it and see', line 215) were important as participants used them to generate new ideas and gain inspiration. As in the previous sequence, such phases refined the

Sequence 2   Non-formal, Girls' Brigade, Group 8 (Dyad)

No.	Turn	Participant	Code	Transcribed discourse
206	2	N	S1	Right we need to add something
207	1	T	S1	Yeah you might need to take one of the clicks off, it's up to you
208	1	N	Q	You, what you want?
209	1	T	A	Leave it if you want
210	1	N	E1a	Unless we move that over there, coz then it keeps going
211	2	N	SUP1	Yeah
212	3	N	Q	And do we want to carry that one?
213	1	T	EM1	That's good, that one,
214	2	T	Q	We got mother ship xxx (referring to sample name)
215	1	N	SUP1	Ah…try it, try it and see
216	1	T	S1	A little bit of scratchin' I expect, but there you, you (i.e., a little scratch would be good)
217	1	N	E1a	I don't know, I don't know if you can do it with this one (i.e., you cannot do scratch with this type of *eJay*)
218	1	T	X	xxx xxx
219	1	N	SUP2	Em, don't know, don't think so
220	1	T	X	xxx
221	1	N	S1	Bit more, over here, after that (searching for sample)… look
222	1	T	SUP1	Yeah
223	1	N	S1	We want something decent (i.e., they need a decent sounding)
224	1	T	S1	'In my land', xxx (s.n.)
225	1	N	S1	'Rhythm' (s.n., they are looking for something decent and just calling out names)
226	1	T	S1	'Keep on' (s.n.)

Note: s.n. = sample name; xxx = non-transcribed word; xxx xxx = non-transcribed utterance composition process, as new suggestions were made, such as to use a 'little bit of scratchin' (line 216) and to add some more 'rhythm' and 'keep on' samples (lines 225 and 226 respectively), which in turn led to further refinements of the compositional structure.

In sum, the creative compositional process was driven and constrained by the results of periods of exploration, where appropriate samples were discovered, and by periods of reflective listening and evaluation, where further critical selection and editing decisions were made.

The mediating role played by the eJay software in the collaborative creative process

As was evident in the previous sequences, in both settings, participants engaged in very similar collaborative creative processes of music making. This was believed to be in part to be due to *eJay*'s strong visual interface, which provided a distinctive 'scaffold' for partners' interactions in both settings, as partners could 'see' their samples and compositions unfold. This was particularly evident in sequences of talk in which participants referred to specific aspects of their compositional structures as they worked. The following examples highlight the specific and unique characteristics of the software that the participants drew on during their creative collaborative process. For example, utterances such as 'we need to put some stuff in there' (Sequence 3, line 91). This utterance demonstrates how the software allowed the participants to playback and listen to what they created, and consequently critically listen to and identify gaps within the compositional structure that they needed to address.

Sequence 3   Formal school context, Group 5 (Triad)

No.	Turn	Participant	Code	Transcribed discourse
91	1	A	S1	We need to put some stuff in there (pointing to last part of composition)
92	1	M	E1a	I know, something sounds crap
93	2	M	Q	Is it that bit in there?
94	1	A	E1a	Yeah, but you need something to carry it on
95	1	M	SUP1	I know, yeah
96	1	P	S1	Like vocal, go to voice (s.t.)
97	1	A	S1	Or that water, or that water, yeah, what's this (s.n.)
98	1	P	S1	Or rap (s.t.)

Note: s.n. = sample name; s.t. = sample type

In contrast, as demonstrated in the previous sequences from more open-ended, exploration phases, where participants scrolled through the bank of pre-recorded samples, the software afforded the participants the option to quickly click, listen to and drag samples to the 'arrange' page, in which they could immediately evaluate the effect and consider whether or not the samples were relevant and worth keeping. In this respect the software not only allowed a fast pace of listening, selecting, and testing and rejecting, it also provided an immediate source of 'reference' sounds. For example, the young people could instantaneously drawn on a wide range of sounds that they otherwise might not have had access to or would have spent a long time searching for or recording. In sum as one of the main features of the task setting, the software provided a shared medium around which the participants organised their creative, collaborative interactions. It enabled them to discuss their ideas and illustrate what they meant visually (via the graphic interface) and provided an immediate, responsive environment through which they could compose spontaneously, and with relative ease.

DISCUSSION AND CONCLUSIONS

Reviewing the results in relation to the existing literature

The aim of this study was to explore participants' creative collaborations using eJay sampling software in a formal secondary school music class and a non-formal youth group in a community centre. Contrary to collaborative learning studies that have found that the task setting and instruction influenced the types of processes engaged in (Bennett & Dunne, 1991; Kumpulainen & Kaartinen, 2000; Van Boxtel et al., 2000), in this study this was not the case. Despite the differences between the two settings, similar types of dialogue occurred most frequently in both settings, namely musical suggestions (S1), musical extensions (E1a), questions (Q) and agreement (Sup1). This finding suggests that any differences between the two settings may be better understood by placing them on Sefton-Green's (2003) formal/non-formal setting continuum, with the formal school setting being one end of this continuum and the community centre setting being in the middle, more similar to semi-formal settings than completely non-formal settings such as at home with the family. In relation to how the settings were *organised*, however, (Sefton-Green's other continuum) the differences may be less, as in both contexts a task was set, using the same technology and within a relatively confined space. In this respect it could be argued that the community centre setting was a semi-formal setting, but organised in a formal-like way. However even taking this into consideration, one might have expected a greater difference in the patterns of interaction occurring. It would appear that in this study the *learning organisation* rather than the *learning setting* played a greater role in understanding how meaning was created and the kinds of interactive patterns that emerged. This raises questions about what kinds of interaction patterns would have been found when the software is used by choice as part of a leisure activity, such as at home. Further research in this area would complement the work carried out in this study.

The quality of the dialogue and its implications for creative thinking

As noted, the most frequently occurring types of talk found in the settings – musical suggestions (S1), musical extensions (E1a), questions (Q) and agreements (Sup1) – were indicative of co-construction and that partners were achieving a shared understanding of the task (Kumpulainen & Kaartinen,

2000; Van Boxtel et al., 2000). However such talk would not necessarily be categorised as exploratory talk, which traditionally has been considered to be the most productive for learning as it engages participants in joint thinking and decision-making through conflicts, challenges, providing justifications and well-argued proposals (Dawes et al., 1992; Mercer, 1994; Mercer et al., 1999; Wegerif & Mercer, 1996). However, it could be argued that such exploratory talk is more a feature of logical, 'closed' tasks where there are well-defined solutions. It is believed that the talk found in this study characterises more creative, open-ended tasks, where there is no fixed or pre-defined solution. In addition, from the qualitative analysis, Webster's (2001, 2002) definition of creativity as a two-fold process that encompasses both divergent and convergent thinking was supported, particularly where participants engaged in cycles of divergent, open-ended exploration and convergent, critical periods of listening, reflecting and editing. Although these periods of critical thinking may have a similar quality to the kinds of dialogues that are often characterised as 'exploratory talk', they function differently as they do not follow the same discursive patterns that are typically found in science- and math-based exploratory talks. Further research in this area, on the kinds of verbal dialogues engaged in when creating in different domain areas, at both novice and expert level, would be worth pursuing (see also Vass, this volume).

The role of eJay software in supporting the collaborative dialogues and creativity

From the qualitative analysis it was clear how important the software was in scaffolding the interactions. *eJay* provided a structured visual interface which enabled all participants, irrespective of the instructions they received, to compose a piece of music. The research indicated that the young people in both settings were engaged in complex dialogical and multimodal (linguistic, musical and gestural) interactions in which they actively appropriated the available technology to create and refine their compositions. *eJay* afforded this experience by providing the young people with the opportunity to become creative, collaborative music-makers and producers. Within the study there was evidence that the immediacy of the software allowed the young people to instinctively, and with minimal effort, produce music collaboratively by selecting, listening and evaluating samples and arranging them on a graphic page, on which they could visualise and discuss their work. The 'click, drag and drop' approach to sample selection and arranging afforded immediate modes of musical composition, while the playback feature allowed the participants to listen and reflect critically on what they had assembled. In addition, the range of samples stored within the software provided instant source material, analogous to a painter's palette from which they could develop their compositional ideas. In sum, eJay scaffolded an ongoing process of production, evaluation and redesigning, from which the young people were continuously communicating, evolving their ideas and defining their task. It would be advantageous to compare *eJay* to other musical software and also examine how young people with different musical backgrounds and expertise use *eJay*; the author is currently investigating these latter questions.

ACKNOWLEDGEMENTS

This work was carried out as part fulfilment of a PhD conducted at The Open University, UK. The author would like to thank all the young people, their teachers and leaders involved in the study; Dr Dorothy Miell and Dr Richard Joiner for their critical support and assistance in this project; and Keri Facer, Learning Director, NESTA Futurelab for her support and comments.

NOTES

1. http://www.ejay-uk.com/. The version used in the study was published in 1997 for Windows 95/98.
2. Girls' and Boys' Brigades are two wings of an international organisation for young people that is similar to Boy Scouts and Girl Guides.
3. MEPA was developed by Gijsbert Erkens (G.Erkens@fss.uu.nl) at the Department of Educational Sciences, University of Utrecht, The Netherlands.
4. Given the nature and scope of this chapter, it was decided to present only a small portion of the statistical analyses carried out for this study. If readers are interested in further elaboraton of the range of analyses conducted, please do not hesitate to contact the author.

REFERENCES

Amabile, T.M. (1983). 'The social psychology of creativity: A componential conceptualisation'. *Journal of Personality and Social Psychology, 45*, 357–376.
Amabile, T.M. (1985). *Social influences on creativity: Interactive effects of reward and choice.* Paper presented at the Meeting of the American Psychological Association, August, Los Angeles, USA.
Barrett, M. (1995). *Children composing: What have we learnt?* Paper presented at the 10th National Conference of the Australian Society for Music Education, Hobart, Tanzania.
Bennett, N. & Dunne, E. (1991). 'The nature and quality of talk in co-operative classroom groups'. *Learning and Instruction, 1* (2), 103–118.
Cole, M. (1997). *Cultural psychology.* Cambridge, MA: Harvard University Press.
Craft, A., Jeffrey, B. & Leibling, M. (eds). (2001). *Creativity in education.* London: Continuum.
Crook, C. (1994). *Computers and the collaborative experience of learning.* London: Routledge.
Csikszentmihalyi, M. (1990). 'The domain of creativity'. In M.A. Runco & R. Albert (eds), *Theories of creativity.* Thousand Oaks: Sage.
Csikszentmihalyi, M. & Getzels, J.W. (1971). 'Discovery oriented behaviour and the originality of creative products'. *Journal of Personality and Social Psychology, 19*, 47–52.
Dawes, L., Fisher, E. & Mercer, N. (1992). 'The quality of talk at the computer'. *Language and Learning* (October), 22–25.
Dillon, T., Joiner, R. & Miell, D. (2001). *An Investigation into Music Technology Practices.* Paper presented at the Research in Music Education Conference, University of Exeter, April.
Eraut, M. (2000). 'Non-formal learning, implicit learning and tacit knowledge in professional work'. *British Journal of Educational Psychology, 70* (1), 113–136.
Facer, K. & Furlong, R. (2001). 'Beyond the myth of the "Cyberkid": Young people at the margins of the information revolution'. *Journal of Youth Studies, 4* (4), 451–469.
Folkestad, G. (1998). 'Musical learning as cultural practice as exemplified in computer-based creative music-making'. In B. Sudin, G. McPherson & G. Folkestad (eds), *Children composing.* Malmö, Sweden: Lund University.
Goodnow, J.J. & Warton, P. (1992). 'Contexts and cognitions: Taking a pluralist view'. In P. Light & G. Butterworth (eds), *Context and cognition, ways of learning and knowing.* New York; London: Harvester Wheatsheaf.

Ireson, J. & Blay, J. (1999). 'Constructing activity: Participation by adults and children'. *Learning and Instruction, 9* (1), 19–13.

Kumpulainen, K. & Kaartinen, S. (2000). 'Situational mechanisms of peer group interaction in collaborative meaning-making: Processes and conditions for learning'. *European Journal of Psychology of Education, 15* (4), 431–445.

Littleton, K. & Häkkinen, P. (1999). 'Learning together: Understanding the processes of computer-based collaborative learning'. In P. Dillenbourg (ed.), *Collaborative learning: Cognitive and computational approaches.* London: Pergamon.

Littleton, K. & Light, P. (1999). *Learning with computers: Analysing productive interaction.* London: Routledge.

MacDonald, R., Miell, D. & Mitchell, L. (2002). 'An investigation of children's musical collaborations: The effect of friendships and age'. *Psychology of Music, 30* (2), 148–163.

Marsick, J. & Watson, K.E. (1990). *Informal and incidental learning in the workplace.* London; New York: Routledge.

McGivney, V. (1999). *Informal learning in the community a trigger for change and development.* England and Wales National Institute of Adult Continuing Education (NIACE).

Mercer, N. (1994). 'The quality of talk in children's joint activity at the computer'. *Journal of Computer Assisted Learning, 10* (1), 24–32.

Mercer, N., Wegerif, R. & Dawes, L. (1999). 'Children's talk and the development of reasoning in the classroom'. *British Educational Research Journal, 25* (1), 95–111.

Mills, J. & Murray, A. (2000). 'Music technology inspected: Good teaching in Key Stage 3'. *British Journal of Music Education, 17* (2), 157–181.

NACCCE. (1999). *All our futures: Creativity, culture and education.* Sudbury: National Advisory Committee on Creative and Cultural Education, DfEE and DCMS.

Pitts, A. & Kwami, R.M. (2002). 'Raising Students Performance in Music Composition through the Use of Information and Communications Technology (ICT): A Survey of Secondary Schools in England'. *British Journal of Music Education*, 19 (61–71).

Prensky, M. (2001). *Digital game-based learning.* New York: McGraw Hill.

Rogoff, B. (1990). *Apprenticeship in thinking: Cognitive development in social context.* London and New York: Oxford University Press.

Sefton-Green, J. (2003). *Literature review in informal learning with technology outside school.* Bristol, UK: NESTA Futurelab.

Smith, M. & Jeffs, T. (eds). (1990). *Using informal education.* Buckingham: Open University Press.

Van Boxtel, C., Van der Linden, J. & Kanselaar, G. (2000). 'Collaborative learning tasks and the elaboration of conceptual knowledge'. *Learning and Instruction, 10* (2), 311–330.

Webster, P. (2001). *Double, double, boil and trouble, Where doth creative thinking bubble.* Paper presented at the 2nd International Research in Music Education Conference, April, University of Exeter, Exeter, UK.

Webster, P. (2002). *Creative thinking and music education: Encouraging students to make aesthetic decisions.* Paper presented at the 10th conference of the European Society for the Cognitive Sciences of Music, April, Liege, Belgium.

Wegerif, R. & Mercer, N. (1996). 'Computers and reasoning through talk in the classroom'. *Language and Education, 10* (1), 47–64.

12
Creative Collaboration in Organisational Settings

Jane Henry

INTRODUCTION

Sustaining creativity across the workforce is often perceived as making a critical difference for an organisation's survival. In addition (unlike typical views of great art or poetry, where the creative product is often seen to emerge from a single individual) most creative and innovative products in organisations clearly emerge from collaboration amongst many different people, as they travel the path from 'bright idea' to the market place.

This chapter discusses ways in which organisations aim to facilitate, develop and sustain creative collaboration. Creative collaboration is examined at four levels, that of the individual, group, organisation and interorganisational levels. The chapter highlights some of the key findings about collaborative creativity at work and discusses how creativity appears to be facilitated at each level.

This chapter considers the effects of ability, style and role on individual contributions to collaborative efforts; the effect of reward systems, reporting structures, and training, especially creativity training, on team processes; the part played by climate, trust and emergent creativity in organisational creativity; and the role of networking, partnership and connectivity in product development across organisations.

Organisations have been under increasing competitive pressure for several decades and nowadays generally seek multi-faceted ways of improving their capacity for collaboration. All four levels can affect creative endeavour and these days the majority of organisations will address all four in some way or other.

INDIVIDUAL PERSON

Until recently much of Western psychological thinking about creativity has assumed that creativity is a quality that emanates from an individual and most creativity research has been framed in line with this assumption (Guildford, 1959; MacKinnon, 1961). For example, the focus on identifying and measuring the characteristics of creative individuals and designing programmes to improve certain aspects of their mental flexibility, such as divergent thinking, thought to be associated with creative endeavour. Much of the work to date has focused on the particular abilities of creative individuals, different styles of creativity shown by individuals with different cognitive styles and the variety of roles, creative and otherwise, found in groups and associated with different personality types. Here we look at the place of individual ability, style and role in creative collaboration.

Ability

Early work on creativity focused on attempts to try and identify the traits associated with more creative individuals and discover what distinguished the exceptionally creative from others who lacked this assumed trait. At this time (in the 1940s and 1950s) there was considerable interest in psychological traits and it seemed natural to view creativity as another trait. The idea of creativity as a trait also found a ready audience in organisations which were attracted to the idea of testing people as a means of refining the fit between individuals' qualities and capabilities and the attributes required for different positions.

Various tests were devised to try and identify the characteristics of 'the creative person' (Guildford, 1959). These studies and other work have shown that creative people tend to have a higher tolerance for ambiguity than the less creative. Though creativity is associated with a novel and apt idea, real world studies have shown that creative people spend more time at the front end of a project settling on the most important question to address – deciding on what is the important question to ask, a phase known as problem finding (Getzels & Csikszentmihalyi, 1976; Perkins, 1981).

Studies of creative individuals in various fields have also shown experience and domain knowledge to be a critical factor (Gruber, 1980; Gruber & Wallace, 1999). One explanation for this phenomenon is that creativity is a form of expert recognition, whereby people develop knowledge in a particular domain and this enables them to chunk information differently from novices leaving them better placed to identify critical questions. Weisburg (1986) argues on the basis of biographical studies of various individuals that it takes a minimum of ten years to produce work of exceptional creativity. Worth's (2001) study of people recognised as creative in their organisation or locale found that this 'local' creativity appears to require a minimum of about three years experience in the field.

The perceived location of creativity as inside the heads of the chosen few is reinforced in narratives about heroic creative endeavours. In the West, creativity tends to be associated with the big idea and the revolutionary breakthrough and these breakthroughs are often glorified in the form of a particular heroic individual who is associated with that breakthrough. We laud Einstein for relativity, Bell for the telephone, and associate Baird with TV and Richard Berners-Lee with the World Wide Web, paying scant attention to their collaborators. The same tendency to glorify a lone hero is seen in our narratives about organisations; we glorify Harvey Jones for turning around ICI, Jack Welch for GM, Ricardo Semler for his metamorphosis of Semco and pay little attention to their colleagues. This is as true in comic books and films, as in science and organisations. We have Superman, Rocky, Mad Max and the Terminator, reinforcing the myth that one man can change the world. It is no surprise that this tendency to glorify particular individuals' roles in creative and other projects is found particularly in individualistic Anglo-Saxon cultures (Reich, 1991).

Style

It has been found that the calibre of individual scientists is important for the success of research, exploratory and development projects in organisations (Zeneca, 1996). However with this exception, many organisations have moved away from the idea that creativity is an ability possessed solely by a small subset of the population and have turned their intention instead to ways of maximising the creativity of the whole workforce rather than a few privileged specialists. This is largely because organisations have been under increased competitive pressure globally from high wage economies and need to find ways to continuously add value to survive. Creativity and continuous improvement seem to offer a means of doing this.

Kirton (1989, 1994) has drawn attention to 'Adaption', a form of creativity that is more concerned with working within existing frames of reference and attending to detail to build and improve on what has gone before to do things better. He contrasts this with 'Innovation' which he sees as a preference for doing things differently by challenging existing ways of doing things, the type of thinking that can lead to the radical breakthrough usually associated with creativity in the West. Adaption and Innovation appear to represent two poles on a dimension of cognitive style. Kirton's (1994) Adaption Innovation inventory is correlated with Openness on a well known personality inventory (Big Five) and also shows moderate correlations with 'judging' and 'perceiving' and 'sensing' and 'intuiting' on the widely used MBTI. Many psychologists now suspect that the five main 'Big Five' dimensions underpin those in numerous other personality tests (Goldberg, 1993). The four MBTI dimensions show correlations with four of the five Big Five dimensions (Bayne, 1994).

On this as on many other inventories, groups of professionals tend to show different profiles that intuitively appear in line with their occupation. For example staff in research and development, where radical ideas might be expected to be more welcome, are more likely to have a preference for innovation. Staff in production, where improvements normally need to work within an existing system, are more likely to have an adaptive preference (Kirton, 1987; Myers & McCaulley, 1988). It is often easier for people with the same cognitive style to communicate with each other than those of different cognitive styles, but in the longer run groups with a mix of personality types are more likely to consider a wider range of options.

Role

Individual cognitive style and role preference also has an effect on the potential for creative collaboration at team level. Teams containing people with a variety of cognitive styles and preferred work roles are known to be more successful than those that are less mixed (Belbin, 1981, 1993; Margerison & McCann,

1990). Belbin lists nine roles, including plant/ideas person, specialist, shaper, resource investigator, team worker, coordinator, implementor, completer, monitor-evaluator. Groups with a number of shapers or competitive task leaders may waste a lot of time deciding who is in charge and groups with a lot of plants – creative people adept at thinking up many new ideas – may not complete the task as set unless the group also includes someone more attuned to the completer-finisher role. Thus even those considered to be creative in the traditional Western sense of the term, i.e. those able to come up with radically new or unusual ideas relatively easily, such as Belbin's plant/ideas person, seem more likely to have these ideas turned into action if they work with people of differing cognitive styles who are better able to complete other parts of the process they tend to have less natural affinity for, such as getting the details right.

Over the life-course of a creative project certain individual roles have been shown to be important for the success of organisational creative collaborations. Three key roles that have been recognised for a long time are those of the inventor who comes up with an idea, the innovator who produces a working prototype and the entrepreneur who is interested in getting the product to market. It appears to be rare to find individuals who fit happily in to all three roles. This is not surprising as the motivation for each appears to be different. The successful inventor and exploratory scientist tend to be motivated by job satisfaction and are happiest in an organisation that affords them considerable freedom. Frequently a working prototype requires the efforts of a team comprising individuals with different knowledge bases who must collaborate to produce a workable product. The team needs to be able to work together. In contrast to the importance of intrinsic motivation to creative inventors, studies of entrepreneurs suggest many are motivated extrinsically and are keen to earn substantial remunerations for the risks they take (Henry, 2001, pp.128–133).

Empirical work suggests that three other roles are critical to the success of organisational creative ventures, that of the champion, the sponsor and technological gatekeeper. The technological gatekeeper is the person who has state of the art of knowledge of key developments, often of a scientific or technical nature, that prove to be an important component in developing some aspect of the creative collaboration (Maidique, 1990). They are more likely to be able to assist creative collaborations if given sufficient freedom and time to keep up with their potentially useful state-of-the-art knowledge. A good idea is not necessarily enough in an organisation, it also needs to wend its way through the company politics and structures. Various studies have shown that a champion and a sponsor are often critical to the success of innovative organisational endeavours. A champion is a senior manager with enough faith in the project to champion it through the company bureaucracy and a sponsor is someone high up enough in the organisation to be able to grant funding, time and resources for the particular creative project in question.

Reward systems

Two common ways in which organisations encourage staff to share creative ideas are suggestion schemes and targeted rewards.

Many companies have in place suggestion and other schemes of continuous improvement in an attempt to harness the creative insights of all employees throughout the organisation. Unless the workforce is so cynical that they do not believe the suggestions will be acted upon, studies of suggestions schemes repeatedly show that employees are full of actionable creative ideas that save substantive sums, time and improve performance. Many suggestions schemes more than pay for themselves in the first year of operation. Organisations often offer financial rewards to those offering the ideas deemed most useful. The ideas keep coming if staff are shown via newsletters, company meetings and the like that a proportion of ideas are implemented.

As regards rewarding staff for good ideas and good work, studies suggest that these work best if they take account of the motivation of the staff concerned. Scientists tend to be motivated intrinsically by personal job satisfaction and so tend to appreciate being given freedom and personal rewards. 3M, a company famous for its continued capacity for innovation, has offered its research and development scientists and engineers up to 15 per cent of their time to work on projects of their own choosing. Staff have also been free to bid for genesis funds to develop ideas arising from such projects (Mitchell, 1991). The ubiquitous post-it pad arose from just such a policy (Nayak & Ketteringham, 1986). 3M is a large organisation with a relatively stable workforce but manages to keep innovating, with something over a quarter of its current products introduced in the last five years. Another policy they have adopted to support collaborative creativity is to provide and encourage frequent opportunities for scientists to network with other scientists and gatekeepers inside and outside the company through, for example, company conferences.

Moving a product from a research idea to a viable prototype almost invariably involves a group of engineers and other scientists with different skills. Zeneca have advocated rewarding inventive scientists involved in exploratory research personally but dividing any rewards offered for developing innovative prototypes equally among members of the team responsible. The logic is that this provides an incentive for an innovative project development team to try to collaborate and share expertise whereas research scientists are often original thinkers better encouraged to follow their own productive lines of enquiry.

Work in organisations suggests individuals naturally play different roles in collaborations, often in accord with their cognitive predispositions. These collaborations appear to have a greater chance of success where the team concerned contains a mix of people with differing styles. Thus individual characteristics are one of the factors that affect the success or otherwise of team collaborations.

Team Process

Teams are central to organisational endeavour and increasingly so as organisations shift to more multi-disciplinary team working and push responsibility down to team level. In addition to questions of appropriate group composition companies face the question of how best to organise such groups, and which reporting structures might best facilitate creative action. Also how to train staff so they can work together effectively and enhance their potential for sustained creativity and innovation. Other questions concern the most useful managerial style and reward systems.

Organising teams

Many organisations have moved from the traditional functional arrangement to a structure that places far greater emphasis on cross-functional collaboration. This is partly because empowered cross-functional teams can react more quickly than traditional hierarchical bureaucratic structures and speed of response is often critical in today's highly competitive world, but also because in manufacturing in particular, cross-functional teams have proved in the long run to be more efficient in many areas.

Innovative product development used to be organised as a relay race with the Research department exploring possibilities and passing the spec to the Design department who compiled a detailed specification for Development, who built a prototype and passed this on to Production to begin manufacture of the product, and then an example would go to Marketing for tests and then on to Sales. Studies in various industries have shown this system to be less efficient than a system employing multi-disciplinary teams comprising say a scientist, designer, various development and production engineers and representatives from marketing and sales who collaborate on creative new projects from conception to marketing (Clark & Fujimoto, 1991). In manufacturing, these multi-disciplinary teams are often grouped into cells housed in divisions based round particular product groups rather than functional divisions. Communication between people from different disciplines, used to speaking in different ways, can be problematic. Job rotation across departments, a common practice in Japan, offers one route to helping staff learn the languages common in different specialisms like design, manufacturing and marketing. This acts as a kind of on the job training which can make subsequent multi-disciplinary team working easier.

Collaborative working and integrated development procedures in and across organisations have been facilitated by the advance in ICTs (information and communication technologies) such as e-mail, video conferencing, mobile phones, the advent of sophisticated laptops, and notably CAD/CAM (computer aided design and manufacturing), which enable distant workers in different departments and organisations to share detailed designs and schedules.

There remains the question as to how best to organise reporting structures for the staff in multi-disciplinary teams. Many organisations bring groups of people together for limited periods to collaborate on particular creative projects. Various different reporting structures have been tried. A team working on a blue sky project may form a venture team and be given resources and line management outside the standard reporting system. An alternative is matrix management where the team member reports both to their line manager and the creative team leader, a situation that can cause problems as staff are pulled both ways (Holt, 1991). Nonaka and Takeuchi (1995) have argued that routine tasks are best organised hierarchically with a parallel network of project teams handling creative projects and staff reporting only to one or the other system for line management purposes not both systems.

In addition to multi-disciplinary teams within organisations some creative industries such as film production are largely based on time-limited creative projects conducted by freelance and other staff brought together for the purpose. Longitudinal studies of such team collaborations suggest that selectors choose staff for each project team principally from a larger group of individuals known to the organisers or recommended to them by peers. This provides a group of people that the organisers know they can trust and that can be matched to make a harmonious team with complementary skills more probable. Such temporary project groupings offer little formal training for staff and some commentators have feared this would make career progression difficult. However industries such as film and advertising offer team participants quite a bit of slack time in which they can observe how others work and perhaps learn on the job (DeFillippi & Arthur, 2002).

In sum, the evidence so far seems to suggest that temporary multi-disciplinary teams can help organisations develop and sustain creativity across the workforce, provided some attention is given to nurturing the group at the outset with little of the downside, such as lack of career progression, feared by some commentators.

Training

Most organisations realise that collaboration normally involves group-level processes that need attention. For example there is an appreciation that teams need time to bond and communication is critical. A widely known mnemonic for team bonding is Tuckman's (1965) sequence of groups first 'forming', then 'storming', and subsequently 'norming' and 'performing'. Team leaders often see it as part of their task to get the group to socialise together so they can begin bonding. Organisations often send teams off-site for a team-building exercise in which team members have a chance to get to know each other informally and begin to develop trust and commitment to the group.

Organisational training also normally gives a fair amount of attention to group process and communication skills such as listening, assertiveness, handling difficult people, conflict resolution and the like. These are designed to help people communicate more effectively when working collaboratively in groups.

Many organisations also offer training designed to enhance employee's potential for creativity. Westerners tend to associate creativity with 'the bright idea', epitomised in the archetypical creativity story of Archimedes. He cried 'eureka' as he realised the potential parallel in measuring the irregular volume of the Kings Crown through displacement of water as he got into his bath (Koestler, 1969). This exemplifies the favoured folk theory of creativity as an idea arising from a novel association between two separate fields, whereby an idea from one field is associated with another to give a new perspective, such as X-rays and food technology leading to the microwave for example. In this view creativity is a mental process in which creative thinking is assumed to be critical; in particular the capacity for divergent thinking and stepping outside the box long enough not to close down on less apparently probable ideas without considering unusual ways forward.

The idea of creativity as a skill that can be taught and transferred accords with the idea of competencies currently dominating thinking about education and training in organisational, education and government fields. Studies of creative endeavour show that mental flexibility is indeed one element present in creative endeavours, along with intrinsic motivation and domain knowledge (Amabile, 1983). The next section considers how creativity training can enhance creative thinking in collaborative projects.

Creativity training in organisations typically involves group-based workshops based around creative problem solving. In the 1960s and 1970s proponents such as De Bono (1971) popularised the idea of training people in lateral and divergent thinking to enhance the capacity for creative thought. In organisations today brainstorming is the most common way of attempting to facilitate group-based creativity. This entails a group of people contributing any idea they can think of, whether sensible or crazy, to the issue at hand, on the assumption that two heads are better than one. A quality idea is expected to emerge from the large quantity of ideas produced if people are stopped from censuring possible lines of enquiry too early by adopting the rule of avoiding any criticism and so deferring judgement (Osbourn, 1953). Some work has suggested that 'brainwriting' produces a greater variety of ideas (e.g. Dunnette et al., 1963). Brainwriting is where people begin by privately writing ideas down before sharing them with the group. It is assumed to avoid 'group think'. Group think can lead to the ideas individuals put forward being influenced by their neighbours' suggestions. For example everyone may suggest a form of container when asked to think of uses for a plastic cup and neglect to mention the idea of the cup as a hat or toy. This process can narrow the range of ideas considered. Brainwriting can avoid runs of variants on a theme within a particular class of ideas such as the plastic cup as pen holder, flowerpot, and cup of water, all examples of the cup as container.

CREATIVE PROBLEM SOLVING

It can be hard to deal effectively with the mass of ideas generated in a brainwriting or storming session, so 'creative problem solving' (CPS) where an idea generation procedure like brainwriting is embedded in a creative problem solving process, is often more productive. Parnes (1967), Rickards (1988) and Henry and Martin (1993) provide examples of this type of approach. CPS entails splitting the stages of thinking. Typically, a creative problem solving framework explicitly encourages people to consider more improbable aspects than they might otherwise, but also to register their favoured ideas from among those put forward. One way of doing this is to alternate between a divergent thinking stage where all ideas are considered and a convergent stage where a smaller subset of favoured ideas are taken forward. Creative problem solving is a common management training activity. It is generally taught to groups as a workshop in which participants may work on problems, issues and opportunities of concern to them. A group brought together for some creative collaboration may be sent off on such a course at the outset or if/when they get stuck in some way and more conventional approaches have failed.

The typical CPS course shares a number of common processes, summarised below:

Creative problem solving processes:
Split the stages of thinking
Accept all ideas, sensible or crazy
Be constructive and positive
Use non-verbal media
Involve all the group
Alternate between divergent and convergent modes of thinking
Use public display of key ideas
Use visual display
Stay open to intuitive hunches and gut feelings
Listen to everyone
Build on others' ideas
Avoid criticism of others' ideas
Avoid closing off options prematurely.

One element is the emphasis on the public display of ideas, typically summarised on flipchart paper. Often the ideas are presented graphically, in large print and in a variety of colours. As visual memory is much superior to semantic memory the use of diagrammatic visual cues, such as mind-maps, causes and consequences diagrams, and concept maps, helps people see and remember the keys issues and ideas at a glance.

The public display of shared opinions through diagrams and non-linear forms of presentation can greatly illuminate and assist meetings to stick to the question at hand and think constructively 'out of the box'. Taking public notes on a mind-map of points being made in a meeting can reduce the meeting time by up to 50 per cent. This normally involves the use of flipcharts or a whiteboard so participants can read the notes. The time saving appears to come from participants unconsciously registering when the notetaker pauses (normally when points are being repeated or are irrelevant to the issue at hand) and curtailing the digression they had or were about to embark on.

Though often advertised as a means of enhancing individuals' creative thinking skills, creative problem solving has many in-built processes designed to facilitate engagement and interpersonal collaboration.

These rules help engage all members of the group and encourage them to contribute. For example brainstorming rules specify that all ideas are accepted, whether sensible or crazy. This helps considerably in preventing people from worrying that their ideas might be crazy and not voicing them and prevents others from criticising their ideas and inhibiting future offerings. The round robin rule is often used at the start of brainstorming to take one idea from each person in turn if they want to give one; if not they are encouraged to pass. This helps to prevent certain individuals from dominating the group with their ideas as they are forced to listen to and take note of everybody's ideas. Another useful facilitative technique which can aid collaboration is the idea of passing the pen. This means encouraging different people to take notes for each technique tried, for example getting two members of the group to do one mind map branch and another two another branch. This encourages all members of the group to take part, so nobody feels left out. Together these strategies help engage participants in a more active collaboration.

Creative problem solving is presented as a series of techniques to help managers and their staff think more creatively. These workshops do indeed help people come up with new ideas, but they also offer a variety of other benefits less explicitly represented in the way they are sold. These include helping participants check that they have considered all possible alternatives, developing a common language for addressing the problem, opportunity or issue at hand and the chance to gain a deeper understanding of their colleagues' ways of perceiving the world.

Another common benefit is a greater respect for other people's points of view. In a CPS session participants are forced to listen to ideas voiced by people they might not respect as well as by those they do. Consciously or unconsciously people come to realise the benefit of giving some time to those who do not see the world as they do. They see that an idea suggested by someone they did not value has been used as a springboard for a productive approach they would not have thought of. As a result participants sometimes become more tolerant and respectful of others. It is perhaps partly for this reason that CPS has become a popular team-building activity. West and Anderson (1996) have pointed out that teams are more likely to explore new territory where they feel safe. The respect and constructive communication encouraged in creativity can help here.

In short, creativity training offers one way of helping all members of a team engage more fully, understand and be tolerant of colleagues, which in turn helps a team collaborate more effectively.

ORGANISATIONAL CLIMATE

We now turn to the place of work. Psychologists have long known that those who feel safe are more inclined to explore new environments and more likely to dare to challenge and question than those who do not feel safe (West, 2000). It is perhaps for this reason that an open organisational climate where people feel free to make mistakes, challenge standard practice and try out different ways of doing things has been found to be a critical factor in the success of creative collaborations in organisations in many sectors/areas (Jelinek & Schoonhaven, 1991).

Open climate

Generally the more creative the organisation the more open the culture tends to be, people will feel free to make mistakes and challenge the status quo, conflicts are out in the open, the company will support risks, take decisions quicker and encourage networking. Less creative organisations are often rule and committee bound, people feel obliged to look busy, do not dare voice their opinion or suggestions for improvement and will cover up mistakes. Table 12.1 elaborates differences in climate that Ekvall (1991) found in the more and less creative organisations he studied in Scandinavia.

Table 12.1   Creative organisational climate

Dimension	More creative	Less creative
Challenge	Enjoyable	Alienated
	Energetic	Indifferent
Freedom	Independent	Passive
	Initiatives taken	Rule-bound
Liveliness	Excitedly busy	Boringly slow
Openness	Trusting	Suspicious
	Failure accepted	Failure punished
Idea time	Off-task play	Little off-task play
Mood	Happy/humorous	Serious/dull
Conflicts	Handled constructively	Handled destructively
Support	People listen helpfully	People are negative and critical
Debates	Contentious ideas voiced	Little questioning
Risk taking	Fast decisions	Cautious, safe decisions
	Risk acting on new ideas	Detail and committee bound

(Source: Based on Ekvall, 1991)

Open-ended cultures where employees have a lot of freedom to determine how they work do not necessarily suit all types. Ekvall (1997) has shown that the type of culture preferred may vary with department, with Research and Development staff tending to favour a looser culture than Production staff.

Given the chance people are more inclined to collaborate on creative ventures with people they trust, because they know, often from personal experience, that the colleague is honourable, knowledgeable, hardworking and/or insightful. Trust is not a given and generally has to be earned through successful close collaboration with colleagues or granted in an open culture where one has faith that disagreements can be dealt with honourably. In reality there is likely to be a limit on the number of people one knows well enough to trust sufficiently to share new creative ideas.

In an effort to kickstart and support more enterprising cultures that would better support collaborative creativity and the sharing of ideas, in the 1990s many organisations tried to change their culture by pushing responsibility down and empowering staff to take more decisions directly (Bowen & Lawlor, 2002). The degree of the transformation has varied, for front end McDonald's staff it means little more than being allowed to vary their greeting slightly but for other companies such as Semco (discussed below) it has meant a fundamental change in how they are run.

It is not a simple or short-term endeavour to change entrenched attitudes and practices among workers and managers. Some rather naive top-down efforts deservedly failed (Legge, 1994) but others do seem to transform their organisations for the better – Jaguar and Rover (before its demise) Dutton and Semco offer cases in point (Semler, 1994; Lewis & Lytton, 2002).

For staff at Semco, a medium size pump manufacturer in Brazil, the transformation meant a gradual shift to a radically different form of organisation with minimal management intervention, upwards appraisal (staff appraising their boss every six months), groups selecting their own staff, setting their own hours, expenses and in some cases share of the profits, and the demise of many traditional corporate departments such as quality, training and personnel (Semler, 1994). At Oticon, a Danish hearing aid manufacturer, creative collaborations are the norm. The bosses trust staff to play a major role in determining which collaboration they choose to work on, a policy which makes it easier to unleash the extra effort found when staff are intrinsically motivated.

Many studies suggest the importance of trust and openness in creative collaboration. Many organisations are aware of these phenomena and though they are not always able to 'walk the talk', have tried to open up their climate with a view to enhancing creativity across the workforce.

Collaborative systems

So far we have looked at creative collaboration from an individual, team and organisational perspective. Some modern management theorists take a wider view and see creativity as a systems-level phenomenon that emerges naturally where it is not blocked (Stacy, 1996; Wheatley, 1994). They draw their inspiration from work on the dynamics of non-linear adaptive systems popularly known as complexity theory. This derives from work studying the collective behaviour of individual agents (be they ants, brain-cells, or people in organisations). Adaptive systems change the way they are organised over time as a result of the collective repetition of certain simple behaviours by the agents in that system. The result of this type of thinking has been applied to situations as diverse as the behaviour of the heart to stock market price movements as well as to creative collaboration in organisations. Several general rules appear to hold across remarkably diverse systems. First, most systems are naturally creative, i.e. useful, timely, novel behaviour emerges which can become embedded over time without 'manipulation' by a manager, for example, to ensure that this comes about. Secondly, systems with some redundancy tend to be more robust over time. A major consequence of this way of framing creative collaboration is that attempts to predict, plan for, and control creativity are seen as doomed to failure. By implication all a manager can do to assist collaboration is to encourage networking among staff who have some form of natural affiliation of interests, wait for creative projects that arise and support those that seem promising. This behoves a more facilitative and supportive form of management that is very different from the traditional manager's attempts to dictate and control the outcome.

On this view creative collaboration appears to work best where managers become part of the team and see their role as supporting and drawing out the creativity of team members.

CROSS-ORGANISATIONAL PRODUCT DEVELOPMENT

A surprising amount of creative collaboration these days occurs across as much as within organisations. This is especially true of much product development, and initiatives across the supply chain. The effect has been to create more permeable organisational boundaries.

Evolutionary vs. radical development

Folklore associates creativity with innovative breakthroughs, but studies on innovative developments show that most innovations arise from collaborations that develop in an evolutionary manner out of what has gone before. The first telephones, TVs and jet planes were not very good; it has taken successive generations of gradual improvements to get them to the sophisticated machines they are today – the colour cellphone with picture messaging and the interactive digital TV are a far cry from their analogue forebears. While Western rhetoric lauds the radical innovative breakthrough and glorifies an individual that comes to be associated with that radical innovation, in privileging innovation it arguably neglects the more evolutionary and adaptive creativity that builds and improves on what has gone before. This blindsight in the Western cultural frame for creativity does not seem to be shared by those in more collaborative cultures. Countries like Japan have an excellent record of continuous improvement in their products and processes, perhaps because they recognise that creativity is very much about collaboration over time and not just breakthroughs by a few individuals. In an attempt to redress this balance some companies have deliberately introduced sporting metaphors, such as playing football, into organisational change programmes in an attempt to present a narrative that is more appropriate to team-based collaboration.

Creative collaboration in organisations can also entail specialists sharing leading edge knowledge, much of which may be tacit. Nonaka and Takeuchi (1995) explain how Japanese firms make a point of encouraging collaborators to share knowledge with their team. They argue that while the West, operating from an information processing paradigm, excels at externalising explicit knowledge, the Japanese, recognising the importance of tacit knowledge, pay more attention to team socialisation and internalising implicit understandings through observation, imitation and reframing. For example Matsushita apprenticing a software designer to a breadmaker to help develop understanding as to how best to program a potential breadmaking machine to knead the dough.

There is some evidence to suggest that collaboration takes a different course at different stages of development. As intimated earlier it appears that the calibre of the individual scientist is important for inventing new products in exploratory research. When it comes to large development projects such as the tilting train, it is extremely difficult for organisations to anticipate the outcome of these capital intensive innovations. Some organisations opt to allow several different teams to work on different approaches to solving the many problems such a large-scale project entails. Each team then presents their chosen way forward at a so called 'shoot-out'. Generally the company can only afford to fund one to fruition. The losing team can easily become demoralised unless this process is seen to be very fair. As regards innovative applications, such as the use of smart cards (card door keys) in hotels, these are best undertaken by a team able to move rapidly. Here an efficient and effective project manager appears to be a key player.

At a cross-organisational level a common innovation cycle has been noted in many fields. A radical invention is introduced and a plethora of companies copy it, until one design comes to dominate the market. Then other players begin to find ways of producing a similar but cheaper and/or better product. There is then some consolidation and only a few leading players remain. In the longer term it is often the cheaper or better copy not the original that comes to dominate the market (Kay, 2002).

Cross-organisational collaboration

Creative collaborations across organisations take many forms including alliances and partnerships. For example Philips' and Sony's alliance to develop CDs (compact discs). Similarly SEAT, Ford and VW market exactly the same MPV or people carrier under different badges. (This arose from a joint venture by Ford and VW to develop a car for this market.) This type of cross-organisational collaboration can save a company money and time and may offer access to new markets. The degree of trust and level of cooperation among the partners seem to have a bearing on the success of the collaboration (Tidd et al., 1997).

Franchises offer another form of highly successful cross-organisational collaboration. The Body Shop and McDonald's have expanded widely through franchised shops. Benetton grew to a company with sales of well over 2 billion dollars, yet it subcontracts 95 per cent of its manufacturing to 700-odd small subcontractors.

Historically manufacturers often granted tenders to the supplier with the cheapest bid. However this practice can produce a high fault rate. Nowadays partnership sourcing is the common practice in the private sector. This is where manufacturers select a group of suppliers and commit to a relatively long-term collaboration with that group. This grants the supplier a more secure source of income and allows them to invest in better technology. Companies may send their own engineers to help a relatively poorly performing supplier improve. This type of arrangement seems generally to produce a more reliable supply of parts on time with a lower defect rate at a reasonable cost compared with 'lowest tender' arrangements (Dyer & Ouchi, 1993).

In addition to collaborating with other organisations, many companies make a point of collaborating with customers in an attempt to develop creative and innovative products. This may be done through focus groups, panel, diary and observation studies that aim to see what customers want, how they tackle tasks, and how they use products in the home and at work. The Apple Powerbook is an example of a product that arose from detailed studies of how consumers used computers. Its innovations included a trackball for right and left handers and a hinge allowing different viewing angles (Tidd et al., 1997, p.246).

In addition to these formal alliances, there also seems to be a synergistic advantage to more informal interactions among a community of people working in broadly the same area in a limited vicinity. Csikszentmihalyi (1996) has commented on the exceptional creative flowering that seems to have happened in certain places at particular points in history – art in Florence in the fourteenth century, pop music in Liverpool in the 1960s, rapid development in South-East Asia in the 1970s and 1980s, and computer development in Silicon valley (USA) in the latter half of the twentieth century. These are just some of the many cases where proximity of colleagues working at the cutting edge in related areas appears to have acted as a stimulus to creative development in the field concerned. The specialised networks and communities of practice that grow up around particular areas may help organisations in that field develop, as film has in Los Angeles and biotechnology is currently doing in Cambridge, England. Fukuyama (1999) suggests that the face-to-face contact, common interests and background allows sufficient trust and social capital to develop for people to be willing to share ideas which in turn provides fertile ground for creative collaboration.

Whilst folklore's conception of the organisation is that of a top-down hierarchy, a number of today's more successful organisations and institutions offering new services have more permeable boundaries. Two of the most successful ever – Visa and the Internet – are distributed interorganisational networks providing collaborative umbrellas for their members. Visa is owned by over 20,000 member organisations. The Internet is not owned by anyone and no one organisation runs it. It makes use of leased lines. For these institutions collaborative connectivity is the critical factor in their success.

In short, open partnership and networking seem to be central to creative collaboration across organisations.

CONCLUSION

Collaboration is essential to creative endeavour in virtually all organisational settings. The ramifications of this truism are ever better appreciated in organisations. Typically work is now organised around multi-disciplinary teams, whether these are brought together as a temporary project group or have a longer life-span.

Long gone are the days where organisations thought it was sufficient to select and appoint a creative individual to 'save the company's bacon' with a great new idea. Organisations are now more likely to attempt to facilitate creative collaboration at a number of different levels: by educating people to appreciate ways of working with those of a differing cognitive style; offering training in creative thinking, facilitating group processes and communication skills; providing opportunities for team-building; attempting to encourage an open climate where people are free to challenge the status quo; putting in place systems to nurture ideas and innovation and engaging in collaborative partnership with organisations with complementary expertise. At the front end of the creative process, creative collaboration seems more likely where people's intrinsic motivation is engaged in the task at hand; they trust those they are working with and they are free to network widely. Together these shifts seem to represent a move towards more mature forms of collaboration both within and across organisations.

REFERENCES

Amabile, T. (1983). *The social psychology of creativity*. New York: Springer Verlag.

Bayne, R. (1994). 'The Big Five versus the Myers-Briggs'. *The Psychologist*, January, 14–16.

Belbin, R.M. (1981). *Management teams why they succeed or fail*, 1st edition. Oxford: Heinemann. 2nd edition 1988.

Belbin, R.M. (1993). *Roles at work: A strategy for human resource management* (2nd edition). Oxford: Butterworth Heinemann.

Bowen, D.E. & Lawlor, E.E. III (2002). 'The empowerment of service workers: What, why, how and when'. In J. Henry & D.T. Mayle (eds), *Managing innovation and change* (pp.243–257). London: Sage.

Clark, K. & Fujimoto, T. (1991). 'Reducing time to market: the case of the world auto industry'. In J. Henry & D. Walker (eds), *Managing innovation*. London: Sage.

Csikszenmihalyi, M. (1996). *Creativity: Flow and the psychology of discovery and invention*. New York: HarperCollins.

De Bono, E. (1971). *Lateral thinking*. Harmondsworth: Penguin.

DeFillipi, R.J. & Arthur, M.B. (2002). 'Paradox in project-based enterprise: The case of film making'. In J. Henry & D.T. Mayle (eds), *Managing innovation and change* (2nd edition) (pp.189–202). London: Sage.

Dunnette, M.D., Campbell, J. & Jaasad, K. (1963). 'The effects of group participation on brainstorming effectiveness for two industrial samples'. *Journal of Applied Psychology, 47*, 10–37.

Dyer, J.H. & Ouchi, W.G. (1993). 'Japanese-style partnerships: giving companies a competitive edge'. *Sloan Management Review*, Fall, 5–63.

Ekvall, G. (1991). 'The organisational culture of idea management: A creative climate for the management of ideas'. In J. Henry & D. Walker (eds), *Managing innovation*. London: Sage.

Ekvall, G. (1997). 'Organisational conditions and levels of creativity'. In J. Henry & D.T. Mayle (eds), *Managing Innovation and Change* (2nd edition) (chapter 8). London: Sage.

Fukuyama, F. (1999). *The Great Disruption*. London: Profile.

Getzels, J.W. & Csikszentmihalyi, M. (1976). *The creative vision: A longitudinal study of problem finding in art*. New York: Wiley.

Goldberg, L.R. (1993). 'The structure of phenotypic personality traits'. *American Psychologist, 48*, 26–34.

Gruber, H.E. (1980). *Darwin on Man: A psychological study of scientific creativity* (2nd edition). Chicago: University of Chicago Press.

Gruber, H.E. & Wallace, D.B. (1999). 'The case study method and evolving systems approach for understanding unique creative people at work'. In R.J. Sternberg (ed.), *Handbook of Creativity*. Cambridge: Cambridge University Press.

Guildford, J. (1959). 'Trends in creativity'. In H. Anderson (ed.), *Creativity and its cultivation*. New York: Wiley.

Henry, J. (2001). *Creativity and perception in management*. London: Sage.

Henry, J. & Martin, J.N.T. (1993). *Creative problem solving*. Milton Keynes: Open University.

Holt, K. (1991). *What is the best way of organising projects?* In J. Henry & D. Walker (eds), *Managing innovation*. London: Sage.

Jelinek, M. & Schoonhaven, C.B. (1991). 'Strong culture and its consequences'. In J. Henry & D. Walker (eds), *Managing innovation*. London: Sage.

Kay, J. (2002). 'Why the last shall be first and the first shall fade away'. In J. Henry & D. Mayle (eds), *Managing innovation and change* (2nd edition). London: Sage.

Kirton, M.J. (1987). *Adaption-Innovation Inventory (KAI) manual* (2nd edition). Hatfield, Herts: Occupational Research Centre.

Kirton, M.J. (1989). *Adaptors and innovators: Styles of creativity and problem-solving*, 1st edition, London: Routledge.

Kirton, M. (1994). *Adaptors and innovators: Styles of creativity and problem solving* (2nd edition). London: Routledge.

Koestler, A. (1969). *The act of creation*. Aylesbury: Pan.

Legge, K. (1994). 'Managing culture: Fact or fiction?' In K. Sisson (ed.), *Personnel Management* (2nd edition). Oxford: Blackwell.

Lewis, K. & Lytton, S. (2002). 'The way forward: partnership sourcing'. In J. Henry & D.T. Mayle (eds), *Managing innovation and change*. London: Sage.

MacKinnon, D.W. (1961). *The creative person*. Berkeley, CA: Institute of Personality Assessment Research, University of California.

Maidique, M. (1990). 'Entrepreneurs, champions and technological innovation'. *Sloan Management Review*, Winter, 59–76.

Margerison, C. & McCann, D. (1990). *Team management*. London: Mercury.

Mitchell, R. (1991). 'Masters of innovation: How 3M keeps its products coming'. In J. Henry & D. Walker (eds), *Managing innovation*. London: Sage.

Myers, I.B. & McCaulley, M.H. (1988). *Manual: A guide to the development and use of the Myers-Briggs Type Indicator*. Palo Alto, CA: Consulting Psychologists Press.

Nayak, R.M. & Ketteringham, J. (1986). '3M's little yellow post-it pads: Never mind I'll do it myself'. In R.M Nayak and J. Ketteringham (eds), *Breakthroughs*. New York: Arthur Little.

Nonaka, I. & Takeuchi, H. (1995). *The knowledge-creating company*. Oxford: Oxford University Press.

Osbourn, A.F. (1953). *Applied imagination*. New York: Scribners.

Parnes, S. (1967). *Creative behaviour handbook*. New York: Charles Scribner.

Reich, R.B. (1991). 'Entrepreneurship reconsidered: the team as hero'. In J. Henry & D. Walker (eds), *Managing Innovation* (pp.62–73). London: Sage.

Rickards, T. (1988). *Creativity at work*. Aldershot: Gower.

Semler, R. (1994). *Maverick*. London: Arrow.

Stacy, R. (1996). *Complexity and creativity in organisations*. San Francisco, CA: Brett-Koehler.

Tidd, J., Bessant, J. & Pavitt, K. (1997). 'Learning through alliances'. In J. Henry & D.T. Mayle (eds), *Managing Innovation and Change*. London: Sage.

Tuckman, B.W. (1965). 'Developmental sequences in small groups'. *Psychological Bulletin, 6*, 384–399.

Weisburg, R. (1986). *Creativity, genius and other myths*. New York: W.H. Freeman.

West, M. (2000). 'Creativity and innovation at work'. *Psychologist, 13* (9), 460–464.

West, M.A. & Anderson, N. (1996). 'Innovation in top management teams'. *Journal of Applied Psychology, 81*, 680–93.

Wheatley, M. (1994). *Leadership and the new science*. San Francisco, CA: Brett-Koehler.

Worth, P. (2001). 'A study of everyday creativity'. Unpublished PhD thesis, Open University.

Zeneca (1996). Presentation by Head of Research at Zeneca to Industrial Society.

13
Creativity and Innovation in Teams

Rosalind H. Searle

Creativity and innovation in teams is a topic that has grown in importance over the last 20 years, reflecting the transition within the workplace towards team-based working practices. Within this chapter, research on both creativity and innovation in teams are reviewed. There is considerable debate within the literature as to their distinctness (King, 1990; Forrester,[1] 2000b), however, the two terms are frequently used interchangeably and so for the purposes of this chapter both creativity and innovation are discussed. The chapter begins by exploring the place of creativity within organisations, before briefly reviewing who is creative, and then examining processes which enable novel ideas to emerge. Finally, the chapter briefly examines the role of context in enabling teams to generate new solutions or products most effectively. (Chapter 12 by Henry explores this aspect in greater detail.) The emphasis in this chapter is on collaboration in terms of the significance of relationships between team members and also the role of context in shaping the success, or otherwise, of these novel ideas.

THE IMPORTANCE OF CREATIVITY FOR BUSINESS

In their drive to develop products more quickly, organisations are increasingly recognising the importance of innovation and creativity. This is a complex undertaking with 'no executive task more vital and demanding' (Nadler & Tushman, 1997). Both the complexity and necessity of promoting innovation and creativity are highlighted in a recent survey of large and medium-sized UK firms which revealed that more than 80 per cent of businesses regarded innovation as critical (Searle & Ball, 2003). This study also assessed the relationship between strategic value and human resource (HR) practices and found that rather than training and developing existing employees, firms' efforts often focused on selecting and recruiting new employees in order to enhance innovation and creativity. Underlying such a strategy is the question of 'who is creative?' Whilst creativity-focused recruitment programmes have an intuitive appeal, they may be limited in the changes they can produce. Let us now explore the implications of asking 'who is creative?'

WHO IS CREATIVE?

Much of the research designed to address the issue of 'who is creative?' is focused at the level of the individual, with limited attention being paid to team working, despite this being increasingly the norm for working practice. In the past, highly creative people were stereotyped as unable to operate within conventional social and organisational norms, and characterised as 'oddballs'. More recently, however, the emphasis has shifted away from such individuals' *style* of behaviour towards a recognition of the potentially productive *outcome* of their work. As a result the notion of an 'innovative employee' has emerged which can be reconciled within the overarching organisational structure.

Research examining key personality dimensions associated with creativity has revealed a wealth of characteristics including: desire for autonomy (McCarrey & Edwards, 1973), high tolerance for ambiguity (Child, 1973), propensity for risk taking (Glassman, 1986); and anxiety (Wallach & Kogan, 1965). One characteristic that clearly resonates with the 'oddball' label is social independence, or the lack of concern for social norms (Kaplan, 1963; Coopey, 1987). Linked to this, Eysenck (1995) revealed some of the more negative characteristics, such as disorderliness, outspokenness, uninhibitedness and quarrelsomeness. However, these studies have tended to concentrate primarily on those involved in creative occupations, such as architects (Mackinnon, 1962) or engineers (McDermid, 1965), rather than focusing on the identification of creative individuals *per se*. Furthermore, they raise questions about causality. For example, we do not know how far anxiety is inherent in the creative process, or whether creativity is actually a means of coping with anxiety. These questions remain unanswered.

In parallel with the work attempting to identify key personality dimensions associated with creativity, a wider debate has ensued concerning the complexity of the 'creativity trait'. Some have argued for a single trait (Guildford, 1958; Kirton, 1976). Kirton, for example, highlighted the bi-polar dimension *adaption–innovation*, in which adaption concerns working more effectively within existing structures, whereas innovation involves a more radical departure with different ways of working. Such work has its critics though: Some consider it to be conceptually flawed (Payne, 1987), or empirically problematic with no clear distinction between the two poles (Egan-Strang & King, 1995). Others argue it is limited due to its omissions of any conception of social and organisational factors (King, 1990). Alternatively a multidimensional four-factor model, the innovation potential indicator (IPI) has been proposed including: challenging behaviour, motivation to change, adaptation and consistency of work style (Patterson, 1999). It was derived from studying those who are innovative regardless of their formal role. The emphasis, however, remains firmly on the individual with little consideration of the application of these traits within a team context.

Team-level knowledge, skills and abilities for innovation

Work on Patterson's IPI instrument within a team context has revealed the complexity of utilising aggregated scores to measure team composition (Forrester, 2001). The study of 100 students randomly divided into 20 teams completing a creative task included a battery of psychometric tests, including the NEO-PI 'big five' personality measure (Costa & McCrea, 1985) and the Typical Intellectual Engagement (TIE) measure (Ackerman, 1994), and information on age and sex. The teams' output was assessed by four independent expert judges for innovation. Only one aspect of innovation, 'radicalness', was found to be significantly related to team composition. A stepwise regression revealed that a combination of aggregated factors, including age, TIE and the personality factor *motivation to change* on the IPI, accounted for 76 per cent of their radicalness. In looking at the beta values only personality was positively associated. This suggests that teams with older and more intelligent members were less radical. However, this is a simplistic way of examining team functioning and more attention is required to understand how aggregated scores relate to how teams actually work together. In order to adequately explore team composition, researchers need to expand their analysis away from simple aggregation to a focus on a range of personality dimensions, including high and low scores and variance for each dimension (Searle & Stern, 2003). Furthermore, studying the behaviour of outliers would help us understand more about team working (LePine et al., 1997). Ultimately, however, we need to develop our understanding of the relationship between individuals' personality and their behaviour within a team context.

Researchers have emphasised the need for diversity within teams, arguing that the inclusion of members with different perspectives and knowledge-bases enables a wider range of ideas to be generated. However, in reviewing research on diversity and team composition, there is limited conceptualisation of diversity within the existing literature, with most studies focusing on observable differences, such as race or gender, or the functional experience of members (Searle & Jarzabkowski, 2003). Whilst obvious differences do play a role in establishing team dynamics at the on-set, evidence suggests that their impact fades, being replaced by more enduring style or behavioural dimensions (Moynihan & Peterson, 2001). A study of 1,222 research and development teams, added to the complexity by suggesting that heterogeneous teams were more effective during creative idea-generating phases, whilst those with homogeneous composition performed best during the idea implementation phase (Andrews, 1979). This suggests more of a dynamic to team composition than initially thought.

In the past, functional experience has been a surrogate for other characteristics such as external contacts. Early innovation work undertaken from an organisational perspective highlighted the significance of personal contacts and consultants (Myres & Marquis, 1969; Utterback, 1982). Individuals fulfilling this role have been variously termed gatekeepers, key communicators, communication stars and linking-pins (see Henry's chapter, in this volume, for more details). Functional diversity is important for innovation precisely because of these external communication networks (Zenger & Lawerence, 1989). Network analysis has indicated the importance of the quality and type of these links, termed 'ties' (Gautam, 2000). There may be an optimum number of ties that enhance creativity which, if exceeded, reduce the benefit, and being on the periphery of a network provides greatest access to external connections (Perry-Smith & Shalley, 2003). None of the current work on individual personality traits for creativity has, however, included an examination of the significance of individuals at the external interface, nor has the quality of contacts been considered at a team level.

Leadership

Although much work has been devoted to leadership, few researchers have considered its significance in team-based creativity research. Any successful management role inherently includes being the external interface for teams, yet the composition of the team and their leader remains under-investigated. When boundaries are managed well, teams' outcomes are enhanced in a number of ways (Ancona, 1990). First, teams' leaders act as ambassadors to smooth the way and ensure support for new ideas. This role is vital, as creativity and innovation often involve a radical departure from the status quo. Failure of the leader to act as ambassador can create fear and anxiety about potential risk (Searle & Wilson, 2001).

Secondly, leaders protect their team from external pressures thereby creating space for ideas to flourish (Pascale, 1990). Although innovation often occurs partly in response to an external threat, excessive demands and threats can act as inhibitors to creativity (West, 2002). For example, the pressure of deadlines increases the rigidity of thinking (Cowen, 1952). A study of 87 teams found high external pressure had the biggest detrimental impact on innovation within larger teams, reducing the quality of their team processes (Curral et al., 2001).

Finally, leaders support teams by lobbying for additional resources (Orpen, 1990). Building good relationships with external bodies can secure extra resources boosting teams' performance (Tushman & Scanlan, 1981). It is clearly beneficial in selecting creative teams to identify someone with sensitivity to this particular role, and yet there is a dearth of research examining team composition, leadership and creativity. It is not as simple as selecting individuals, nor is it about aggregating personality dimensions; we need a more sophisticated approach to studying diversity in team composition and leadership, their behaviours and subsequent creative outcomes.

CREATIVITY AS PROCESS?

Team processes are an important factor in promoting or inhibiting creativity and innovation. Within the creativity literature much work has been focused on understanding the outcome of a creative process, such as typologies of creativity (Sternberg, 1999). Whilst this approach is not without value, it offers only a partial insight into creativity as it ignores the creative processes themselves. A further complication surrounds the study of unconscious aspects of process, such as the role of incubation in problem-solving, which remain largely ignored at the team level. In this section four key aspects of team processes are explored: participation, trust, conflict resolution and wider support.

Participation

Recent emphasis has been placed on understanding decision-making processes involved in the selection of creative ideas. Within a team context this has concentrated on participation, or empowerment and gaining collective commitment in any form of decision-making (Locke et al., 1997). Participation, however, involves a number of discrete elements. For example, it can be the means by which new ideas are shared and novel combinations generated (Porac & Howard, 1990). Without active participation, composition diversity would fail to reap any positive outcome. Teams can also provide feedback, evaluate ideas and enable social comparison to occur, which provides information about norms and the standards required by the team and/or organisation (Paulus, 2000). Participation in a project enables resistance to novel ideas to be reduced, with members feeling they had influenced and contributed towards the final outcome, thus providing an investment in the outcome (Kanter, 1983).

There is also a negative impact from participation (Latané et al., 1979; Steiner, 1972). Termed 'process loss' this is produced either from freeloading within the team context, or the reduction in the volume and quality of ideas generated within a team (Paulus et al., 2000). As a result, early idea-generation may be more effective if done alone, with team members bringing their initial thoughts to a subsequent meeting, rather than commencing with collective brainstorming. Recent evidence has also shown how team-based idea-generation effectiveness can be enhanced through the use of computer mediated exchange or facilitation, which assists in the collection and management of team members' novel suggestions (Paulus, 2002).

Trust

A key factor affecting participation in any creative task is the level of trust between team members. Innovation involves a departure from the status quo and therefore has an inherent risk and vulnerability associated with it, with the potential of ridicule or rejection for those who suggest radical ideas. In order to enhance innovation a safe environment is required in which vulnerability is minimised (Edmondson, 1999; Nystrom, 1979). During idea-generation, trust and perceptions of safety can be enhanced if suggestions are not questioned, challenged, ridiculed or ignored (Prince, 1975). Through using these simple steps outlandish ideas can still be aired and evaluated later within the team.

Part of any creative process requires creative self-efficacy, which is related to role competence. Team members must be confident that they can have novel ideas of value and which can have positive outcomes. Self-efficacy is influenced by factors such as previous relevant job experiences, educational attainment, personal explanatory style and the availability of information systems offered by proximal others (peers, superior and subordinates) (Farr & Ford, 1990). The behaviour of others, and the trust which emanates from our relationships with them, emerges as a significant factor in whether or not we regard ourselves as creative and determines the level of persistence following rejection or failure (Ford, 1996). Recently a significant relationship between self-perception and creativity has been found, in that creative self-efficacy was more significant than job self-efficacy in producing creative performance (Tierney & Farmer, 2002). Creativity is a volitional activity, and low self-esteem or confidence are the hallmarks of less creative individuals (Feist, 1998). Therefore the impact of trust should not be overlooked, as it boosts current levels of teams' performance, but also has an enduring impact on perceptions of their members' future creative potential. The creation of a safe team-space appears vital.

Conflict resolution

Conflicting and competing perspectives are fundamental for creativity to occur (Nemeth & Owens, 1996; Tjosvold, 1998). However it is not conflict *per se*, but *informational conflict* which is necessary for productive team-working. Indeed organisations with high internal strife and conservatism constrain creativity (Kimberly, 1981). Searle and Jarzabkowski (2003), however, suggest that informational conflict promotes top teams' decision-making and strategy development, freeing team members to consider novel and diverse perspectives.

Functional and dysfunctional conflict are distinct (Amason, 1996). Dysfunctional conflict is confined to interpersonal aspects and has an emotional element (Simon & Peterson, 2000). In contrast, functional conflict focuses on information or task-related aspects. The latter is characterised as 'constructive conflict', allowing the exploration of opposing perspectives and a more complete analysis of the evidence (Tjosvold & Johnson, 1977; Tjosvold, 1998). Constructive conflict, however, is only found in a cooperative setting where there are mutually beneficial objectives and super-ordinate goals enabling the team to see the wider value of their task-related differences. This suggests a relationship between such contexts and the aforementioned climate required for trust.

Minority dissent is often a significant factor in productive conflict. The success of any minority influence requires the confident, consistent and persistent presentation of arguments (Nemeth & Owens, 1996). Without these qualities opinion change within a wider team is unlikely. Productive dissent in teams requires high levels of interaction, information-sharing and participation in decision-making (De Dreu & West, 2000). The link between a team climate conducive to both trust and constructive conflict is obvious, but it is yet to be explicitly explored within a team innovation context. While the connection between diversity of composition and productive aspects of process is evident, a paucity of research focused on this relationship remains.

Support for innovation

The final aspect of process that enhances creativity is wider support. Research indicates that support comprises a number of distinct elements. For example, both Amabile (1983) and Kanter (1983) emphasise the importance of rewarding rather than punishing creativity. Whilst this appears to have clear links into behavioural conditioning, the issue is more complex. Although the rewards suggested by Amabile are derived by the individual from doing the task, others (e.g. Kanter, 1988 and Sundstrom et al., 1990) suggest the need for coherence in wider-organisational reward and recognition schemes (see Chapter 12 for further discussion). However, formal organisational schemes can inadvertently undermine team-level innovation if they are overly individual in their focus (Forrester, 1995).

More consistent evidence emerges for the role of support from managers, as highlighted earlier. This type of support can take two forms: 'articulated support', which involves the acceptance of creativity within the workplace, and more tangible 'enacted support' in the form of providing time, money, equipment or expert advice (Andrews & Farris, 1972; Schroeder et al., 1989). Support can be provided from a variety of routes: through technical expertise which involves others' insights into the problem or potential solutions based on their experiences (Mintzberg, 1979; McCall & Kaplane, 1985); previous training (Simon, 1986); identification and adoption of existing solutions (Rogers & Shoemaker, 1971); or by talking to customers (Waterman, 1988).

The behaviour of others can be vital in creating behavioural norms denoting the value of creativity. In her study of student and health teams, Zhou (2003) identified how creative co-workers acted as models, enhancing others' observational learning by providing examples of creativity-relevant skills and strategies, such as how to identify problems, generate solutions, evaluate and refine ideas. This process was not simply about mimicking others, but derived from individuals modelling such behaviours within their own jobs. Creative co-workers can actively stimulate their less creative colleagues. It was this, rather than direct supervisory feedback, that enhanced creativity.

More laterally, support for novel ideas can be provided through broadening participation levels in teams. Pascale (1990) argued that the success and speed of the introduction of new products within the Japanese automotive sector has been achieved through the work of multi-disciplinary teams. (Chapter 12, by Henry, discusses issues relating to multi-disciplinary teams in more detail.) Let us now consider studies focusing more holistically on teams' processes.

FORMAL MODELS

Building on the previous literature a four-phase climate model of team innovation has been devised, commencing with identification of the problem, then moving to idea generation, support for innovation, and finally, evaluation (Anderson & West, 1994). This model can be a useful tool in assisting organisations to identify which aspects of climate need to be improved in order for innovation to flourish. Whilst this model does indicate the importance of context in shaping the direction of innovation, its measure of innovation is a simplistic frequency count of the number of ideas generated, rather than their quality. Work aimed at understanding in more detail the working processes within teams was undertaken by Gersick (1988, 1989). She identified a rapid transition around the mid-point of a team's activity with a 'punctuation' point resulting in the departure from earlier ideas and leadership, but also creating an ideal point for any external intervention to occur. Unfortunately her rich work focused solely on final ideas and failed to consider creativity in its entirety; for example, did the team just generate that one idea, or were there a series of ideas later brought together? This is an important issue if we are to assist teams in being more creative.

Gersick's observational approach has recently been utilised to examine the complete idea generation and implementation process (Forrester, 2000b). This research has also considered the impact of different types of constraints on teams' innovative outcomes. In considering this, the research builds on King & Anderson's (1990) characterisation of three distinct team conditions. In the first condition – 'emergent' – there was no limit placed on the team's ideas, whereas those operating under the 'imposed' condition were required to incorporate certain specific elements into their design. The final condition – 'imported' – provided information about other campaigns which the team were free to use or adapt to suit their purpose.

The study revealed that teams followed distinct processes. Those operating with a pre-determined output ('imposed') showed the lowest levels of innovation. In analysing their behaviour these teams failed to consider or utilise the full range of external resources available to them, especially concerning external advice and information sources. The imposition of an external constraint on the outcome affected both the team's working processes and their outcome. In contrast, highly innovative teams showed more open sharing of task-based information. This finding concurs with the aforementioned significance of a participative style and knowledge-creation enquiry process (Kylen & Shani, 2002). It supports constructive task-focused controversy as important for innovation, whilst pressure appears to reduce creative processes. Those teams with highly innovative outputs spent time clarifying what was being asked of them by their external task setter. This supports the value of boundary sensitivity with innovative teams ensuring they are meeting the requirements of users. Innovative teams created a supportive climate, by giving each other positive feedback about each others' ideas. Surprisingly there was no difference found between innovation levels and the time that teams spent in setting goals, the volume of ideas generated, their attention to formatting their final ideas or the directive behaviour of leaders.

STUDYING PROCESSES

In studying teams' creative processes recall and questionnaire-based approaches dominate offering, Paulus (2002) argues, limited scope for objective performance measures. Inevitably through the use of such methodologies inaccuracies in the reporting of creative processes can ensue. It is thus vital to observe teams actually working on projects together. This can, however, pose practical problems as much important activity may occur outside the teams' formal meeting time. Moreover, researchers have tended to restrict their attention to teams with successful outcomes, thus producing a partial view by failing to consider creative activities regardless of their success. We are beginning to understand which processes are important for teams' creativity and to a more limited extent some of their connections with team composition, but this neglects a third significant issue – that of the contexts for creativity.

CREATIVITY IN CONTEXT

The previous sections have alluded to contextual factors which are associated with the enhancement of creativity. However, whilst context is a major factor in sustaining and developing creativity, it is a factor which is frequently omitted from studies. When reviewing which type of organisation is most conducive with respect to creativity no clear picture emerges regarding its size (Mohr, 1969; Rogers, 1983); nor centralisation/decentralisation (Zaltman et al., 1973; Kimberly, 1978). The devolution of power is a significant element (Cummings, 1965; Kanter, 1983) and is associated with increased team autonomy.

One of the most significant aspects of context is organisational climate, which refers to the general atmosphere within an organisation. Whilst Kaplan (1963) was the first to recognise the necessity of a receptive context, Ekvall (1991) has conducted the most comprehensive study. Perhaps not surprisingly, there are resonances with team-level findings, with elements such as freedom (autonomy), trust, commitment and diversity of staff emerging as significant positive factors (see Chapter 12 for further discussion of this point).

Ekvall (ibid.) notes the importance of open relationships between co-workers and organisational support for new ideas in enhancing innovation and creativity, particularly the role of leaders in the constructive handling of conflict and actively listening to staff. Leaders and management, as found earlier, have a particular part to play in the management of external boundaries, in the clarification of goals (Bailyn, 1985) and in providing supportive feedback (Amabile, 1983). However, recent evidence suggested the impact of co-workers may be greater than that of leaders (Zhou, 2003).

Kaplan (1963) identified tolerance of risk as important for stimulating innovation, and argued for staff freedom in choosing problems they work on, and the benefits of management's acceptance of the working styles of highly creative people. Furthermore it is evident that participative decision-making enables risk to be shared whilst fostering autonomy (Allen et al., 1980; Kanter, 1983). The bending and breaking of rules often occurs in product development teams, especially where processes to limit risk, such as operating a 'stage-gate' model in which projects had to pass certain criteria at each stage, have been adopted (Olin & Wickenberg, 2001).

Organisations sometimes have to achieve a precarious balance between maximising their competitive advantage and minimising risk (Colewell, 1996). Evidence indicates that the more radical the idea the higher the strategic risk, with risk at its highest when ideas require a completely new way of thinking, breaking with continuity and resulting in the crossing of an 'innovation boundary' (ibid.) or the adoption of 'new logic' or paradigm (Bouwen et al., 1992). In trying to minimise the negative impact of such transition many firms have tried to stimulate incremental, rather than radical change, but such reluctance to embrace novelty may inevitably curtail creativity. A range of different policies have been devised to assist organisations in managing risk. For example in one US automotive firm they managed risk by ensuring innovation was undertaken only by a technically-elite group, whilst a Japanese counterpart restricted the duration of any projects (Forrester, 2000a). A further manifestation of risk management concerns how mistakes are managed; mistakes can present either an opportunity for review and learning or they are hidden away, stifling creativity (Edmondson, 1999).

More recently organisations have considered how physical context can promote creativity. For example, organisational consultants 'IF' have promoted the development of 'play-spaces' designed specifically to foster and support innovation and creativity. Sundstrom et al. (1990), in their model of team effectiveness, identified a space, or 'turf', which differentiated a particular team from the rest of the organisation. They argued that detachment enabled more radical ideas to be entertained, but that boundaries needed to be actively managed to ensure that the work of teams remained aligned with the firm's objectives. There can be a tension between these two aspects. While the generation of generic creative spaces has been adopted by a number of organisations, paradoxically it may represent the failure to promote a more pervasive creative context. The introduction of such designated 'creativity' spaces may be indicative of an aversion to risk and stereotypic views of creativity as being out-with, rather than as an integral part of the day-to-day workplace. Teams clearly do not operate in a vacuum and it is important that studies consider the role of the wider context in shaping the creativity of teams.

SUMMARY

Through exploring these three elements of team creativity – composition, process and context – the interrelationships between them becomes more apparent. Recognising that more work needs to be undertaken regarding precisely what constitutes innovation or creativity, the chapter highlights that large gaps remain in our understanding of creative and innovative teams. Some organisations might perceive that they have techniques which enable them to identify creativity, however such techniques are typically concerned with the identification of creative individuals and we need to develop our understanding of crucial issues relating to the composition of teams. Although some attention has been paid toward creative processes, this has been restricted to examining successful outcomes and few studies have considered why creative ideas fail. Nor has there been sufficient attention paid to temporality and its relationship to the adoption of ideas. Research into teams has revealed that participation, trust, task-based conflict resolution and external support are vital factors in creating a conducive atmosphere for creativity. Leaders, as well as co-workers, have significant roles to play in both the recognition and acknowledgement of creativity, and in providing models of good practice.

This chapter has shown that a firm which seeks to enhance innovation by merely recruiting new 'creative' staff will fail unless they also pay attention towards promoting constructive team-working processes and fostering a supportive context. Creativity is a collaborative process which involves both social and task-related elements, and requires a working environment in which staff feel able to take risks by thinking differently and in the knowledge that their efforts will not be sanctioned or ridiculed. Further study is required into how composition, process and context are interconnected if we are to truly assist organisations towards developing and promoting the creativity and innovation of their teams. It is clear that both researchers and organisations need to adopt a more holistic approach if they are to increase their appreciation of how to enhance creative outcomes at the team level. Such efforts are likely to be rewarded not just with economic growth, but also with improved job satisfaction and well-being amongst team members.

NOTE

1. Former name of current author.

REFERENCES

Ackerman, P.L. (1994). 'Intelligence, attention and learning: Maximal and typical performance. Current topics in human intelligence'. In D.K. Detterman (ed.), *Theories of intelligence*, Vol. 4 (pp.1–27). Norwood, NJ: Ablex.

Allen, T., Tushman, M. et al. (1980). 'R&D performance as a function of internal communication, project management, and the nature of work'. *IEEE transactions, 27*, 2–12.

Amabile, T.M. (1983). *The social psychology of creativity*. New York: Springer-Verlag.

Amason, A.C. (1996). 'Distinguishing the effects of functional and dysfunctional conflict on strategic decision making: Resolving a paradox for top management teams'. *Academy of Management Journal, 39* (1), 123–148.

Ancona, D.G. (1990). 'Outward bound: Strategies for team survival in an organization'. *Academy of Management Journal, 33* (2), 334–365.

Anderson, N. & West, M. (1994). *Team climate: Measuring and predicting innovation in groups at work*. Paper presented at the Annual Occupational Psychology Conference of the British Psychological Society, Birmingham.

Andrews, F.M. (1979). *Scientific Productivity*. Cambridge: Cambridge University Press.

Andrews, F. & Farris, G. (1972). 'Time pressure and performance of scientists and engineers: A five-year panel study'. *Organisational Behaviour and Human Performance, 8*, 185–200.

Bailyn, L. (1985). 'Autonomy in the industrial R&D laboratory'. *Human Resource Management, 24*, 129–146.

Bouwen, R., De Visch, J. & Steyaert, C. (1992). 'Innovation projects in organisations: Complementing the dominant logic by organisational learning'. In N. Anderson (ed.), *Organisational change and innovation: Psychological perspectives and practices in Europe* (pp.123–148). London: Routledge.

Child, D. (1973). *Psychology and the teacher*. Holt-Rhinehart.

Colewell, J.B. (1996). 'Quiet change, big bang or catastrophic shift: At what point does continuous improvement become innovative?' *Creativity and Innovation Management, 5* (1), 67–73.

Coopey, J. (1987). *Creativity in complex organisations*. Paper presented at the Annual Occupational Psychology Conference of the British Psychological Society, University of Hull.

Costa, P.T. & McCrea, R.R. (1985). *The NEO Personality Inventory Manual*. Odessa, FL: Psychological Assessment Resources.

Cowen, E. (1952). 'The influence of varying degrees of psychological stress on problem-solving rigidity'. *Journal of Abnormal and Social Psychology, 47*, 420–424.

Cummings, L. (1965). 'Organisational climate for creativity'. *Academy of Management Journal, 8*, 220–227.

Curral, L.A., Forrester, R.H., Dawson, J.F. & West, H. (2001). 'It's what you do and the way that you do it: Team task, team size and innovation-related group processes'. *European Journal of Work and Organisational Psychology, 10* (2), 187–204.

De Dreu, C.K.W. & West, M. (2000). 'Minority dissent and team innovation: The importance of participation in decision-making'. *Journal of Applied Psychology, 68* (6), 1191–1201.

Edmondson, A.C. (1999). 'Psychological safety and learning behaviour in work teams'. *Administrative Science Quarterly, 44* (2), 350–382.

Egan-Strang, C. & King, N. (1995). Review of Kirton Adaptation-Innovation Inventory (KAI). *Review of personality assessment instruments (level B) for use in occupational settings.* Leicester: British Psychological Society.

Ekvall, G. (1991). 'The organisational culture of idea management: A creative climate for the management of ideas'. In J. Henry & D. Walker (eds), *Managing innovation* (pp.73–79). London: Sage.

Eysenck, H. (1995). *Genius: The natural history of creativity.* Cambridge: Cambridge University Press.

Farr, J.L. & Ford, M. (1990). 'Individual innovation'. In J.L. Farr (ed.), *Innovation and creativity at work: Psychological and organisational strategies* (pp.63–80). Chichester: Wiley.

Feist, G. (1998). 'A meta-analysis of the impact of personality on scientific and artistic creativity'. *Personality and Social Psychological Review, 2,* 290–309.

Ford, C.M. (1996). 'A theory of individual creative action in multiple social domains'. *Academy of Management Review, 21,* 1112–1142.

Forrester, R.H. (1995). 'Implications of lean manufacturing for human resource strategy'. *Work Study, 44* (3), 20–24.

Forrester, R.H. (2000a). 'Capturing learning and applying knowledge: An investigation of the use of innovation teams in Japanese and American automotive firms'. *Journal of Business Research, 47* (1), 35–46.

Forrester, R.H. (2000b). 'Innovation in teams: A qualitative and quantitative study of team behaviours'. *Work Psychology.* Birmingham: Aston Business School.

Forrester, R.H. (2001). *Constructing the perfect team: Innovation potential individuals and teams examined.* Lyon, France: European Group of Organisation Studies Conference.

Gautam, A. (2000). 'Collaboration networks, structural holes, and innovation: A longitudinal study'. *Administrative Science Quarterly, 45* (3), 425–456.

Gersick, C. (1988). 'Time and transition in work teams: Towards a new model of group development'. *Academy of Management Journal, 31,* 9–41.

Gersick, C. (1989). 'Marking time: Predictable transitions in task groups'. *Academy of Management Review, 32* (2), 274–309.

Glassman, E. (1986). 'Managing for creativity: Back to basics in R&D.' *R & D Management, 16,* 175–183.

Guildford, J.P. (1958). 'Traits of creativity'. In H.H. Anderson (ed.), *Creativity and its cultivation.* New York: Wiley.

Kanter, R. (1983). *The change masters.* New York: Simon and Schuster.

Kanter, R. (1988). 'When a thousand flower bloom: Structural, collective and social conditions for innovation in organisation'. *Organisation Behaviour, 10,* 169–211.

Kaplan, N. (1963). 'The relation of creativity to sociological variables in research organisations'. In F. Barron (ed.), *Scientific creativity: Its recognition and development.* New York: J. Wiley & Son.

Kimberly, J. (1981). 'Managerial Innovation'. In W. Starbuck (ed.), *Handbook of organisational design.* Oxford: Oxford University Press.

Kimberly, J.R. (1978). 'Organisational site and the structuralist perspective. A review, critique, and proposal'. *Administrative Science Quarterly, 21,* 571–597.

King, N. (1990). 'Innovation at work: The research literature'. In J. Farr (ed.), *Innovation and creativity at work: Psychological and organisation strategies* (pp.15–59). Chichester, England: Wiley.

King, N. & Anderson, N. (1990). 'Innovation and creativity in working groups'. In J. Farr (ed.), *Innovation and creativity at work: Psychological and organisation strategies* (pp.81–100). Chichester, England: Wiley.

Kirton, M.J. (1976). 'Adaptors and innovators: A description and measure'. *Journal of Applied Psychology, 6,* 622–629.

Kylen, S.F. & Shani, A.B. (2002). 'Triggering creativity in teams: An exploratory investigation'. *Creativity and Innovation Management, 11* (1), 17–30.

Latané, B., Williams, K. & Harkins, S. (1979). 'Many hands make light work: The causes and consequences of social loafing'. *Journal of Personality and Social Psychology, 37,* 822–832.

LePine, J.A., Hollenbeck, J.R., Ilgen, D.R. & Hedlund, J. (1997). 'Effects of individual differences on the performance of hierarchical decision-making teams: Much more than g'. *Journal of Applied Psychology, 82*, 803–811.

Locke, E., Alavi, M. & Wagner, J.A. (1997). 'Participation in design making: An information exchange perspective'. *Research in Personnel and Human Resource Management, 15*, 293–331.

Mackinnon, D.W. (1962). *The personality correlates of creativity: A study of American Architects.* Proceedings of the Fourteenth Congress on applied psychology, Copenhagen.

McCall, M.W. & Kaplane, R. (1985). 'Whatever it takes'. In *Decision makers at work*. New York: Prentice-Hall.

McCarrey, M.W. & Edwards, S.A. (1973). 'Organizational climate conditions for effective research scientists role performance'. *Organizational Behaviour and Human Performance, 69*, 439–459.

McDermid, C.D. (1965). 'Some correlates of creativity in engineering personnel'. *Journal of Applied Psychology, 49*, 14–19.

Mintzberg, H. (1979). *The structure of organisations: A synthesis of the research.* Eaglewood Cliff, NJ: Prentice-Hall.

Mohr, L.B. (1969). 'Determinants of innovation in organisations'. *American Political Science Review, 63*, 111–126.

Moynihan, L.M. & Peterson, R.S. (2001). 'A contingent configuration approach to understanding the role of personality in organisational groups'. In R. Staw (ed.), *Research in Organisational Behaviour* (pp.327–378). San Francisco: Jai Press.

Myres, S. & Marquis, D.G. (1969). *The evolutionary theory of economic change.* Cambridge, MA: The Belkap Press of Harvard University Press.

Nadler, D.A. & Tushman, M.L. (1997). 'Implementing new designs: Managing organisational change'. In P.Anderson (ed.), *Managing strategic innovation and change: A collection of readings.* Buckingham: Open University Press.

Nemeth, C. and Owens, P. (1996). 'Making work groups more effective: The value of minority dissent'. In M. West (ed.), *Handbook of Work Group Psychology* (pp.125–142). Chichester, England: John Wiley.

Nystrom, H. (1979). *Creativity and Innovation.* Chichester: Wiley.

Olin, T. & Wickenberg, J. (2001). 'Rule breaking in new product development – Crime or necessity?' *Creativity and Innovation Management, 10* (1), 15–25.

Orpen, C. (1990). 'Measuring support for organizational innovation: A validity study'. *Psychological Reports, 67*, 417–418.

Pascale, R. (1990). *Managing on the Edge.* London: Penguin Books.

Patterson, F.C. (1999). 'Assessing innovation potential'. Unpublished thesis, University of Nottingham, submitted December 1998.

Paulus, P. (2000). 'Groups, teams and creativity: The creative potential of idea-generating groups'. *Applied Psychology: An international review, 49*, 237–262.

Paulus, P. (2002). 'Different ponds for different fish: A contrasting perspective on team innovation'. *Applied Psychology: An international review, 51* (3), 394–399.

Paulus, P.B., Larey, T.S. & Dzindulet, M.T. (2000). 'Creativity in groups and teams'. In M. Turner (ed.), *Groups at work: Advances in theory and research* (pp.319–338). Hillsdale, NJ: Lawrence Erlbaum.

Payne, R.L. (1987). 'Individual differences and performance amongst R&D personnel: Some implications for management development'. *R & D Management, 17*, 153–161.

Perry-Smith, J.E. & Shalley, C.E. (2003). 'The social side of creativity: A static and dynamic social network perspective'. *Academy of Management Review, 28* (1), 89–106.

Porac, J.F. & Howard, H. (1990). 'Taxonomic mental models in competitor definition'. *Academy of Management Review, 2*, 224–240.

Prince, G. (1975). 'Creativity, self and power'. In J.W. Getzels (ed.), *Perspectives in creativity* (pp.249–277). Chicago: Aldine.

Rogers, E. & Shoemaker, F. (1971). *Communication of innovations: A cross cultural approach.* New York: Free Press.

Rogers, E.M. (1983). *Diffusion of innovations.* New York: Free Press.

Schroeder, R., Van de Ven, A., Scudder, G.D. & Polley, D. (1989). 'The development of innovative ideas'. In A.V. de Ven (ed.), *Research on the management of innovation*. New York: Harper & Row.

Searle, R.H. & Ball, K.S. (2003). 'Strategy, human resource policy and innovation practice: Evidence from the UK'. *Journal of creativity and innovation management, 12* (1), 1–10.

Searle, R.H. & Jarzabkowski, P. (2003). 'Diversity + trust = enhanced top management team performance'. In H.K. Avallone (ed.), *Identity and diversity in organisations*. Milan Italy: Guerini Studio.

Searle, R.H. & Stern, P. (2003). 'Team composition and performance'. Paper presented at the European Association of Work and Organisational Psychology conference, Lisbon: Portugal.

Searle, R.H. & Wilson, D.C. (2001). *A step too far: The role of mistrust in the failure of a radical project team refereed*. EIASM Workshop on trust within and between organisations, Amsterdam, Holland.

Simon, H.A. (1986). 'How managers express their creativity'. In *Across the board*. London: Merdi.

Simon, T. & Peterson, R. (2000). 'Task conflict and relationship conflict in top management teams: The pivotal role of intragroup trust'. *Journal of Applied Psychology, 85*, 102–111.

Steiner, I.D. (1972). *Group processes and productivity*. New York: Academic Press.

Sternberg, R.J. (1999). 'A propulsion model of types of creative contributions'. *Review of General Psychology, 3*, 83–100.

Sundstrom, E., De Meuase, K. & Futrell, D. (1990). 'Work teams: Applications and effectiveness'. *American Psychologist, 45* (2), 120–133.

Tierney, P. & Farmer, S.M. (2002). 'Creative self-efficacy: Its potential antecedents and relationship to creative performance'. *Academy of Management Journal 45*, 1137–1148.

Tjosvold, D. (1998). 'Co-operative and competitive goal approaches to conflict: Accomplishments and challenges'. *Applied Psychology: An International Review 47*, 285–342.

Tjosvold, D. & Johnson, D.W. (1977). 'The effects of controversy on cognitive perspective-taking'. *Journal of Education Psychology, 7*, 679–685.

Tushman, M.L. & Scanlan, T.J. (1981). 'Boundary spanning individuals: Their role in information transfer and their antecedents'. *Academy of Management Journal, 24*, 289–305.

Utterback, J.M. (1982). 'Innovation in industry and the defusion of technology'. In W.L. Moores (ed.), *Readings in the management of innovation* (pp.29–41). Boston, MA: Pitnam.

Wallach, M.A. & Kogan, N. (1965). 'A new look at the creativity-intelligence distinction'. *Journal of Personality, 33*, 348–369.

Waterman, R. (1988). *The renewal factor*. London: Bantam.

West, M. (2002). 'Sparkling fountains or stagnant ponds: An integrative model of creativity and innovation implementation in work groups'. *Applied psychology: An international review, 51* (3), 355–424.

Zaltman, G., Duncan, R. & Holbeck, J. (1973). *Innovations and organisations*. New York: Wiley.

Zenger, T. & Lawerence, B. (1989). 'Organizational demography: The different effects of age and tenure distribution on technical communication'. *Academy of Management Journal, 32*, 353–376.

Zhou, J. (2003). 'When the presence of creative co-workers is related to creativity: Role of supervisor close monitoring, developmental feedback, and creative personality'. *Journal of Applied Psychology, 88*, 413–422.

14
Thinking Outside the (Music) Box: Collaborations Between Composers and Architects
Tim Sharp and Jim Lutz

INTRODUCTION

Music and Architecture – at first thought no two disciplines could be more different: music, dynamically unfolding in the ephemeral medium of sound, and architecture, defining itself through its rooted materiality. How can a collaborative effort possibly exist between artists working in these two seemingly very different media? Historically, however, these disciplines have in fact held much in common, each frequently providing the creative impetus or theoretical underpinning for the other. The architect Louis Kahn once described great architecture as that which starts with the immeasurable, proceeds through the measurable, and returns to the immeasurable (Martin, 1994, p.16). The same can be said for great music, and although music and architecture have different phenomenal presences, the underlying organisation of their respective formal structure and colloquialisms are similar. The first half of this chapter, written by a performing musician, focuses on the emergent synergistic collaboration that takes place between fixed architectural space and the music that is chosen to be performed in that space. Such collaboration becomes the primary parameter at work as repertoire is considered for concerts to be performed by purposefully exploring how music and architecture synergistically enhance each other in collaboration. In the second half of this chapter, an architect explores three specific examples of direct collaboration between an architect and a composer. These examples demonstrate that music and architecture can each provide the immediate artistic inspiration and conceptual foundation for the other.

EMERGENT SYNERGISTIC COLLABORATION

The collaboration of sound and space contributes significantly to experienced meaning as musical performance meets architectural structure. As performance space is considered for the presentation of a choral or orchestral work, space participates in the performance as significantly as a piano's sounding board participates in the playing of a piano sonata or the skull's resonating chambers participate in creating human vocal tone. The convergence of sound

189

and space create an environmental collaboration, even though the architectural space is fixed.

In the publication *Architecture as a Translation of Music*, Elizabeth Martin proposes a novel and helpful concept as we consider the special meaning that comes as sound and space collaborate. Martin suggests the presence of something she terms a '*y*-condition' between music and architecture:

> Let's say, simply for a point of departure, that there exists a definable membrane through which meaning can move when translating from one discipline to another. What I mean by membrane is a thin, pliable layer that connects two things and is, in this case, the middle position of music + architecture. The membrane is similar perhaps to the role of a semi-tone or semi-vowel in the study of phonetics. A semi-tone is a transitional sound heard during articulation linking two phonemically contiguous sounds, like the *y* sound often heard between the *I* and the *e* of qu*ie*t. I am suggesting that something similar occurs, a *y*-condition, in the middle position of music + architecture when translating one to the other. (Martin, 1994, p.16)

This '*y*-condition' implies more than the physics of the reverberation of sound in architectural space. As music and architecture utilise their most basic means of expression through notes, meters, tones, lines, colours, and forms, meaning as a result of the collaboration of music and architecture is carried on by their respective systems of artistic and imaginative composition, design and execution. Within the setting of a live performance, these means of expression assist music and architecture as they individually and together create environmental collaboration and thinking. Superimposed layers of architectural structure and ornament in a Renaissance building have parallels in the stacking of voices in a Renaissance motet. Heavily decorated and twisting lines in a Baroque column have parallels in the ornamented counterpoint of a Baroque fugue; symmetry in a Rococo parlour have parallels in the sonata-allegro form of a Classical-era string quartet. Architecture moves from a frozen to a liquid state as music embodies the lines, colours, and forms of the performance space. As a particular architectural space is studied, an emergent synergistic musical parallel may be suggested.

Throughout history, architects and musicians have collaborated directly by this shared sense of form, style, and even language. Music begins, develops, and concludes, and through this process takes the performer and listener on a journey through time. Architecture visually symbolises this journey through its various properties. The intersection of architecture and music produce Martin's *y*-condition as the two collaborate with each other and become something new in relationship. In concert presentations of music chosen for and suggested by the architectural space in which it is performed, meaning is compounded for the listener and performer in at least two ways as sound and architectural space collaborate – a new dimension in acoustic and aesthetic meaning.

ACOUSTICAL COLLABORATION

Physical interaction between music and the materials of architecture provides the first layer of meaning in this collaborative process. This first layer of meaning is an interaction related to the property of sound energy. When a musical work is performed in a room there are two sources of sound-energy density at the point where the listener receives the audible performance, namely, direct and reflected sound (Olson, 1967, p.273). According to Harold P. Geerdes, author of *Music Facilities: Building, Equipping, and Renovating*, there is an optimum acoustical environment for every genre of musical performance. Speaking directly to choral performance space, Geerdes states: 'while there are other acoustical factors to be considered, the most important is the reverberation time at middle frequencies…' Many rooms are built primarily for speech and drama presentation. According to Geerdes, these activities require about one second reverberation time. Music in general requires reverberation time of one and a half to two seconds or more. However, according to Geerdes, unaccompanied choral music requires two to three and a half seconds of reverberation time. This is more than twice the amount of reverberation time required for normal speech or music (Geerdes, 1987, p.51). Therefore the first question that must be asked of a performance space in which choral music will be performed is this: does this room provide the ideal amount of reverberation time for the musical genre to be performed?

Sound is actually produced when air is set into motion by any means whatsoever. In choral music sound is produced by the intermittent throttling of an air stream in the human larynx by a community of voices. When a sound wave is produced, it then moves forward toward any receptive, listening ears. As a sound wave encounters large rigid walls, the sound wave will be reflected backward. The reflected sound wave is the same as that which would be produced by the image of the sound source. As a result of this collaboration, the listener hears both direct sound and reflected sound. For unaccompanied choral music, the ideal is for this sound to linger in the performance space for two to three and a half seconds. As musicians perform, the fixed architecture passively collaborates in the performance by providing this reverberation time.

When a performer or ensemble starts a sound in a room, the energy does not build up instantly, but builds as the sound waves grow, enter and proceed through the performance space. This is similar to the waves made from the point where a pebble is thrown into a body of still water. The wave expands as it moves further from the beginning point. Each layer of sound that is sent out by the sound source is reflected many times from the partially absorbing walls of the room before it is ultimately dissipated. The energy in the direct sound is greater than the reflected sound because of the smaller distance and the absence of absorption by the walls which occurs in reflected sound. The reflected sound suffers a reduction in energy at each reflection; therefore, the succeeding increments of reflected sound become smaller and smaller and are ultimately dissipated. As in the case of the growth of sound, some time is required for the sound energy to be completely absorbed. This reverberation time may be reduced by the introduction of porous materials that absorb sound. Such materials typically include carpets, tapestries, rugs, drapes, upholstered furniture, and seats filled with people (Riedel, 1986).

As sound energy is completely absorbed by the space after the source is stopped, a finite decay of sound is heard. Owing to this finite decay time, the sound energies of the various sounds overlap. The overlapping becomes more pronounced as the reverberation time of the room is increased. Reverberation of an optimum value in unaccompanied choral music is desirable, because the prolongation and blending of musical tones due to reverberation produce a more pleasing musical performance. Composers have been well aware of this phenomenon and have intentionally factored in reverberation time in their concept of harmonic movement, horizontal and vertical voice movement, tempo, rests, and many other musical elements of composition. As composers factor in reverberation time in the design of their compositions, again, collaboration is taking place between musician and architecture.

Sound takes an interesting path from sound source to source of reflection on its way to the listener. Sound will pass around the corner of a building, around a column, over a wall, and through an open window. Low frequencies bend around obstacles more easily than do high frequencies. The larger the ratio of the wavelength to the dimensions of the obstacle, the greater the diffraction. In the case of an echo, there occurs a very late reflection of the sound source with nothing in-between to reflect or absorb a tone. If a reflected sound arrives at the listener more than .06 seconds after the initial sound arrives, an echo is perceived. This becomes an acoustical fault which is not desirable, neither is a 'hot spot' which is a point of low sound intensity, nor a 'dead spot' which is a point of no sound intensity, nor a sound 'flutter' which is a closely repetitive echo. As a conductor considers a performance space, attempts are made to avoid acoustical faults such as these.

The primary function of a building naturally dictates the selection of components and furnishings for the building. As performance space is considered, particularly buildings that were not necessarily designed for musical performance, the ideal placement of performing forces will have performers close together and in a direct line of sight to the listeners. In spaces with axial geometry (longer than wide), music will project with good distribution throughout the space if the performers are located high at the end of a major axis. Regarding various components existing in the space, attention is given to the size and absorbent qualities of such items. When these factors are taken into consideration, performing spaces such as the more conventional concert halls, churches, museums, public buildings, as well as the less-conventional spaces including warehouses, hangers, hotels, lobbies, banks, or any large structure can become collaborators in the performing process.

Regarding the materials that make up the space, too many absorbing materials in the space will remove desirable sound energy from the environment. The floor is typically the building surface that is largest and nearest to musicians. It is important that the floor be reflective of sound. Appropriate floor materials include slate, quarry tile, sealed wood, brick, stone, ceramic tile, terrazzo, and marble. Durable, hard-surfaced walls and ceiling are essential for good acoustical reflections. The ceiling is potentially the largest uninterrupted surface and therefore should be used to reinforce tone. Appropriate wall and ceiling materials include hard plaster, gypsum wallboard, sealed woods, glazed brick, stone, filled and painted concrete block, marble, and rigidly mounted wood panelling. Walls, floors, and doors should retard the transmission of noise into the space from adjoining rooms, from the outdoors, or via structure-borne paths.

The geometric components of the space also exert great influence on the acoustical success of the room. The angle of sound energy incident on a surface equals the angle that sound reflects off a surface. This allows the distribution of reflected sound to be highly controlled, which is important in the control of reverberation in general, echoes, hot spots, dead spots, and flutter.

The amount of reverberation time is the single most important factor in locating a desirable acoustical condition for a performance space. Specifically, reverberation is the amount of time in seconds that sound energy will take to drop 60 decibels after the source has ceased producing a tone. A reverberation period that is too short will leave music dull and lifeless and without tuning stability. Reverberation time differs in low, middle, and high range frequencies. The two to three and a half seconds of desired reverberation time mentioned earlier refers to mid-range frequencies. Conditions influencing the reverberation period include the surface area of all materials and furnishings in the room, the relative sound reflecting or absorbing qualities of all materials and furnishings, and the cubic volume of the space. In summary, three critical issues relate to the significant collaborative issue of reverberation – surface materials, reflection/absorption quality of those materials, and volume of space.

Consider a concert performance of a set of Renaissance choral motets that took place at St Mary's Episcopal Cathedral, a neo-Gothic structure in Memphis, Tennessee. Elements of the cathedral's architecture amplified and carried the musical sounds, physically participating in the actual musical performance by the reverberation and prolongation of the choral sounds. The listening community heard the motets from the performing ensemble collaborating with the architectural space during the performance. The reverberation time of the cathedral was three to four seconds in duration, creating a highly desirable acoustical collaboration between sound and space (Rhodes Singers, 2001).

AESTHETIC COLLABORATION

Music and architecture share the aesthetic expression of human experience. Architecture has been described as 'built myth', linked to the psyche and its need for spiritual orientation, wholeness, and transcendence (Barrie, 1996, p.11). Themes of trial and redemption, tension and release, rise and fall, life and death, light and darkness find expression in the lines, structure and form which make up musical and architectural expression. Not only do music and architecture share a common language and means of expression, music and architecture work together and interact as an overt representation of the artistic goals of each medium.

It is tempting to either condemn or idealise the past based upon our modern perspective. We either look backward with an air of superiority and perceived progress, or we look backward with a sense of nostalgia and perceived cultural erosion. We behave in a way that seems to think that our modern time is in some way unrelated and separated from the past. While this is true in time, it is not true in spirit. The musical troping of a Gregorian chant finds parallels in architectural elaboration as lines are built up in layers in a Gothic arch. The building of a Renaissance chord finds parallels in the geometrical shapes found in the structure of a fifteenth-century cathedral. The densely ornamented lines of a Baroque fugue find an analogue in the twisted and highly decorated turns of a Baroque column. Classical sonata form has an architectural parallel in the Rococo buildings of the late eighteenth century. Wagner's operas were so complex that they required the building of a specific opera house for their performance. The structure of space and the structure of music have commonalities that participate in the meaning of the works in collaboration. Both are metaphors for life, themes that are both visible and audible. As Carl Jung argues: 'The psyche is not only of today. It reaches back to prehistoric ages' (Laszlo, 1958, p.xiii).

Both architectural space and musical composition and performance are visible and audible interpretations of human aesthetic expression. Emotion and meaning is embodied in each means of expression, but fuller meaning is possible as a result of the relationship between architecture and music when experienced in collaboration. Architecture, in addition to directly symbolising human expression, in essence acts as a stage that accommodates and facilitates the sound enactment of the expressive elements in musical performance. The space has been so designed as to keep outside noise out, and to participate in the sounds produced inside the space. As composed sound interacts with walls, columns, beams, arches, domes, vaults, un-cut and cut glass, fresco, and sculpture, both audibly and visually, the intersections of the combined experience interpret the expressions of the community. If architectural space is studied, compositions appropriate to the artistic expression of the space can be paired. Such collaboration allows the architecture to suggest the musical programme.

As performing forces present Stravinsky's *Symphony of Psalms*, Rachmaninov's *Vespers*, Bach's *Mass in B Minor*, or Beethoven's *Choral Fantasy*, story and belief are not only retold, but are offered with a 'feelingful' dimension through the artistic sounds produced. When successfully combined, emotion and interpretation is added to the telling of the myth. 'Built myth' embodied by architectural space collaborates with 'sounded myth' embodied in performed music.

Consider a performance that took place recently at a chapel designed by Fay Jones in Bella Vista, Arkansas. The chapel consists of 15 primary arches, each incorporating three or four subsidiary arches, joined together by 31 tons of steel and 4,460 square feet of glass, creating both a feeling of weightlessness and an aura of strength. Light streams into the space from every direction. The music chosen for performance in this modern space was contemporary American composer Morten Lauridsen's extended orchestral/choral work *Lux Aeterna*, based upon the text of the requiem mass, along with other Latin texts (Rhodes MasterSingers Chorale, 2004). The theme of light penetrates the work's chosen texts which in turn inspires the composer's musical setting. The same themes are present in both the music and architectural space in which the music was performed. The music collaborates with the structure in a performance that shares similar artistic themes and shared myth and meaning.

Story and belief are not only expressed by both composer and architect, but are offered with an added collaborative dimension through the sounds taking place in the particular space. Architecture and artistic sound are symbols of the continuity of the belief systems of a community needed to symbolise permanence, even when, as in music, they appear ephemeral. As architecture and music collaborate, elements of architecture amplify and carry the sound as architectural elements physically participate in the actual musical performance by the reverberation and prolongation of the sound. The listening community hears the music, but also sees and hears the architectural space collaborate in the performance. Once again, when a musical work is performed in a room there are two sources of sound – energy at the point where the sound is produced, and energy where the sound is reflected from architectural elements. The listener benefits from both sources of sound energy. Whether the listener realises it or not, there are two performers present in the room – the musicians, and the material space. While it is true that the material space is fixed and performs something of a passive role in terms of collaboration, it is nevertheless a serious aspect of the performance, producing 'chamber music' in the most literal sense of the word. To the sensitive performer, the physical space begins the process of collaboration, and the performer learns to both look and listen to what the room is saying in terms of programming and performance acoustical preferences.

However, there can also be instances in which the emergent information provided by the architectural space does not suggest an apparent musical collaboration. On a solely acoustic determination, the amount of reverberation time or the acoustic faults present in the space can suggest the consideration of a new programme direction, or cause the space to be ruled out entirely for musical presentation. When the requisite reverberation time in a space is less than one and a half to two seconds, classical musical performance in the space may be ruled out altogether. As defined earlier, too many absorbing materials in the space will actually remove desirable sound energy from the environment. Since the primary objective is the hearing of the music, unfortunately, aesthetic collaboration is often less important in the determination of a programme. Bland terms such as 'performance space' and 'black box' are used to describe acoustically appropriate but aesthetically deprived performance locations. Even more problematic, there are instances where the physical space could actually be discordant with a particular programme. For example, a lively orchestral work performed in a space with three to four seconds reverberation would end up audibly overlapping itself within the space, causing a cacophony of undesired dissonance. A chamber work designed as a parlour piece could be overwhelmed by a civic auditorium. Vocal masterpieces could find their texts incongruous with certain architectural settings.

Meaning is compounded as sound and space productively collaborate in a concert. The two work together as both attempt to move the immeasurable to the measurable. The structure of sound and the structure of space have commonalities that participate in the construction of meaning of the works in combination. Both organised sound and organised space are visible and audible interpretations of human experience. As both performer and audience experience sound and space together, compounded meaning is the result of the carefully considered collaboration.

INTERMEZZO

The process of emergent synergistic collaboration is possible when one artist follows on and thoughtfully responds to the completed work of another, finding within the previously realised opus opportunities to augment or perhaps critically comment upon it. In the following material, three architectural works are cited – the Philips Pavilion, the setting for *Prometeo*, and the Swiss Music Box. In these examples sound and space inform one another through a vocabulary shared by musician and designer.

The second half of this chapter posits that these trans-generic efforts are possible in part because 'isomorphic correspondences' exist between these two allied arts at a fundamental level. A concept taken from Gestalt psychology, architectural historian Stephen Grabow describes isomorphic correspondence as 'similar structural relationships occurring in different media. [It is] the relationship between our experience of order in space and the distribution of underlying dynamic processes in the brain' (Grabow, 1993, p.438). To this end, principles such as structure, rhythm, harmony/dissonance, time, etc., provide a compositional vocabulary shared by architecture and music that facilitates collaboration. Music and architecture further find a common language in the discipline of mathematics. The architect Frank Lloyd Wright summarised this relationship saying, 'It seems to me that music is a kind of sublimated mathematics. So is architecture a kind of sublimated mathematics, and in the same sense. There lies the great relationship and warm kinship between music and architecture. They require very much the same mind' (Lucas, 1998).

In support of this thesis, three examples of collaborations between architects and musicians are offered:

1. The Le Corbusier / Iannis Xenakis / Edgard Varèse joint-effort on the Philips Pavilion at the 1958 Brussels World's Fair.
2. The Renzo Piano / Luigi Nono collaboration in 1983–84 that produced the purpose-built performance space for the opera *Prometeo*.
3. The Peter Zumthor / Daniel Ott project for the Pavilion of the Swiss Confederation at Expo 2000 in Hanover, Germany.

These works span a period of 44 years, from 1956 to 2000, and represent perhaps the most significant examples of collaboration between architects and composers in recent time. Each project illustrates a different way in which architects and composers have been able to work together, melding aspects of art and science together to produce a synergistic result.

THE PHILIPS PAVILION (1956–58)
LE CORBUSIER / IANNIS XENAKIS / EDGARD VARÈSE

In the winter of 1956, Philips, the Dutch electronics manufacturer, approached the nearly 70-year-old Swiss-French architect Le Corbusier with an offer to design a pavilion for their company at the world's fair to be held in Brussels in 1958. One might think that a relatively small 6,500-square-feet temporary structure would hold little interest for one of the world's most famous architects, especially when he was then immersed in completing the new capital city for the Indian state of Punjab. Since the end of the Second World War, however, Le Corbusier had grown increasingly interested in exploring aspects of the fourth dimension in his work, specifically how to address the concept of a space–time continuum in architecture. Philips, as one of the world's foremost manufacturers of electronic equipment for illumination and sound reproduction, offered to provide him with access to some of the most advanced electronic technology available. Provided with this incentive, and the fact that the company did not want a traditional 'showroom' exhibition space, but rather one where the capabilities of their products could be demonstrated rather than simply displayed, Le Corbusier accepted the commission.

As originally envisioned by Le Corbusier, the temporary structure was to serve as the venue for an eight-minute-long multimedia presentation he entitled *Poème électronique*. The work was to feature a film montage designed by the architect synchronised with coloured lights and coordinated with a specially commissioned, pre-recorded musical work. Regarding his concept and its proposed musical component, the architect wrote to his future musical collaborator stating:

> My idea is that music should have a part in this. […] It is a scenario to be created wholly from relationships; light, plasticity, design and music. […] It will be the first truly electric work and with symphonic power. (Treib, 1996, p.6)

Music was intended to be a salient feature of the work from its inception. Philips had initially recommended that the architect work with Benjamin Britten for the music, but Le Corbusier insisted that Edgard Varèse was the composer that he wished to collaborate with on the project. Corbusier had met Varèse while in New York in 1935 and had attempted to work with him in 1954 on the pilgrimage church he designed at Ronchamp. Varèse would write in response to Corbusier's offer to participate in the Philips project: '…I want to let you know immediately that I find your project superb and that I accept with great pleasure your offer of collaboration' (Treib, 1996, p.6).

While the structurally ambitious and technologically complex nature of the project required many collaborators – film editors, structural and electrical engineers, acoustic consultants, and the like – one individual played a key role in the conceptualisation and realisation of the project. Iannis Xenakis is today known to most as a composer, but he was for twelve years employed in the office of Le Corbusier as an engineer and project manager. During his tenure in Corbusier's office, he would spend any rare moments of free time composing. In this discussion Xenakis provides a critical link between the worlds of music and architecture. He played a pivotal role in the design and development of the Philips pavilion, the project that would precipitate a bitter break between himself and his friend and mentor, and which would eventually lead him to largely abandon architecture and to devote himself to music.

Because of the very tight schedule for the project and the pressing need for Le Corbusier to spend extended periods of time in India attending to his ongoing work there, a great deal of the responsibility for the Philips project fell to Xenakis. In seeking a form for the Brussels building, Xenakis made a connection between his musical score for a composition he had previously written entitled *Metastasis* (1953–54) and a possible concept for the Philips building.

About this Xenakis writes:

[...] *Metastasis* was the source of [...] the Philips Pavilion [...] which I designed and made out of ruled surfaces much like my fields of string *glissandi*, which suddenly and for the first time in the history of music opened the way to the continuity of sound transformations in instrumental music. (Xenakis, 1987, p.45)

Xenakis' unequivocal claim of ownership of the design concept proved to be a major point of contention between him and Le Corbusier, bringing forward one of the potential pitfalls of the collaborative process: that of disputes over authorship. This disagreement was no doubt exacerbated by the employer–employee relationship between the two. Along similar lines, architectural historian Marc Treib raises another point of relevance to authorship inherent in complex technological undertakings, asking:

Can Varèse be credited with the work [music] entirely, given the amount of collaboration provided by [the Philips engineers]? Or does one regard this contribution as one would a virtuoso violinist or conductor who might consult on the limits of what can be performed on the instrument? (Treib, 1996, p.250)

Despite the friction that developed between Le Corbusier and Xenakis over the architectural component of the project, there was certainly none to be found between Corbusier and Varèse. After completion of the project, the architect wrote to the composer expressing his: 'great satisfaction with your brilliant collaboration [...]. You will have to agree that I did not bother you, but I must say that you yourself have been the structure for this Poème with your magnificent music' (Treib, 1996, p.211).

While the technical demands of the cutting-edge work delayed its opening, during the six months that the pavilion was open to the public more than 1 million visitors had the opportunity to experience the work. The collaborative venture was critically lauded, Varèse's biographer describing it as: 'a music box for the twentieth century, [...] the meeting of two sculptors in space, one working with "solids", the other with the ephemeral' (Bredel, 1984).

In this instance the collaborative process allowed for the realisation of ideas long-held by the project's three major contributors: Corbusier's interest in space–time, Varèse's notion of 'spatial music' and Xenakis' desire to translate music into three-dimensional space.

ARCHITECTURAL SETTING FOR THE OPERA
PROMETEO (1984) – RENZO PIANO / LUIGI NONO

Following the Philips pavilion by some 25 years, the architect Renzo Piano and composer Luigi Nono collaborated to create a purpose-built musical space for Nono's opera (or 'non-opera' as it has sometimes been characterised) – *Prometeo*. Nono's *Prometheus: A Tragedy in Listening* [*Prometeo: Tragedia dell'ascolto*] (1984), to give its full title, came some nine years after another of his operatic works, *Al gran sole carcio d'amore* (1975), a work that was known for its extremely elaborate and complex staging. *Prometeo* initially began along similar lines, but by the late 1970s Nono had decided to move in the opposite direction, forgoing any theatrical sets whatsoever, at least in the traditional sense, instead envisioning his work performed within a bespoke minimalist framework. Regarding these changes Nono said:

After *Gran sole* I needed to rethink my whole work and my whole existence, not only as a musician but as an intellectual in today's society in order to discover new ways of seeing things and new opportunities for creative endeavor. Many concepts and ideas have become hackneyed so that it is now absolutely necessary to give the greatest possible prominence to the imagination. (Stenzl, 1995, pp.49–50)

He later states: 'We must learn to live with the plurality of times and spaces, with multiplicities and with differences' (Stenzl, 1995, p.50). The representation of the 'prominence of imagination' and the 'plurality of times and spaces' are central concepts underpinning not only the musical work, but its original architectural environment as well.

Technically, *Prometeo* incorporates compositional elements previously used by Nono in others of his works: fragmented and dislocated texts and sounds (in this instance sources as disparate as Hesiod, the biblical book of Genesis, and Walter Benjamin) and electronic technology to alter and augment live vocals and instruments. It is in his conceptualisation of the performer–audience relationship, however, that architecture becomes an essential component of the piece. Like other members of the Darmstadt School – Karlheinz Stockhausen and Pierre Boulez in particular – had done before him, Nono sought to cultivate the potential for interaction between sound and space. In this operatic work, the composer sought to subvert the traditional spatial arrangement of performers and audience, placing the listener in the central space and integrating the musicians and singers around, above, below and alongside them. Reclining and swivelling seating was designed in order to facilitate the audience's new relationship to the players. Performers moved through the space to envelop the listeners in a dynamic and constantly changing sonic environment. As architect Renzo Piano describes: 'The music in *Prometeo* is not projected into perspective, over the heads of the audience as in a traditional opera house, but instead inundates the audience, which becomes fully immersed in the performance' (Buchanan, 1993, p.87).

Not only were the staging requirements called for by Nono's production challenging in their own right, for example the dispersed arrangement of the musicians required the use of closed circuit video monitors in order for them to follow the conductor, but they were made even more complex by external factors. First presented in Venice as part of the *Biennale* in 1984, the production premiered at the church of San Lorenzo. Several months later, a revised version of the opera was mounted in a disused factory in Milan utilising the same performance environment. The internal requirements of the work, coupled with the demands and limitations of mounting the production in very different types of venue, plus the technological challenges associated with orchestrating dozens of perambulating singers and musicians, called for a collaborative effort that went well beyond that typically found between composer and set designer. When characterising his approach to the design of performance spaces, Piano uses a musical metaphor saying: 'The most beautiful adventure for an architect is to build a space for music. Perhaps it is more beautiful for a luthier to design a violin, but both are about building instruments' (Ferrari, 2003). The architectural 'instrument' created by Piano for the opera relates both to the instruments of the performing musicians through form, material and action (various curved wooden panels could be adjusted to 'tune' the space) and the setting as an 'instrument', or tool, essential to the realisation of Nono's artistic vision.

The critical contribution of the architectural setting to the success of the opera's intent can, in this instance, be demonstrated. A later production of *Prometeo* in Brussels presented the work in a conventional opera house, staged in a more traditionally dramatic manner. In the words of director André Richard, a frequent collaborator of Nono's: '[…] neither the performances nor the production was any good. The whole show was a failure. The visual direction interfered with the performances; for a fact, the performers told me it ruined their performances' (Asada et al., 1998). We find in the collaborative effort of Luigi Nono and Renzo Piano a synergistic relationship where each art is informed by the other. Here architecture gives form to conceptual notions of time and space while addressing the pragmatic demands of the production, while the instruments of the musicians provide the inspiration for the architectural expression.

PAVILION OF THE SWISS CONFEDERATION (2000) PETER ZUMTHOR / DANIEL OTT

Its creators conceived the pavilion representing the Swiss Confederation at the world exposition held in Hanover, Germany in 2000, as a *gesamtkunstwerk* (total work of art) for the new millennium. The structure was intended as a truly collaborative effort that brought not only architecture and music together in a meaningful way, but lighting, fashion and the culinary arts as well to create an environment engaging all of the senses. Not unlike Renzo Piano's environmental setting, the Swiss Sound Box as it was dubbed (*Klangkörper*: literally 'sound body'), finds much of its inspiration in the materials and structural concepts of the musical instruments that are used to fill its spaces with sound. Peter Zumthor, the Swiss architect and individual responsible for establishing the project's overall concept, was initially trained as a cabinetmaker and the realisation of the building form reflects an appreciation of wood as a primary material in both the architecture and musical instruments native to his country. The temporary structure is composed of walls formed of stacked lumber, not unlike the manner that wood is set out to cure in a luthier's workshop. These timber members are held together solely by compression, without nails or bolts, utilising steel rods pre-stressed by large tension springs that adjust to the swelling and shrinking of the wood. Tectonically these assemblies poetically reference instruments like the violin and dulcimer in their use of wood and metal.

Daniel Ott, the composer (or musical curator as he is officially credited), shared in developing the concept for the project. Responsible for creating the sonic component of the environment, Ott writes: 'I had this idea of "spatial music" with mobile musicians inside a continually changing sound space. [...] One of the aims is to complement/cross the musical flow, to intervene and disrupt constructively' (Hönig, 2000, p.45). This desire to 'disrupt constructively' can find an architectural parallel in the purposefully disorienting, labyrinthine layout of the enclosure. Both the structure and the music are further united through their use of numbers as organisers. The numerical relationship between the architecture and the musical programme is described in the publication written to detail the various aspects of the project thus:

The composer has attempted to convert the number that he gathered from the Swiss Sound Box enterprise into a composition and in turn to convert the rows of numbers and proportions produced by the composition into sound and time-based structures. For example, architectural numbers: twelve stacks, three courts, the number of beam layers within a stack (4, 5, 6, 8, 10, or 11), proportions of the floor plan, etc. (Hönig, 2000, p.175)

In other words, the composer is here taking physical elements of the architecture as the source of inspiration for his compositions. Using the language of mathematics as the common denominator, numbers found in the building itself establish the sonic and temporal parameters for the improvisational musical performances occurring within the space. Both architect and composer have worked together to consciously establish a quantifiable link between the physical and sonic realms. Daniel Ott has further extended this notion of creative collaboration through the nature of his compositions, providing opportunities for self-expression on the part of individual performers. Relative to this kind of collaboration, or musicians as 'joint composers' as he characterises the relationship, he writes: 'The idea was not to produce a bunch of random elements but to create a *gesamtkunstwerk* that benefits from the diversity of the participating musicians: integrating the performers as co-authors, as people and not just executing robots' (Hönig, 2000, p.167). Peter Zumthor and Daniel Ott found common ground for fruitful collaboration through numerical relationships common to both music and architecture. Issues of materiality (wood, metal) and structure (tension, compression) shared by buildings and musical instruments became additional concepts that united sound and space – the building itself becomes an instrument played upon by nature.

CONCLUSION

As presented in the first half of this chapter, we have seen that the collaboration of sound with space produces a type of 'chamber music'. By this we infer that the real experience of the sounds and meaning of music is captured within all of the participating elements of the performance 'chamber'. Physically, participation takes place as acoustically reflective surfaces contribute to the reverberation of the musical sound – pitches combined to convey melody, harmony, rhythm, timbre, texture, form, and text. Visually, participation takes place as reflective surfaces such as glass, stone, plaster, wood, and metal are artistically turned into elements of design which mirror the ideas and beliefs of a community. Sound and space converge at that moment to create meaning through a condition unique to the collaboration of architecture and music.

As outlined in the second half of the chapter, we see that architects and composers have historically collaborated with synergistic results. In the case of Le Corbusier, Xenakis and Varèse, we find that despite being separated by vast distances geographically (New York, Chandigarh, Paris and Eindhoven), collaboration was possible because the three artists were closely joined in their aesthetic intent. The true spirit of the Philips pavilion literally was formed in the final few days prior to opening as architecture, sound and cinema were united to form a transcendent environment. Renzo Piano's work with Luigi Nono, on the other hand, deferentially placed architecture in a supporting role to music. Rather than seeking a direct translation of music into architectural form as Xenakis did, the structure presented itself as a neutral instrument brought to life only when 'played' during the musical experience for which it was built. In a somewhat different form of interaction between sound and space, the collaborative effort between Peter Zumthor and Daniel Ott manifested the give-

and-take exchange of improvisational artists. The composer restated themes borrowed from the architecture, while the designer drew inspiration from the tools and tropes of musicians. All of these constructions were purpose-built, temporary structures. In essence, the buildings became as ephemeral as the music performed within them. As the dialogue using the shared vocabularies of compositional systems and mathematics continues it is logical to assume that collaborative ventures between practitioners of these allied arts will continue. Through an analysis of the processes used by architects and composers to develop these works it is possible not only to gain a deeper insight into the nature of collaboration, but also to extrapolate the potential for applications across other disciplinary boundaries.

REFERENCES

Asada, A., Choki, S., Isozaki, A. & Lachenmann, H. (1998). *Luigi Nono and Prometeo* (transcript of symposium panel discussion) www.ntticc.or.jp/pub/ic_mag/ic027/html

Barrie, B. (1996). *Symbols, structures and rituals.* London: Shambhala Publications.

Bredel, M. (1984). *Edgar Varèse.* Paris: Editions Mazarine.

Buchanan, P. (1993). *Renzo Piano Building Workshop: Complete works.* London: Phaidon Press Limited.

Ferrari, G. de (2003). 'Piano Forte'. *Travel + Leisure* (magazine), December 2003, p. 84.

Geerdes, H. (1987). *Music facilities: Building, equipping, and renovating.* Reston, VA: MENC Publications.

Grabow, S. (1993). 'Frozen music: The bridge between art and science'. In B. Farmer & H. Louw (eds), *Companion to contemporary architectural thought.* London and New York: Routledge.

Hönig, R. (ed.). (2000). *Swiss sound box.* Basel: Birkhäuser.

Laszlo, V.S. de (1958). *Psyche and symbol: A selection of the writing of C.G. Jung.* New York: Doubleday Anchor Books.

Lucas, S. (ed.). (1998). 'Eye music' (uncredited author). *The Frank Lloyd Wright Quarterly, 9* (2), 8.

Mâche, F. (2001). *Portrait(s) de Iannis Xenakis.* Paris: Bibliothèque nationale de France.

Martin, E. (1994). *Architecture as a translation of music.* New York: Princeton Architectural Press.

Olson, H.F. (1967). *Music, physics and engineering* (2nd edition). New York: Dover Publications.

Piano, R. et al. (2002). *Architecture and music – Renzo Piano Building Workshop.* Milan: Edizioni Lybra Immagine.

Riedel, S.R. (1986). *Acoustics in worship space.* St Louis, MO: Concordia Publishing House.

Stenzl, J. (1995). *Prometeo – Tagedia dell'ascolto.* Köln: EMI Electrola GmbH.

Treib, M. (1996). *Space calculated in seconds.* Princeton, NJ: Princeton University Press.

Varga, B.A. (1996). *Conversations with Iannis Xenakis.* London: Faber and Faber.

Xenakis, I. (1987). 'The Monastery of La Tourette'. In H.A. Brooks (ed.), *Le Corbusier* (pp.142–162). Princeton, NJ: Princeton University Press.

AUDIO RECORDINGS

Lauridsen, Morten. (2004). *Lux Aeterna* (Rhodes MasterSingers Chorale, Timothy Sharp, conductor). Memphis, TN: Rhodes College.

Nono, Luigi. (1995). *Prometeo – Tragedia dell'ascolto.* Köln: EMI Electrola GmbH.

Ott, Daniel. (2002). *Klangkorperklang.* Zurich: Migros-Genossenschafts-Bund.

Varèse, Edgard (1998). 'Poème électronique'. In *Edgard Varèse – The complete works.* London: London Records.

Various composers. (2001). *Motets of the Italian renaissance* (Rhodes Singers and MasterSingers Chorale, Timothy Sharp, conductor). Memphis, TN: Rhodes College.

Xenakis, Iannis. (1999). 'Concrete PH'. In *Early modulations – Vintage volts*. New York: Caipirinha Music.

Xenakis, Iannis. (2000). 'Metastasis'. In *Xenakis – Orchestral works and chamber music.* Salzburg, Austria: col legno.

List of Contributors

Cordelia Bryan originally studied music and performing arts before embarking on a career spanning 25 years in three sectors of education. Her most recent research arises from *Assessing Group Practice*, a collaborative project involving a consortium of six Higher Education Institutions which she directed from the Central School of Speech and Drama in London. For the past 12 years Cordelia has led other successful Higher Education projects enhancing different aspects of learning and teaching at University of North London, Anglia Polytechnic University and as an independent consultant. She has lectured and published widely on educational development within HE.

Maarten de Laat conducts research on e-learning in both educational and organisational contexts. His interests include describing, theorising and supporting networked learning and knowledge management practices. Besides working for the e-Learning Research Centre based at the University of Southampton, he works for the Centre for ICT in Education at IVLOS, University of Utrecht. He is co-founder of KnowledgeWorks, a software company that develops software to support networked learning and knowledge management and he facilitates a Dutch online workshop on the foundations of Communities of Practice in collaboration with Cpsquare.

Teresa Dillon. Teresa's main interests are in the application of new and emerging technologies within the performing arts and education. Working across both disciplines, she is currently based at NESTA Futurelab, Bristol, UK where she researches and carries out prototype development and evaluation on the design of new technologies for learning.

Jane Henry is an applied psychologist based at the Open University Business School. She developed and chairs the OU Creativity, Innovation and Change Masters Programme and has written extensively on creativity and development, as well as designing a number of creativity CD-Roms, websites, and audio-visual programmes. Her books include *Creativity and Perception in Management* and *Creative Management* (2nd edition) (both 2001), and *Managing Innovation and Change* (2002), all published by Sage. Her research interests include work on the relationship between cognitive style, creativity and development. She regularly advises various public, private and not-for-profit organisations on ways of developing collaborative creativity.

Gabrielle Ivinson is a lecturer in the School of Social Sciences, Cardiff University. Her areas of interest are: cognition and culture; schooling, knowledge and pedagogy and gender and education. She is a social and developmental psychologist who draws on socio-cultural theory and social representation theory. Her doctoral thesis, *The Construction of the Curriculum*, investigated elements of the curriculum as social representations. Latterly she has been studying how students in secondary schools construct subject knowledge with an emphasis on social gender identity. She has developed an interest in art and national identity in post-devolution Wales.

Vera John-Steiner has been a leading scholar of creativity and socio-cultural studies for more than 30 years. Her book, *Creative Collaboration*, describes the dynamic partnerships from which some of Western culture's most important ideas were born. Her book, *Notebooks of the Mind: Explorations of Thinking*, won the 1990 William James Book Award from the American Psychological Association. She is Presidential Professor of Linguistics and Education at the University of New Mexico.

Mathilda Marie Joubert is a part-time research associate in psychology at The Open University studying collaborative creativity and she is also an independent consultant, researcher and trainer on creativity, education and the arts to a number of clients from the business, arts, education and voluntary sectors, including Synectics Europe where she is a Partner in Innovation. Mathilda previously trained and worked as a classical musician and as a teacher across all sectors of the education system. She was Research Officer to the National Advisory Committee on Creative and Cultural Education (NACCCE) which published the 1999 report *All Our Futures: Creativity, Culture and Education* and she is the author of *Challenging Convention: Creativity in Organisations* (2002).

Vic Lally is a researcher, educator, and consultant in collaborative e-learning in higher education and he is Director of Learning and Teaching for the Faculty of Social Sciences at the University of Sheffield (UK). He has directed many national and international research programmes in e-learning and collaboration, and produced over 60 publications in the field. Current projects include 'E-China' with Huang Ronghuai of the School of Networked Education at Beijing Normal University, 'Theorising Learning' with Maarten de Laat at Southampton University, and 'Creative Collaborations' with Maarten de Laat and Maddy Sclater of Glasgow University.

Karen Littleton is a Senior Lecturer in Developmental Psychology in the Educational Dialogue Research Unit at The Open University, UK, and Visiting Professor at the University of Helsinki. She has researched collaborative learning, often with reference to new technologies and gender, and has published extensively in this area. Karen Littleton co-edited *Learning with Computers* (1999) with Paul Light, *Rethinking Collaborative Learning* (2000) with Richard

Joiner, Dorothy Faulkner and Dorothy Miell, and *Learning to Collaborate, Collaborating to Learn* with Dorothy Miell and Dorothy Faulkner (2004). She is the co-author, with Paul Light, of *Social Processes in Children's Learning* (1999). From 1994–99 she was senior scientist in the European Science Foundation's 'Learning in Humans and Machines' programme. She is currently the lead editor for the international book series *Advances in Learning and Instruction.*

Jim Lutz is an assistant professor in the Architecture Program at the University of Memphis. He received his degrees from the University of California, Berkeley and Syracuse University. He was a practising architect for 20 years before entering academic work.

Dorothy Miell is a Senior Lecturer in Psychology in the Faculty of Social Sciences, The Open University, UK and a member of the University's Centre for Research in Education and Educational Technology. Her research interests lie in studying close relationships, particularly the effects of such relationships on identity development and on the nature of collaborative working in creative tasks such as music making. She has recently edited (with Raymond MacDonald and David Hargreaves) *Musical Identities* (2000) and *Musical Communication* (forthcoming for 2005, both Oxford University Press), and she is on the international editorial boards of *Journal of Social and Personal Relationships, Psychology of Music,* and *International Journal of Teaching for Thinking and Creativity.*

Seana Moran is an advanced doctoral student in Human Development and Psychology at the Harvard University Graduate School of Education. Her dissertation work takes a lifespan, dynamic systems perspective on how people develop commitment to a line of work/career, especially to work that is creative and transforms the domain. She has written about Vygotsky's contribution to a developmental view of creativity (with Vera John-Steiner) and about the development of extraordinary/creative achievements in art, science, leadership and moral excellence for the sixth edition of the *Handbook of Child Psychology* (with Howard Gardner), as well as several teacher-resource guides for developing entrepreneurship and creativity.

Stephen O'Hear is currently a fellow for the National Endowment for Science, Technology and the Arts (NESTA) where he is developing innovative and practical uses of digital technologies within education. He has developed and taught on a range of digital media courses at WAC Performing Arts and Media College and has consulted on numerous e-learning projects including developing the BETT short-listed website *Moving Words* as part of a major Open University research project.

Rosalind H. Searle is a Chartered Occupational Psychologist and lecturer in Psychology at The Open University. Prior to becoming an academic she worked as a consultant for General Motors and completed her PhD in innovation in teams in 2000. Her research spans two main areas: team composition and processes (where she is particularly interested in social processes, such as trust, and their role in change); and selection and assessment (where she is interested in the impact of new technologies). She is currently Chair of the British Psychological Society Division of Occupational Psychology.

Fred Seddon is a research lecturer in Psychology at The Open University. His research investigates collaborative creativity in jazz performance and in collaborative computer-based music composition. He studied Music Psychology at the University of Keele between 1997 and 2001. His PhD investigated adolescent computer-based composition in relation to instrumental experience.

Julian Sefton-Green is the Head of Media Arts and Education at WAC Performing Arts and Media College – a centre for informal training and education – where he directs a range of digital media activities for young people and coordinates training for media artists and teachers. He has researched and written widely on many aspects of media education, new technologies and informal learning, including *Cultural Studies Goes to School* (with David Buckingham) (Taylor and Francis 1994), *Digital Diversions* (UCL Press 1998), *Creativity, Young People and New Technologies* (Routledge 1999) and *Evaluating Creativity: Making and Learning by Young People* (Routledge 2000). He has directed research projects for the Arts Council of England and the British Film Institute and has spoken at a number of conferences around the world.

Timothy Sharp is a professor of music and chair of the Department of Music at Rhodes College, Memphis, TN (USA). He holds the Elizabeth G. Daughdrill Chair in the Fine Arts at Rhodes. He has conducted ensembles in renowned spaces such as Carnegie Hall, Coventry Cathedral, St Mark's Cathedral, and a variety of innovative concert locations matching programmes to appropriate architectural space. Timothy Sharp and Jim Lutz teach a course at Rhodes College entitled 'Seeing Music, Hearing Architecture'.

Helen Storey trained as a fashion designer and having graduated from Kingston University in 1981 she served an apprenticeship with Valentino in Italy returning to London to set up her own label in 1984. Helen was awarded 'Most Innovative British Designer' in 1990; she received an industry award for Best Exporter in the same year and was nominated for British Designer of the Year in 1990 and 1991. She was a member of the National Advisory Committee on Creative and Cultural Education (NACCCE), appointed by the Secretaries of State for Education and Employment; and Culture, Media and Sport. Since 1997 Helen has widened her perspective whilst working on cross-disciplinary collaborative creative projects. She is currently visiting professor and senior research fellow at the University of the Arts, London; Kings College, London and Heriott-Watt University, Scotland. For further information on the work of Helen Storey see: www.helenstoreyfoundation.org

Eva Vass completed doctoral and postdoctoral research at The Open University, researching issues concerning creativity and collaboration in educational settings. She is now a lecturer at the University of Southampton. Her doctoral research examined the nature of productive group work in the context of computer-supported collaborative creative writing. The study was based on naturalistic observations of ongoing classroom activities and explored the beneficial effects of friendship pairing in the development of creative writing skills. She is the author of 'Friendship and collaborative creative writing in the primary classroom'. *Journal of Computer-Assisted Learning*, 2002, 18 (1), 102–110.

Sini Wirtanen is an assistant and doctoral student in the Research Centre for Educational Psychology at the University of Helsinki, Finland. Her work focuses on understanding the processes of teaching-learning. She has particular research interests in collaborative learning and the identity work of piano-solo students.

Index

Compiled by Stephanie Johnstone